First Part

[6] His birth (God's mercy be upon him)

According to information we have heard from the tongues of reliable sources who traced it and on its basis eventually constructed his horoscope by the dictates of the art of astrology, his birth took place during the months of the year 532 [1137-8] and in the castle of Takrīt.[1] His father, Ayyūb ibn Shādī (God have mercy on him), who was governor there, was a noble, generous man, mild and of excellent character. He had been born in Dvin.[2] Later it came about that he was transferred from Takrīt to the city of Mosul, and his child moved with him and there resided until he came of age. His father was a respected commander, as was his father's brother, Asad al-Dīn Shīrkūh, in the service of the Atabeg Zankī.[3]

His father then chanced to be transferred to Syria (may God preserve it) and was given Baalbek, where he remained for a while. His son moved to Baalbek and lived there in the service of his father, being educated under his wing and imbibing[4] his good morals and manners, until signs of good fortune became visible in him and marks of leadership and lordship were manifest. Al-Malik al-'Ādil Nūr al-Dīn Maḥmūd ibn Zankī (God have mercy on him) advanced him, relied on and looked to him, and made him a favoured intimate. It continued to be the case that, each time he was advanced, he would demonstrate further cause to require his promotion to a higher position. Then came the time for his uncle, Asad al-Dīn, to make his expedition to attack Egypt. We shall give a clear and detailed account of that in the proper place, God willing.

---

1 Situated on the River Tigris, north of Baghdad.

2 Situated near Tiflis and at this period ruled intermittently by the Kurdish dynasty of the Shaddādids (see *EI*^{2}, ii, pp. 678-681).

3 'Imād al-Dīn Zankī, the son of Sultan Malikshāh's senior mamluke, Āqsunqur, ruled in Mesopotamia (with a capital at Mosul) and in northern Syria. He was officially Atabeg, that is guardian/regent for a Seljuq prince and was killed in 541/1146. His son Nūr al-Dīn succeeded him, initially in Aleppo and later in Mosul too. See Elisséef, *Nūr al-Dīn.*

4 Literally, 'sucking the breast of'.

[7] Account of his adherence to religious beliefs and observance of matters of Holy Law that we have witnessed (God have mercy on him).

In the genuine Hadīth from the Prophet (may God bless him and give him peace) he said, 'Islām is built on five things: testimony that there is no god but God, performance of the prayers, the giving of alms, fasting in Ramaḍān, and the Pilgrimage to the Sacred House of God.'[1]

His creed was good and he was much mindful of God Almighty. He took his creed from proof by means of study with the leading men of religious learning and eminent jurisconsults. He understood of that what one needs to understand, such that, when disputation occurred in his presence, he could contribute excellent comments, even if they were not in the language of learned specialists. Consequently he gained a creed free from the defilement of anthropomorphism but his studies did not dig too deep to the extent of denying the divine attributes or misrepresentation.[2] His creed followed the straight path, agreed with the canon of true discernment and was approved by the greatest of the ulema.

The leading Shaykh Quṭb al-Dīn al-Naysabūrī[3] (God have mercy on him) had compiled for him a creed which gathered together all that was needed in this field. In his intense devotion to it he used to teach it to his young children so that it became fixed in their minds from infancy. I have seen him going over it with them, while they recited it from memory in front of him.

Prayer

He was extremely assiduous in the performance of prayer communally. Indeed, he mentioned one day that for years he had only prayed in company. If he fell ill, he would summon the imam on his own and force himself to stand and pray in company. Over the years he used to practise the daily devotions of the mystic.

[8] If he awoke at any time in the night, he had a series of prayers he would perform or otherwise he would complete them before the dawn prayer. While he remained in possession of his faculties he never neglected to perform his prayers. I saw him (may God sanctify his spirit) standing to pray during his fatal illness and he only missed prayers during the three days when his mind wandered. If ever prayer time found him travelling, he would dismount and pray.

---

1 With slight differences this tradition is found in Bukhārī, *al-Jāmi' al-ṣaḥīḥ*, i, p. 10.

2 Instead of *tamwīh* it is tempting to propose, as a plausible emendation, *al-tanzīh* (lit. 'declaring God free of impurity', that is, acknowledging God's attributes but holding them to be above human understanding).

3 Born 505/1112, died 578/1183, Abū'l-Ma'ālī Mas'ūd ibn Muḥammad of Nishapur had an eminent career as scholar and teacher in Iraq and Syria (under Nūr al-Dīn and then Saladin). See *Sanā'*, pp. 70-71 and Ibn Khallikān, *Wafāyāt*, v, pp. 196-197.

Alms
When he died, he possessed nothing for which he owed any alms. As for superogatory charity, that exhausted all the property he owned. He ruled all that he ruled, but died leaving in his treasury in gold and silver only forty Nāṣirī dirhams and a single Tyrian gold piece. He left no property, no house, no estate, no orchard, no village, no farm, not a single item of property of any sort.

The Ramaḍān Fast
He fell a little short in respect of fasting on account of illnesses that he successively suffered in numerous Ramaḍāns. Qāḍī al-Fāḍil[1] undertook to keep a record of those days and he began (God have mercy on him) to fulfil those missed obligations at Jerusalem the year he died. He strictly kept the fast for more than a month, for he had missed some Ramaḍāns which illness and also prosecution of the Jihād had prevented him from keeping. Fasting did not agree with his constitution, but God inspired him to fast to make up what he had missed. As he fasted, I kept the tally of the days he fasted, because the Qāḍī was absent. His doctor criticised him but he would not listen, saying, 'I do not know what the future may bring.' It was as though he were inspired to discharge his obligation (God's mercy on him), and he continued until he had fulfilled what was due.

[**9**] *Pilgrimage*
He always intended and planned it, especially in the year of his death. He confirmed his determination to perform it and he ordered preparations to be made. Provisions were got ready and all that remained was to set out. However, he was prevented because of lack of time and the unavailability of what was proper for such a person. He therefore put it off till the next year, but God decreed what He decreed. Everyone, high and low, knew about this.

He loved to listen to readings of the Glorious Koran. Indeed, he would choose[2] his imam and stipulate that he should be a person learned in the sciences of the Koran with a solid knowledge of it by heart. He used to ask whoever was present with him at night, when he was in his 'tower',[3] to recite two, three or even four sections, while he listened. In his public sessions he would ask those who commonly did this to recite a verse or up to twenty or even more than that. Once he passed by a youngster who was reciting the Koran before his father. He admired his recitation and showed him favour, appointing him a share from his private table and endowing him and his father with a portion of arable land. He (God have mercy in him) was emotionally

---

1 Abū 'Alī 'Abd al-Raḥīm ibn 'Alī al-Baysānī, Saladin's senior administrator and a celebrated prose stylist (born 529/1135, died 596/1200), was known as 'the Learned Qāḍī' (see *EI*^{2}, iv, pp. 376-377).

2 Reading with B *yastakhīr* instead of *Nawādir*'s *yastakhbir*.

3 A wooden security sanctum erected in the sultan's complex of tents.

sensitive and easily moved to tears. Whenever he heard the Koran, his heart was touched and his eyes would fill with tears on most occasions.

His desire to hear Ḥadīth[1] was intense. Whenever he heard of a shaykh whose sources were of high authority and whose knowledge was extensive, if he was one of those who attended his court, he would summon him and hear Ḥadīth from him, then ensure that those present with him in that place, his children or his personal mamlukes, would also hear it. He would order people to sit when listening to Ḥadīth to show honour to it. If the shaykh in question was one one of those who did not frequent the courts of sultans and scorned to be present in their councils, he himself would go to him and study with him. He visited al-Ḥāfiẓ al-Isfahānī[2] at Alexandria (may God Almighty protect it) and he transmitted many *ḥadīth*s on his authority. [**10**] He was fond of reading Ḥadīth in private. He would summon me in his private moments, produce some books of Ḥadīth and himself read them. When he came across an *ḥadīth* that contained a moral lesson, his heart would melt and his tears flow.

He was full of reverence for the cult practices of the religion, believed in the resurrection of the body and that the righteous would be rewarded with Paradise and the evil-doers with Hellfire, accepted the truth of the provisions contained in the Holy Law, with a heart at ease with that, and hated the philosophers, those that denied God's attributes, the materialists and those who stubbornly rejected the Holy Law. He once ordered his son, al-Malik al-Ẓāhir, the lord of Aleppo, to execute a young man that came forward, called al-Suhrawardī,[3] of whom it was said that he rejected the Holy Law and declared it invalid. His son had arrested him because of reports about him that he heard. He informed the sultan of this, who ordered his execution and his body to be publicly displayed for some days. This was done.

His belief in God was right and proper (God sanctify his spirit), his trust in him was great, as was his spirit of repentance. One of the results of this which I witnessed I shall now relate. The Franks (may God forsake them) were camped at Bayt Nūbā, a place near Jerusalem the Noble (may God Almighty protect it), less than a day's march distant. The sultan was in Jerusalem, having posted a detachment to watch and maintain contact with the enemy and having sent spies and intelligence gatherers to them. A series of reports told of their strong determination to march up to Jerusalem, besiege it [**11**] and mount an assault. The Muslims were very frightened at this, so he summoned the emirs and informed them of the disaster that threatened the Muslims, consulting them

---

1 The vast corpus of reported sayings and doings of the Prophet Muḥammad.

2 The Hadith scholar Abū Ṭāhir Aḥmad ibn Muḥammad al-Silafī (born in Isfahan about 472/1079) came to Alexandria in 511/1117, where he died in 576/1180 (Ibn Khallikān, *Wafāyāt*, i, pp. 105-107). For a list of extant writings, see Brockelmann, *Geschichte*, supplement i, p. 624.

3 This noted Sufi, Shihāb al-Dīn Yaḥyā al-Suhrawardī, was executed in 587/1191 at the age of 38 (see Trimingham, *Sufi Orders*, pp. 8-9).

about whether to remain in Jerusalem. They came up with some specious reply whose inner meaning was quite other than the apparent. All insisted that there was no advantage in his staying there in person. This would expose Islam to great danger. They said that they would stay while he left with a part of the army which could surround the enemy, as had been the case at Acre. He himself and the troops with him would be engaged in interrupting the enemy's supplies and pressing hard on them, while they would be engaged in holding and defending the city. The session of the council broke up at that juncture, with the sultan still insisting on staying in person, because he knew that, if he did not, no-one would. When the emirs had dispersed to their houses, some people came from them to declare that they would only remain if his brother al-Malik al-'Ādil or one of his children stayed to be in authority and the person whose orders they could take. He realised that this was a hint on their part that no-one should stay. He was upset, his thoughts were in turmoil and he was extremely troubled in mind.

That night - it was the eve of a Friday - I sat in attendance on him from the beginning of the night until near dawn. It was the winter season and we two were alone apart from God. We were making dispositions of companies and arranging for each what was required. Eventually, I was overcome with concern for him and fear for his health, for 'dryness' was dominating his humours. I pleaded with him to lie down in the hope that he would sleep for a while. He said, 'Perhaps you are sleepy.' Then he rose [for the day]. I had hardly arrived at my quarters and attended to some of my affairs before the muezzin made the call to prayer and dawn came up. On most occasions I used to pray the dawn prayer with him, so I went to him again, as he was pouring water over his hands and feet. He said, 'I did not get any sleep at all.' I replied, 'I know,' to which he said, 'How so?' 'Because I did not sleep and there was no time left for sleep.' [**12**] Then we occupied ourselves with our prayers, before sitting together as we had been. I said to him, 'Something has occurred to me, and I think it useful, God willing.' 'What is it,' he said. 'Perfect reliance on God, repentance and trust in him to clear up this worrying matter.' 'How should we act?' he asked. I replied, 'Today is Friday. Let my lord wash himself when he leaves and pray as normal at the Aqsa Mosque, the site of the Night Journey[1] of the Prophet (God bless him and give him peace), and let my lord command that some alms be given secretly through someone he trusts and let him perform two *rak'a*s[2] between the call to prayer and its commencement

---

1 The Prophet was carried on the winged horse Burāq from Mecca to 'the furthest mosque', early interpreted as Jerusalem. This incident (the *isrā'*) is generally considered separate from Muḥammad's ascension into the heavenly spheres. For a full discussion, see *EI*^{2}, vii, pp. 97-105, s.v. *mi'rādj*.

2 A *rak'a* is a series of ritual movements, bowing, prostrating etc., repeated a set number of times at different prayer times during the day.

and call upon God in his prostration, for there is a genuine *ḥadīth* about this, and say in your heart, "My God! my earthly means have been devoted to the aid of Your religion. There is nothing left but to trust in You, hold fast to Your rope[1] and rely on Your goodness. You are my sufficiency and what an excellent trustee!" God is too generous to allow your purposes to founder.'

He did all that and I prayed at his side as normal. He prayed two *rak'a*s between the call to prayer and its commencement, and I watched him as he prostrated himself with his tears running over his gray beard and on to his prayer mat, although I could not hear what he was saying. Before that day was over a message arrived from 'Izz al-Dīn Jūrdīk, who was in command of the screening detachment, in which he reported that the Franks were on the move. That day their whole army had ridden off into open country. They halted until full midday, and then returned to their tents. On Saturday morning there came a second message reporting the same. During the course of the day a spy arrived with news that they were in disagreement. The French were of the opinion that they had to besiege Jerusalem, whereas the king of England and his followers held that he should not endanger the Christian cause and launch them into this upland when there was no supply of water, for the sultan had polluted all the wells around Jerusalem. They had assembled for a council, it being their custom to meet on horseback to debate questions of war. They had appointed ten persons and made them the judges. Whatever they advised, they would not be opposed. [**13**] On the Monday morning a messenger came with the good news that they had retired in the direction of Ramla. This is one of the effects that I witnessed of his reliance on God Almighty and trust in Him.

Account of his justice (God's mercy upon him)

Abū Bakr the Righteous[2] (God be pleased with him) related that the Prophet (God bless him etc.) said, 'The just ruler is God's shadow on His earth. Whoever gives sincere aid to him personally or in his dealings with God's servants, God will shelter him beneath His throne on the day when there is no shelter but in Him; but whoever betrays him personally or in his dealings with God's servants, God will forsake him on the Day of Resurrection. Every day the good works of sixty righteous men, each of whom is a true worshipper striving for the good of his own soul, are credited to [the benefit of] the just ruler.'

Saladin was just, gentle and merciful, a supporter of the weak against the strong. Each Monday and Thursday he used to sit to dispense justice in public

---

1 Reading *bi-ḥabli-ka* as in B, with reference to Koran iii, 103, 'Hold fast to God's rope all together'.

2 The first caliph in Medina, who died Jumādā II 13/August 634 (*EI*², i, pp. 109-111).

session, attended by the jurisconsults, the Qāḍīs and the doctors of religion. The door would be opened to litigants so that everyone, great and small, senile women and old men, might have access to him. That was his practice both at home and abroad. However, at all times he would accept petitions presented to him, to discover what injustices were reported to him. Every day he collected the petitions,[1] and then used to sit with his clerk for a while, either at night or during the daytime, and minute each petition with whatever God put into his heart.[2]

[14] No-one ever appealed to him without his stopping, hearing his case, discovering his wrong and taking his petition. I have seen him, when a man called Ibn Zuhayr from Damascus appealed to him against Taqī al-Dīn, his nephew, send for him to be brought to the court of justice. Saladin only released him after he had called two reputable court witnesses of accepted probity to testify that he had appointed as his proxy in the court case and dispute the Qāḍī Abū'l-Qāsim Amīn al-Dīn, the Qāḍī of Ḥamā. The two witnesses appeared and established their testimony before me in his court (God be pleased with him) claiming that the proxy had been legally appointed and contesting the case. When his proxy status had been established, I ordered Abū'l-Qāsim to be treated on equal terms with the claimant. This was done, although the former was a courtier of the sultan, and then the dispute between them was heard. The opportunity to take the oath was directed to Taqī al-Dīn, and thereupon the court ended its session. The onset of night prevented us from summoning him - and Taqī al-Dīn was one of those whom Saladin held most dear and respected, but he did not favour him in the matter of justice.

More impressive than this anecdote and something that proves his justice is a case he was involved in with a merchant called 'Umar al-Khilāṭī. I was one day in the court of justice at Jerusalem when a handsome old man, a well-known merchant called 'Umar al-Khilāṭī, came in with a court document which he asked to be admitted as evidence. I questioned him: 'Who is your opponent?' He replied, 'My opponent is the sultan. This is the seat[3] of the Holy Law and we have heard that you do not show favour.' 'In what matter is he your opponent?' I asked. 'Sunqur al-Khilāṭī was my mamluke and remained my property until he died. He held large sums of money, all of which were mine. He left them when he died and the sultan seized them. I am now

1 At this point *Nawādir* adds from the 1317/1899 Cairo edition the following (absent from B): 'and he would open the door of justice and not send away anyone seeking him out because of certain events or judgments.'

2 Text which is absent in B is here added in *Nawādir* from the 1317 A.H. Cairo edition: 'He never sent away a petitioner, claimant or applicant and in addition he was continually mindful of God and constantly reading scripture (God's mercy upon him). He was merciful to his subjects, a champion of religion, an assiduous reader of the Glorious Koran, both knowing well and practising what is in it, never offending against it.'

3 Literally, 'carpet'.

claiming them from him.' I replied, 'Old man! what kept you inactive until now?' to which he answered, 'Rights are not invalidated by delay. This court document declares that he was my property until he died.'

[15] I took the document and perused its contents, which I found to contain a personal description of Sunqur al-Khilāṭī and that he had been purchased from so-and-so the merchant in Arjīsh[1] on such-and-such a day of the month and year there specified, that he remained his property until he ran away in such-and-such a year and that the witnesses to this document were unaware that he had in any way ceased to be his property. The document was properly drawn up throughout. I was astonished at this affair and said to the man, 'It is only possible for me to hear this case when the other party is present. I will let both him and you know what the situation is.' The man accepted that and hurried away.

When I happened to wait upon the sultan during the remainder of the day, I informed him of the situation, and he declared it all highly unlikely, saying, 'Did you read the document?' I replied, '[Yes], I read it and I found it properly issued and approved from Damascus. It was inscribed "Court document from Damascus" and reputable witnesses testified to it through the Qāḍī of Damascus.' 'Very well,' he said, 'we shall summon the man and go to law with him, doing in the case whatever the Holy Law requires.' Later, when he chanced to be sitting in private, I said to him, 'This litigant keeps coming. We shall have to hear his claim.' He answered, 'Appoint a proxy for me who will hear the claim. Let the witnesses establish their testimony. Delay the reading of the document until the man is present here.' I did this and then he summoned the man and bade him approach so that he took his seat before the sultan and I was at his side. Then the sultan left his throne to be on an equal footing with the other. He said, **[16]** 'If you have a claim, speak out.' The man made his case as initially stated, and the sultan answered, 'This Sunqur was my mamluke. He remained my property until I freed him. He then died and left what he left to his heirs.' The man said, 'I have evidence to support what I have claimed.' He then asked for the document to be read into court, which I did and found it to be as I have described.

When the sultan heard the date, he said, 'I have people who will testify that at that date this Sunqur was my property and in my possession in Egypt, and that I had bought him with eight others at a date a year earlier than that, and that he continued in my possession until I freed him.' He then summoned a number of leading emirs of the military who testified to that, telling the story as he had and mentioning the date he claimed. The man was nonplussed. I said to Saladin, 'My lord, he has done this only to seek the clemency of the sultan. He has come before our lord and it is not good that he should leave disappointed.'

---

[1] A town near Khilāṭ, on the NE shore of Lake Van in Armenia (*EI*^{2}, i, p. 627).

'That is a different matter,' the sultan said. He ordered a robe of honour for him and a substantial sum, the amount of which escapes me. Consider the wonderful and extraordinary themes to be found in the context of this affair, his humility, his compliance with the truth, his self-effacement and his generosity instead of punishing when he had a perfect right to do so (may God show him abundant mercy).

[17] Remarkable examples of his generosity

[The Prophet] (God bless him and give him peace) said, 'When a generous man stumbles, God takes him by the hand.'[1] There are [many] *ḥadīth*s concerning generosity.

Saladin's generosity was too public to need to be recorded and too famous to need to be recounted, and yet we will give an indication of it in general terms. He ruled all that he ruled and, when he died, in his treasure chest were found only forty-seven Nāṣirī dirhams of silver and a single Tyrian gold coin, the weight of which was unknown to me. He would give away whole provinces. Having conquered Āmid,[2] he was asked for it by Ibn Qarā Arslān[3] and gave it away to him. When a number of envoys had gathered at his court in Jerusalem, at a time when he had planned to depart for Damascus, but there was nothing in his chest to give the envoys, I kept on about them, raising their subject, until he sold a village that belonged to the Treasury and distributed the money he received for it amongst them. Not a single dirham was left over.

In times of shortage he would be generous, just as he would in easy circumstances. The officials of the Royal Chest used to hide a certain amount of money from him, as a precaution in case some crisis surprised them, because they knew that, if he learnt of it, he would spend it.

[18] In the context of some *ḥadīth* that was mentioned, I heard him say, 'It is possible that there are people who look upon money as dirt.' It is rather as if he had himself in mind.

His gifts were beyond what any petitioner hoped for. I have never heard him say, 'We have already given to so-and-so.' He used to give large gifts and he would smile no more on those to whom he gave than he would on those to whom he gave nothing.

---

1 Not traced in the canonical collections.

2 An important town in Diyār Bakr, the upper Tigris basin. It took the name of the district (i.e., Diyarbakir) from the early modern period (*EI*², ii, 343-347).

3 Nūr al-Dīn Muḥammad ibn Qarā Arslān was a member of the Turkish Artuqid dynasty which ruled in parts of Diyār Bakr from the end of the 11th to the beginning of the 15th century A.D. (*EI*², i, pp. 662-667). He died in 581/1185-6 (Ibn al-Athīr, *al-Kāmil*, xi, p. 514).

He would give and be generous beyond measure. The people knew this, so they used to be always asking him for more. I never heard him say, 'I have given several times more. How much more can I give?' Most approaches on such matters were made verbally through me or by my hand. I was ashamed at the amount that they asked for, but not embarrassed before him at the frequency of my requests for them because I knew that he did not blame one for that. Everybody who ever served him was dispensed with the need to ask anyone else for anything.

As for counting up his gifts and all their variety, then there is no hope of really getting to the truth. The head of his administration said to me, when we had a conversation about his generosity, 'We totalled up the number of horses that he gave away on the plain of Acre alone, and it came to 10,000.' Those who have witnessed his giving will consider this figure on the small side.

O God, You inspired in him this generosity, but You are the more generous one. Generously bestow Your mercy and good pleasure upon him, O most merciful of the merciful.

[19] Account of his bravery (God sanctify his spirit)

It is related from the Prophet (God bless him and give him peace) that he said, 'Verily, God loves bravery, even in the killing of a snake.'[1]

Saladin was one of the great heroes, mighty in spirit, strong in courage and of great firmness, terrified of nothing. I have seen him camped opposite a huge number of Franks, when their reinforcements were constantly arriving and their forces successively gathering, though he was growing in nothing but strength of heart and steadfastness. In a single evening seventy odd ships of theirs came to Acre, as I was counting them from the afternoon prayer until sunset, but he only grew stouter in spirit. At the beginning of winter he would grant leave to depart and remain himself with a small squadron, facing their vast numbers.

I once asked Balian, son of Barisan,[2] one of the great princes of the coast, while he was sitting before Saladin on the day peace was concluded, about their total numbers. The dragoman conveyed his answer: 'The lord of Sidon' - also one of their wise rulers - 'and I were making our way to our army from Tyre. When we came in sight of them we both estimated their numbers. He estimated that they were 500,000 and I thought 600,000.' Possibly he put it the other way round. I replied, 'How many of them perished?' He said, 'In combat about 100,000, but by natural causes or drowning, we have no idea.' Of this multitude only a minority returned.

1 Not found in Wensinck's *Concordance*.
2 In Arabic Bāliyān ibn Bārizān, i.e., Balian II of Ibelin, the castle built at Yubnā. He is called 'ibn Bārizān' from Barisanus, a latinised name for his father Balian I.

Every day, when the sultan was in close contact with them, he had to make a circuit around the enemy once or twice. When the battle was fierce, he would ride between the two battle lines, accompanied by one page leading a spare mount, and cross between the armies from right to left, disposing the battalions and ordering them to advance or halt in positions that he thought fit, all the time observing the enemy at close quarters.

[**20**] Once a portion of Ḥadīth was recited to him between the battle lines. This was because I said to him, 'Ḥadīth has been heard in all honourable situations, but it has never been recorded that it has been heard between the battle lines. If our lord were of a mind to have that related of him, it would be excellent.' He gave permission for that, summoned part of a collection and on the spot summoned someone who was authorised to transmit it. The text was then read to him, while we were on horseback between the battle lines, ambling at times and halting at others.

I have never at all seen him consider the enemy too numerous nor exaggerate their strength. However, he was sometimes deep in thought and forward planning, dealing with all departments and arranging what was required for each without any onset of bad temper or anger.

During one of the fiercest engagements on the plain of Acre the Muslims were routed, even the centre and the sultan's guard. The drums and the banner fell, while he (God be pleased with him) stood firm in a small troop. He had withdrawn to the hill, to rally the men and to stop their flight, to shame them into resuming the battle. He persisted until the Muslim army was victorious over the enemy that day. About 7,000 of them were killed, both foot and horse.

He continued to resist them steadfastly, though they were in great numbers, until the weakness of the Muslims became evident to him. He then made peace at their request, for their weakness and losses were greater, although they were expecting reinforcements and we expected none. There was an advantage to us in making peace, and that became clear when circumstances and fate revealed what they had kept concealed.

He was sometimes ill but would recover. Disturbing circumstances were overwhelming him, though he was full of endurance, face to face with the enemy and with both sets of camp fires visible to each other. We could hear the sound of their bells and they could hear our call to prayer. Eventually the situation was resolved in the best and most favourable manner (God sanctify his spirit and illuminate his tomb).

[21] Account of his zeal for the cause of Jihad

God Almighty said, 'Those who strive in the Jihad on Our behalf, We shall verily guide their paths. God is with those that do good.'[1] Texts concerning the Jihad are numerous.

Saladin was very diligent in and zealous for the Jihad. If anyone were to swear that, since his embarking on the Jihad, he had not expended a single dinar or dirham on anything but the Jihad or support for it, he would be telling the truth and true in his oath. The Jihad, his love and passion for it, had taken a mighty hold on his heart and all his being, so much so that he talked of nothing else, thought of nothing but the means to pursue it, was concerned only with its manpower and had a fondness only for those who spoke of it and encouraged it. In his love for the Jihad on the path of God he shunned his womenfolk, his children, his homeland, his home and all his pleasures, and for this world he was content to dwell in the shade of his tent with the winds blowing through it left and right. One blustery night on the plain of Acre his tent collapsed on him. Had he not been in his 'tower', it would have killed him, but that only added to his eagerness, steadfastness and zeal.

If anyone wished to gain his favour, he would urge him to perform the Jihad or relate some of the traditions of Jihad. Numerous books on the Jihad were composed for him. I, too, am one of those who compiled a book on it for him. I brought together its practices and every Koranic verse or *ḥadīth* that has been transmitted concerning it, and I explained anything unusual. He frequently used to peruse it and in the end his son, al-Malik al-Afḍal, studied it with him.

[22] I shall relate something I heard him say. He had taken Kawkab in Dhū'l-Qa'da in the year 584 [January 1189] and given the troops leave to depart. The Egyptian army had begun to return to Egypt, commanded by his brother, al-'Ādil, and he journeyed with him to see him on his way and to benefit from praying at the Feast in Jerusalem (God Almighty protect it). We travelled in his retinue. After he had celebrated the Feast in Jerusalem, it occurred to him that he would proceed with them to Ascalon and take his leave of them there, then return by the coastal route to investigate the state of the coastal territories as far as Acre and to arrange their administration. They advised him not to do so, for when the troops departed we would be left in small numbers, while all the Franks were at Tyre and this was a great danger. However, he paid no attention and took leave of his brother and the armies at Ascalon.

---

1 Koran xxxix, 69.

We travelled in his service along the coast, making for Acre. The weather was very wintry and the sea was raging terribly with 'waves like mountains', as God said.[1] My experience of seeing the sea was very recent. The thought of the sea was terrible to me, so much so that I imagined that, had someone with the power said to me, 'If you cross one mile of the sea, I will make you king of the world,' I would not have done it, and I considered those who put to sea in the hope of gaining a dinar or a dirham to be quite stupid and I approved of the opinion of those who would not accept the testimony of a seafarer.

All this came to my mind because of the great dread which I experienced from the motion and billowing of the sea. While I was thinking this, he turned to me and said, 'Shall I tell you something?' 'Of course,' I said. He went on, 'I have it in mind that, when God Almighty has enabled me to conquer the rest of the coast, I shall divide up the lands, make my testament, take my leave and set sail on this sea to their islands to pursue them there until there no longer remain on the face of the earth any who deny God - or die [in the attempt]'. These words had a great effect on me since they totally contradicted the thoughts I was having. I said to him, **[23]** 'There is no-one on earth more courageous than our lord and none stronger of purpose than he to aid the religion of God.' 'How so?' he asked. I replied, 'Because, as for courage, the state of this sea and its terrors do not frighten our lord, and, as for aiding the religion of God, our lord will not be satisfied with uprooting God's enemies from a particular place on the earth until he has purified the whole earth of them.'

I asked him leave to tell the thoughts that came to my mind. He granted leave, so I told him as follows: 'This is surely an excellent purpose, but let our lord dispatch troops by sea. He is the bastion and bulwark of Islam and it is not right that he should risk his person.' He said, 'I shall ask your legal opinion. What is the noblest of deaths?' 'Death on the path of God,' I said. He continued, 'What aim compares with my dying the noblest of deaths?' Consider this mind, how pure it was, and this soul, how courageous and gallant! O God, You know that he bestowed his efforts to aid Your religion, in the hope of Your mercy, so show him mercy.

[24] Remarkable examples of his endurance and his winning credit in Heaven

God (Almighty and Glorious is He) said, '[For those who] ... then strove and endured, your Lord later is forgiving and merciful.'[2]

On the plain of Acre I saw Saladin overcome by an extremely poor state of health on account of numerous boils which had appeared on his body from his

---

1 Cf. Koran xi, 42.
2 Koran xvi, 110.

waist to his knees, so that he was unable to sit down. He would simply lie on his side if he was in his tent, and he refused to have food served him because of his inability to sit. He ordered it to be distributed to the troops. Nevertheless, he had taken his station in his campaign tent close to the enemy and had disposed the troops as left wing, right wing and centre, in battle formation. Despite all, he rode from early morning till the noonday prayer, going the rounds of the battalions, and also from late afternoon until the sunset prayer, enduring the intense pain and the violent throbbing of the boils, while I expressed my amazement at that. He would say, 'When I ride, the pain goes away, until I dismount.' This is divine solicitude.

When we were at al-Kharrūba he was ill, having retired from Tell al-'Ajūl[1] on account of his illness. The Franks got to hear of this and sallied out, desirous of gaining some advantage over the Muslims. This was the engagement at the river. They advanced a day's march as far as the wells which were below the hill. Saladin ordered the baggage to be prepared for departure and a withdrawal towards Nazareth. The lord of Sinjār, 'Imād al-Dīn,[2] was **[25]** also in poor health and Saladin gave permission for him to withdraw with the baggage, but he himself remained. The following day the enemy rode out to attack us. Despite pain, he mounted his horse and drew up the army in battle formation to meet them. He placed on the extreme right wing al-'Ādil and on the extreme left Taqī al-Dīn. His two sons, al-Ẓāhir and al-Afḍal, he stationed in the centre. He himself took position beyond the enemy with his troop. As soon as he descended from the hill, a Frank who had been taken prisoner was brought before him. He ordered his head to be cut off, which was done in his presence, after the man had been offered Islam and had rejected it. Whenever the enemy moved, aiming for the head of the river, he circled around behind them to cut them off from their tents, riding for a while and then dismounting to rest, shading himself with a kerchief on his head from the severe effect of the sun but not erecting any tent for himself so that the enemy would not spy any weakness.

He so continued until the enemy camped at the head of the river while he camped opposite them on a hill overlooking them until nightfall. Then, on his orders, the armies of Islam returned to a defensive stance, instructed to spend the night under arms. He himself retired, with us attending upon him, to the summit of the hill, where a small tent was pitched for him. The doctor and I spent the whole of that night tending and distracting him, while he slept fitfully

---

1 *Nawādir* reads al-Ḥajl, as does Bodleian Ms. Marsh 515, fol. 13a. There is a lacuna in B at this point. Wilson, *Saladin*, p. 28: '[it] seems to be near *Tell el-'Ajjûl* noticed later'. This is the only mention of Tell al-Ḥajl and the situation described here appears to be the same as on p. 135 below, where Tell al-'Ajūl is given. I have emended accordingly.

2 'Imād al-Dīn Zankī, a nephew of Nūr al-Dīn Maḥmūd, died in 594/1197 (Ibn al-Athīr, *Kāmil*, xii, p. 132).

until dawn broke. The trumpet sounded and he along with the troops mounted up and surrounded the enemy, who moved back to their tents on the west back of the river. That day the Muslims pressed them terribly hard.

Also on that day, to win credit in heaven, he sent forward his sons, al-Ẓāhir, al-Afḍal and al-Ẓāfir, and all who were with him. He continued to send forward everyone with him until only the doctor and I remained in attendance along with the Inspector of the Army and the pages with flags and banners in their hands, nothing more. Anyone looking from a distance would have thought that a vast host stood beneath them, but there was only one man, worth a vast host. The enemy remained on the move, suffering losses the while. Whenever a person was killed they buried him, and if anyone was wounded they carried him so no-one would be left behind to reveal the number of their dead and wounded. They marched on while we observed them. In the end their situation became very serious and they camped at the bridge. Whenever the Franks dismounted and made camp the Muslims despaired of gaining any success over them because in their dismounted state they defended themselves very strongly.

With the troops on horseback, he remained in his position facing the enemy until the end of the day and then ordered that they should spend the night [**26**] as they had yesterday. We returned to our camping spot of the previous night and passed the night as we had before. At dawn we resumed our close pressure on the enemy. They broke camp and moved off as before, fighting and suffering losses, until they came near to their tents, from where extra support joined them, and so they managed to reach their tents.

Consider this endurance and zeal for heavenly credit and what heights this man attained! O God, You inspired in him endurance and zeal and You gave him his success. Do not deprive him of his reward, O most merciful of the merciful.

I saw him when he received the news of [the death of][1] a son of his, already past puberty or approaching it, called Ismā'īl.[2] He read the letter but told nobody (we did not know about it until we heard it from others) and showed no affect of that on his face, apart from the fact that, when he read the letter, his eye shed a tear.

One night at Ṣafad when he was besieging it, I was with him when he said, 'Tonight we shall not sleep until we have erected five trebuchets.'[3] He assigned

1 This addition is found in the text as quoted in *Rawḍ*, ii, p. 222.

2 For this son of Saladin who predeceased him, see Sibṭ ibn al-Jawzī, *Mir'āt*,

3 The Arabic term is *manjānīq*. pl. *majānīq*. There is an extensive schola[illegible] typology, terminology and dating of mediaeval siege weapons, summarised in Rogers, *Latin Siege Warfare etc.*, Appendix III: [illegible] The likelihood is that the *majānīq* met with in this text [illegible] characterised by a traction-operated lever or beam. See [illegible] 1973, pp. 99-116. Trebuchets were described in a tre[illegible]

men to each one who would be responsible for setting it up. All night long we were in attendance on him (God sanctify his spirit) in a most pleasant humour and delightful companionship, while messengers were coming one after another to announce that such-and-such had been erected on this trebuchet and this-and-that on another, until there came [27] the dawn and everything had been finished, except that all that remained was to fit their 'sows'.[1] It had, moreover, been one of the longest nights and one of the coldest and wettest.

I also observed him at the time when the news of the death of Taqī al-Dīn 'Umar, his nephew, came to him. We were facing the Franks without our baggage train at Ramla. Every night there would be shouts, the tents would be struck and the troops be in the saddle until dawn. In our position at Ramla there was only a gallop between us and them. He summoned al-'Ādil, 'Alam al-Dīn Sulaymān ibn Jandar, Sābiq al-Dīn ibn al-Dāya and 'Izz al-Dīn ibn al-Muqaddam and he ordered the men to be driven away from near his tent, so that no-one remained closer than a bow-shot. Then he produced the letter, read it and wept so bitterly that he reduced us to tears without our knowing the cause. Choked by his tears, he said, 'Taqī al-Dīn is dead.' He and the company wept bitterly, but I recovered myself and said, 'All ask pardon of God for this response. Consider where you are, what you are about, and ignore all else.' Saladin said, 'Yes, I ask pardon of God,' which he took to repeating, finally saying, 'No-one must learn of this.' He requested some rose water and washed his eyes, then he had some food brought. His staff attended and no-one knew about it until the enemy retired to Jaffa and we withdrew to Latrun, where our heavy baggage was based.

Saladin (God have mercy on him) was greatly fond of and solicitous for his young children, though he bore parting with them manfully and accepted their absence from him. He endured bitter and harsh conditions of life, although fully able to live differently, to gain credit with God. O God, he gave up all that in his desire for Your good pleasure, so be pleased with him and show him mercy.

'Alī, which has been studied and translated by Cahen, 'Un traité etc.'. An English translation will be found in Lewis, *Islam etc.*, i, pp. 218-223.

[1] *Khanāzīr* , sing. *khinzīra* 'sow', the term for the axle, on which the beam of the trebuchet pivots (see Cahen, 'Un traité etc.,' pp. 141-142; 157-1588). Al-Khwārizmī, *Mafātīḥ al-'ulūm*, p. 249, described the *khinzīra* as 'part of the mechanism [of the trebuchet], something like a pulley except that it is oblong in shape.' In the illuminating article by Chevedden, 'The Hybrid Trebuchet', fig. 4 shows the installation of a trebuchet: 'The chief engineer is guiding the axle bearings of the rotating beam onto the journal blocks surmounting the two trestles.'

[28] Some random remarks on his forbearance and clemency

God (Almighty and Glorious is He) said, '... and those who forgive people, for God loves those that do good.'[1]

He was forbearing, forgiving and rarely angry. I was in attendance on him at Marj 'Uyūn before the Franks marched upon Acre (may God facilitate its conquest). It was his custom to be out on horseback at the normal time for that, later to dismount for food to be served. He would eat with his staff, and then go to a personal tent to sleep. Later, when he awoke, he would pray and then relax in private, with me in attendance, when we would read a little Ḥadīth or a little canon law. He studied with me a digest by Sulaym al-Rāzī[2] which contained the 'four quarters' of law.[3]

One day he dismounted as usual, food was served, then he made as though to rise, but he was told, 'It is nearly time for prayer,' so he sat down again. 'We shall pray and sleep afterwards,' he said. He sat conversing, rather out of sorts, having dismissed all except his close courtiers. An old mamluke, much respected by him, approached and presented him with a petition on behalf of one of the warriors. Saladin said, 'I am tired now. Keep it for a while.' Taking no notice, he thrust the petition close to Saladin's dear face and opened it so that he could read it. His eye fell on the name written at the head of the petition and he recognised it. 'A worthy man,' he said. The mamluke said, 'Will the lord then endorse his petition?' to which the sultan answered, 'I do not have my pen-box to hand at the moment.' Saladin was sitting at the entrance to his tent, so placed that no-one could enter. The pen-box was by the back wall of the tent, which was a big one. The man who had addressed him said, 'There is the pen-box at the back of the tent.' This could mean nothing but 'Fetch it.' Saladin turned around, saw the pen-box and said, 'By God, he's right.' **[29]** Then, leaning back on his left arm, he stretched out his right and reached it. He endorsed the petition, and I said, 'God Almighty said concerning his Prophet, "Verily you are of a noble character."[4] I can only think that our lord shares the same character with him.' He replied, 'We were not put out in any way. We settled his business - and the reward [in Heaven] is ours.'

Had some persons and certain individuals had this happen to them, they would have been furious. Who could address his superior in such a way! This is the ultimate in kindness and forbearance, and God does not neglect to reward those that do good.

---

1 Koran iii, 134.

2 *Nawādir* reads 'Sulaymān' but Sulaym is given in B and in the quotation found in *Rawḍ*, ii, p. 223. Abū'l-Fatḥ Sulaym ibn Ayyūb was a Shāfi'ī lawyer who settled in Tyre and died in 447/1055 (Ibn Khallikān, *Wafāyāt*, ii, pp. 397-399).

3 Presumably the reference is to the four 'roots' of Islamic legal knowledge, the Koran, the Sunna, the 'consensus' (*ijmā'*) and analogy (*qiyās*).

4 Koran lxviii, 4.

His cushion was sometimes trodden on when people crowded in on him to present petitions, but he was not at all affected by that. One day my mule shied away from the camels while I was riding in attendance on him, and it pressed painfully on his thigh, but he was smiling. On a windy and rainy day I preceded him into Jerusalem, when it was very muddy. My mule spattered him with mud, so that it ruined all he was wearing, but once again he was laughing. I wanted to drop behind him on that account, but he would not let me.

From those that sought his help or those that complained to him he would listen to the strongest language that could be heard and meet it with a complaisant smile. There follows an anecdote the like of which is rarely to be recorded.

The brother of the king of the Franks (may God forsake them) had set out for Jaffa, for our troops had withdrawn some distance from them and fallen back to Latrun, which is a place two days march from Jaffa for troops on a forced march but three for normal travelling. Saladin assembled his forces and proceeded to Caesarea to confront their reinforcements in the hope of gaining some success over them. The Franks who were in Jaffa learnt of this. It was the king of England who was there with a number of troops. He sent most of those he had with him in ships to Caesarea, fearing for the reinforcements that some disaster might happen to them. The king himself remained with a small force because they knew that the sultan and his troops were far away from them.

When Saladin arrived at Caesarea and saw that the reinforcements had already arrived and were safely within the walls, he realised that he would not achieve what he planned, so he immediately travelled all night long and came to Jaffa in the morning. The king of England, leading seventeen knights and three hundred foot-soldiers, was camped in a tent outside the town. Our troops offered him battle that morning. He, the accursed one, got to horse (for he was brave, valiant and expert in battle) and stood his ground, not entering the town. The Muslim army surrounded them except in [**30**] the direction of the town and was drawn up in battle formation. The sultan ordered the troops to charge, to seize this opportunity, but some of the Kurdish emirs answered with rough words, the nub of which was a reproof because of the insufficiency of their feudal grants. The sultan tugged on his horse's reins like a man in anger, because he knew that they would do nothing that day. He left them and went away. He commanded his tent which had been erected to be dismantled. Everyone melted away from the enemy, convinced that the sultan would probably gibbet and execute several persons that day.

Saladin's son, al-Ẓāhir related to me that on that day he was so fearful of him that he did not dare fall into his sight, although he had charged deeply [into the enemy] that day and even been restrained by the sultan. Saladin kept going and eventually camped at Yāzūr, which was a short stage. A small tent was pitched for him there, which he occupied, while the troops camped beneath small bivouacs,[1] as was customary at that time. There was not a single emir who did not shake with fear and believe that he was about to be arrested and reprimanded. Al-Ẓāhir said, 'I could not persuade myself to attend on him, such was my anxiety, until finally he called for me. I came into his presence just after a lot of fruit had arrived from Damascus. He said, "Fetch the emirs so that they can eat some." My worries were dispelled and I went to seek the emirs, who presented themselves very fearfully, but they found him in a happy and relaxed mood which restored their confidence, trust and contentment. They left him planning to break camp, just as if nothing at all had happened.'

Consider such forbearance which is not met with in times like these nor related of men of his position in previous generations (God's mercy be upon him).

[31] Account of his observance of chivalrous behaviour

The Prophet (God bless him and give him peace) said, 'I was sent to perfect noble qualities of character.'[2]

Whenever the Prophet shook hands with someone he would not let go his hand until that person had taken the initiative to do so. The sultan too was a paragon of chivalry, generous, extremely modest and had a welcoming face for any guests that arrived. He would not countenance any guest leaving him until he had been fed, nor that anyone should approach him on any matter without his seeing to it.

He received graciously anyone that came to him on a mission, even if he were an infidel. The prince, lord of Antioch, visited him, and the first he was aware of this was when he was standing at the door of his tent in the month of Shawwāl 588 [October 1192], this being after peace had been made, when he was returning from Jerusalem to Damascus. The prince confronted him during his journey and made a request. The sultan gave him al-'Amq,[3] which is territory he had taken from him the year the coast was conquered, that is, 584 [1188].

When the lord of Sidon visited him at Nazareth, I saw how the sultan honoured him and received him graciously, ate a meal with him and, in addition, proposed that he should convert to Islam, telling him of some of its special excellencies and urging him to take the step.

He used to receive with honour the scholars, the men of learning and letters, and individuals of high reputation that came to him, urging us not to overlook

1 Dozy gives the singular *ṣīwān*, which is from the Persian *sāyabān* 'tent, parasol'.
2 This *ḥadīth* is found, with a small variation of wording, in Mālik, *al-Muwaṭṭa'*, p. 382.
3 Literally 'the Depression', the alluvial plain north-east of Antioch (see *EI²*, i, pp. 109-111).

any noted scholars that passed by our tents without bringing them to him so that he could reward them with his liberality.

In the year 584 [1188-9] we were visited by a man who encompassed both religious learning and mystic devotion. He was a man of high repute, whose father was the former lord of Tabrīz. He rejected his father's calling and occupied himself with learning and good works. He went on pilgrimage, then came to visit Jerusalem. Having satisfied his pious wishes and seen the results of the sultan's efforts there, he conceived a wish to visit him, and so came to us at the royal camp. The first I knew of him was when he entered my tent. I received him and made him welcome, then asked the reason for his coming. He told me and said that he especially desired to visit the sultan because of the excellent and admirable good works of his that he had seen. I informed the sultan that **[32]** night of this person's arrival and he summoned him. The sultan heard an *ḥadīth* from him, thanked him on behalf of Islam and urged him to do good. Then we left together and he spent the night with me in my tent. After we had prayed the dawn prayer, he started to say goodbye to me, so I upbraided him for going without taking leave of the sultan, but he paid no attention and ignored my words. He said, 'I have completed my business with him. I have no aim apart from seeing and visiting him,' and he departed immediately. Several nights later the sultan questioned me about him and I told him what he had done. His face showed signs of vexation that I had not informed him of his departure. 'How may such a man come visiting,' he said, 'and leave us without a touch of our benevolence?'

He was severely critical of me for that and I found I could not avoid writing a letter to Muḥyī al-Dīn,[1] the Qāḍī of Damascus, in which I charged him with enquiring after the man and delivering a note to him which I enclosed in my letter. I told him of the sultan's disapproval of his leaving without meeting him, and I urged him to come back, for the friendship between us demanded no less. The next I knew he had returned to me, so I wrote a note and informed the sultan of that. He wrote in reply, 'Please bring him with you [to see me],' which I did. He welcomed him in a friendly manner, saying how much he had wished to see him again. He kept him for several days and then rewarded him with a fine robe of honour, gave him a fitting mount and much apparel to take to his family, his servants and neighbours, and money for his needs. The man then took his leave, full of gratitude and sincere blessings on the sultan's reign.

I was present once when there had been brought before him a Frankish prisoner, who was awestruck, so much so that signs of his fear and dread were obvious. The dragoman said to him, 'What are you fearful of?' God prompted his tongue to say, 'I was fearful before I saw this blessed face. After seeing him

---

1 This is Muḥyī al-Dīn Muḥammad ibn Zakī al-Dīn 'Alī, born 550/1155-6 and died 598/1202, who preached the first khutbah in Jerusalem after the reconquest, which is quoted in his biographical entry in Ibn Khallikān, *Wafāyāt*, iv, pp. 229-237.

and coming before him, I am convinced that I shall see nothing but good.' The sultan relented towards him and graciously freed him.

One day I was on horseback in attendance on him face to face with the Franks when one of the forward pickets arrived with a woman in great distress, bitterly weeping and continually beating her breast. The man said, 'This woman has come out from the Frankish lines and asked to be brought to you, so we have done so.' The sultan ordered the dragoman to question here about her business. She said, 'Muslim thieves [**33**] entered my tent yesterday and stole my daughter. I spent all night until this morning pleading for help. I was told, "Their prince is a merciful man. We shall send you out to him to ask him for your daughter." So they sent me to you, and only from you will I learn of my daughter.' The sultan took pity on her. His tears flowed and, prompted by his chivalry, he ordered someone to go to the army market to ask who had bought the little girl, to repay what had been given for her and bring her back, having heard something about her early that day. Hardly an hour had passed before the horseman arrived with the little girl over his shoulder. The moment the woman's eye lighted on her, she fell to the ground, besmirching her face with earth, while all around wept for what she had suffered. She was lifting her eyes to heaven, although we did not know what she was saying. Her daughter was handed to her, then she was taken off and restored to their camp.

The sultan thought it not right to ill-treat those in his service, even if they seriously betrayed him. Two bags of Egyptian gold coins in his treasure chest were replaced by two bags of copper coins. He did nothing with the officials except dimiss them from their jobs, nothing more.

Prince Reynald,[1] the lord of Kerak, came before him with the king of the Franks on the coast, after both had been taken prisoner at the battle of Ḥaṭṭīn during the year 583 [1188]. The battle is famous and will be described in its proper place, God willing. He had given orders for both to be brought before him. This accursed Reynald was a monstrous infidel and terrible oppressor, through whose land a caravan from Egypt (God defend it) had passed when there was a truce between the Muslims and the Franks. He seized it treacherously, maltreated and tortured its members and held them in dungeons and close confinement. They reminded him of the truce, but he replied, 'Tell your Muḥammad to release you.'

When Saladin heard what he had said, he vowed that, when God gave him into his hands, he would personally slay him. After God had delivered him into his power on that day, he was fully determined to kill him in fulfilment of his vow. He summoned him with the king. The king complained of thirst, so the sultan had a glass of sherbet brought for him, from which he drank. Then Reynald took it, at which the sultan said to the dragoman, 'Say to the king,

---

1 In Arabic: Arnāṭ. This is Reynald (or Reginald) of Châtillon, sometime prince of Antioch and lord of Transjordan.

"You are the one who gave him the drink. I give him no drink nor any of my food.'" What he meant was 'If anyone eats my food, chivalry would demand that I harm him not.' Later he struck off his head with his own hand to fulfil his vow.

When he took Acre, he released all the prisoners from their narrow confinement. There were about [**34**] 4,000 of them. To each of them he gave expenses to allow them to reach their home town and their family. I heard this from the lips of several of them, because I was not present on that campaign.

The sultan was very sociable, well-mannered and of a pleasant wit. He knew by heart the genealogies of the Arabs and their [ancient] battles and was knowledgeable about their past histories and ways. He knew the pedigrees of their horses and had studied the wonders and rarities of this world, so that anyone who conversed with him could gain knowledge of things that could be heard from no-one else.

In his kindness of heart he would ask one of our number about his health, what treatment he was having, his diet and drinks, and how his affairs progressed. His gatherings were decent and respectable. Nothing but good was ever mentioned about anyone in his presence. He disliked gossip, not wishing to hear anything but good of a person. His language was pure, for I never saw him fond of cursing. His pen was also pure, for he never wrote anything to harm a Muslim. He was loyal and faithful. No orphan was ever brought before him without his blessing the dead relative, expressing his distress and giving him the fief of the departed. If the orphan had an elder relative on whom he could depend, he would entrust him to that person, but if not, he would maintain for the orphan sufficient of the fief to meet his needs and hand him over to someone who would take care of his upbringing and act as his guardian. He could never see an old man without feeling pity and giving him generous gifts. He never changed these ways until God received him into His mercy seat and the abode of His favour.

These are some random remarks on the excellencies of his character and his noble qualities which I have limited myself to for fear of prolixity and wearying [the reader]. I have only recorded what I witnessed or what trustworthy sources told me which I have checked. This is a portion of what I learnt during my service with him. It is negligible compared with what others learnt who accompanied him for a long time and who were earlier in his service. However, this amount will suffice an intelligent person as evidence of the purity of these morals and qualities of his.

Since this part is completed, we shall now embark on the second part of the book concerning his changing fortunes and his battles and victories (may God sanctify his spirit and illumine his tomb with the light of His mercy).

Second Part

containing

an exposition

of

his changing fortunes,

his battles

and his victories

in their chronological order

(God sanctify his spirit

and

illumine his tomb)

Second Part

[36] Account of his first expedition to Egypt in the company of his uncle, Asad al-Dīn

The reason for this was that a man called Dirghām had rebelled against Shāwar, the vizier of the Egyptians,[1] desiring his office and position. Dirghām gathered many troops, which Shāwar was unable to withstand, and so was defeated and expelled from Cairo. Dirghām killed his son, seized Cairo and assumed the vizierate.

If any person overcame the holder of the office and the holder of the office was unable to resist him, and people realised his inability, it was the custom of the Egyptians to recognise the victor by assigning him the position and giving him control, for their power came through the forces of their vizier, who in their manner was titled 'sultan'. They did not believe in enquiring too closely and their aims and practices had followed this established pattern from the beginning of their rule.

When Shāwar had been defeated and expelled from Cairo, he was eager to make for Syria, planning to attend upon Nūr al-Dīn ibn Zankī to seek his aid and the support of his troops against his enemies. Nūr al-Dīn ordered Asad al-Dīn Shīrkūh to leave for Egypt to perform their obligations towards a visiting suppliant and to spy out the land and learn its state of affairs. That was in the year 558 [1163]. Asad al-Dīn Shīrkūh made his preparations and then departed for Egypt, taking with him Saladin, although he was reluctant, because Asad al-Dīn so relied on him. He made him commander of his forces and his adviser. They set out and came to Egypt, along with Shāwar, on 2 Jumādā II 558 [8 May 1163].

Their arrival in Egypt had a great effect and terrified the population. Shāwar was victorious over his rival and Asad al-Dīn restored him to his office and rank and firmly established his position and power. He also saw the country first hand and learnt its current state. He withdrew with an ambition to win the land implanted in his heart and having learnt that it was a land without men, where the system continued by mere delusion and in impossible ways.

---

1 By 'Egyptians', the Fatimid caliphs are meant.

[37] He began his withdrawal from Egypt to return to Syria on 7 Dhū'l-Ḥijja in the above-mentioned year [6 November 1163]. He decided nothing and settled no matter without Saladin's advice and opinion, because of the signs of an auspicious future and sound ideas that he discerned in him. All that he did was crowned with success. Asad al-Dīn remained in Syria, laying his plans and thinking how to return to Egypt, dreaming of this and preparing the basis for this with al-'Ādil Nūr al-Dīn until the year 562 [1166-7].

Account of his return to Egypt and the reason for it. This is noted for the Battle of al-Bābayn[1]

Asad al-Dīn continued to talk about this amongst people until it came to the hearing of Shāwar, who was obsessed by fear of a Turkish invasion. He realised that Asad al-Dīn was ambitious to seize the country and that he would inevitably attack it. He therefore wrote to the Franks and agreed with them that they would come to Egypt, maintain him in full control and aid him to extirpate his enemies so that his foot[2] would be firmly established there. This came to the ears of Asad al-Dīn and al-'Ādil Nūr al-Dīn, who feared greatly that the infidels would take Egypt and gain control of all its land. Asad al-Dīn therefore made his preparations. Al-'Ādil Nūr al-Dīn sent troops with him and compelled the sultan (may God have mercy on him) to accompany him despite his being very unwilling.

They set out during the month of Rabī' I 562 [December 1166-January 1167] and they arrived in Egypt simultaneously with the Franks. [38] Shāwar acted in concert with the Franks and all the Egyptians against Asad al-Dīn. There were many engagements and fierce battles, and then the Franks withdrew from Egypt as did Asad al-Dīn. The reason for the Franks' departure was that Nūr al-Dīn sent his troops into their lands, where he took Munayṭira. Hearing of this, the Franks feared for their lands and so withdrew. The reason why Asad al-Dīn withdrew was the weakness of his army, because of the alliance of the Franks and the Egyptians and because of the hardships endured and the terrible things witnessed. However, he did not withdraw until he had reached an agreement with the Franks that they would all retire from Egypt.

He returned to Syria in the remainder of the year, having added to his strong desire to win the country an intense fear that the Franks might seize it, as he now knew that they had reconnoitred it as he himself had and they had got to know it in the same way that he had. He remained in Syria most reluctantly and with an

1 The site, near al-Ashmunayn, where Shirkūh defeated a combined Fatimid and Crusader force.

2 Reading with B and the text of *Rawḍ*, i, p. 367: *qadamuhu* (instead of *qalbuhu*, 'his heart').

anxious heart, while fate was drawing him towards something that was [in fact] destined for another, although he was quite unaware of that.

In Rajab 562 [April-May 1167] Nūr al-Dīn took the castle of Munayṭira[1] after Asad al-Dīn's departure and destroyed the castle of Akāf in the hinterland north of Damascus.

In Ramaḍān this year [June-July 1167] Nūr al-Dīn with his brother Quṭb al-Dīn and also Zayn al-Dīn assembled at Ḥamā for a raiding expedition. They entered Frankish territory and destroyed Hūnīn in Shawwāl [July-August 1167].

In Dhū'l-Qa'da this year [August-September 1167] Asad al-Dīn returned from Egypt, and Qarā Arslān died in Diyār Bakr.

Account of their return to Egypt for the third time, which is when they conquered it, and other events that occurred in the year 564 [1168-9]

This came about because the Franks (God forsake them) gathered their foot and their horse and marched towards Egypt, breaking all the terms of the peace that had been agreed with the Egyptians and Asad al-Dīn, in their eagerness for the country. When Nūr al-Dīn and Asad al-Dīn heard of that, they could not tolerate it, but hastened to send an expedition.

Nūr al-Dīn provided money and men but did not go in person because he feared the Franks would attack his lands and because his attention was drawn **[39]** towards Mosul by reason of the death of Zayn al-Dīn 'Alī ibn Baktakīn[2] (God have mercy on him), who died during Dhū'l-Ḥijja 563 [September-October 1168][3] and surrendered all the castles that he possessed, apart from Irbil, to Quṭb al-Dīn Atabeg, for he had held them all from the Atabeg Zankī. For this reason, Nūr al-Dīn developed ambitions in that direction and sent troops.[4] Asad al-Dīn, however, went in person and provided money, family and manpower. The sultan once said to me, 'I was the most unwilling of men to leave [for Egypt] on this occasion. It was not by my own choice that I left with my uncle.' The words of God Almighty, 'It is possible for you to dislike a thing, though it is the best for you,'[5] are apposite here. When Shāwar had become aware that the Franks had set out for Egypt as described, he sent to Asad al-Dīn to request his aid and support. The latter left hurriedly and arrived at Cairo during the month of Rabī' I in the year 564 [December 1168].

---

1 A fortress in Mt Lebanon guarding the pass from Baalbek to the sea. Akāf, mentioned just below, is unidentified.

2 The emir of Irbil.

3 See Ibn Khallikān, *Wafāyāt*, iv, p. 114.

4 B adds a phrase: *hādhā al-sabab fīhi al-fikr*, 'There is some doubt about this reason'.

5 Koran ii, 216.

This year, that is 564, in Muḥarram [October 1168] Nūr al-Dīn gained the castle of Ja'bar, which he bought from its lord, Ibn Mālik, after his capture, in return for Sarūj, Bāb Buzā'a and al-Malūḥa. This same month Yārūq died after whom al-Yārūqiyya takes its name.[1]

After the Franks had learnt of Asad al-Dīn's arrival in Egypt by agreement of the latter and the locals, they withdrew, retracing their steps. Asad al-Dīn took up residence there with Shāwar coming to visit him from time to time. Shāwar had promised them substantial monies in return for the sums they had expended, but he did not deliver anything to them. Asad al-Dīn's grasp on the land tightened, for they knew that if the Franks found an opportunity, they would seize the country and that their own coming and going each time was useless, that Shāwar was playing with them and the Franks alternately, and that the country's rulers were notorious followers of a false creed.[2] While Shāwar survived they knew that there was no way they could take over the land. Therefore they concerted their plan to seize him if he visited them. They frequently waited upon him without Asad al-Dīn, while Shāwar would on some occasions go to meet Asad al-Dīn.

[**40**] Shāwar used to ride in the fashion of their viziers, with drums, trumpets and banners, and only the sultan himself was bold enough to seize him from amongst his retinue. In fact, when Shāwar came riding towards them, Saladin met him on horseback and rode at his side. He caught hold of his collar and ordered his troops to seize his followers. The latter fled and were robbed by the soldiers. Shāwar was arrested and placed in a separate tent. Straightaway there came a warrant from the Egyptians by the hand of a palace eunuch, saying, 'We must have his head,' following their custom in the matter of viziers to establish the position of anyone who gains the upper hand over his rival. Shāwar's neck was severed and his head sent to them.

The vizieral investiture robe was sent to Asad al-Dīn, who donned it, then proceeded to the palace where he was installed as vizier. This was on 17 Rabī' II 564 [18 January 1169]. He remained the ultimate authority, ordering and forbidding, while the sultan dealt with and settled daily affairs, since the responsibility for ordering and forbidding was entrusted to him because of the level of his competence, his knowledge and his good judgement and governance, until 22 Jumādā II of the above year [22 March 1169].

---

1 The castle of Ja'bar on the left bank of the Euphrates north of Raqqa (see *EI*^{2}, ii, p. 354, s.v. Ḳal'at Dja'bar). It had been held by emirs of the Uqaylid clan since the time of the Seljuq Malikshāh. Sarūj is the modern Sürüc just in Turkey (*EI*^{2}, ix, pp. 68-69). Bāb Buzā'a is the modern Bāb, about 40 km east of Aleppo, a western extension of the ancient Buzā'a (*EI*^{2}, i, pp. 1357-1358). Al-Yārūqiyya was a suburb of Aleppo, previously called al-Ḥāḍir and largely settled in the Zengid period by Turkomans led by Yārūq (Elisséef, *Nūr al-Dīn*, iii, p. 870).

2 That is, Ismā'īlī Shiism.

Account of Asad al-Dīn's death and the passing of authority to the sultan

It was the case that Asad al-Dīn was a great eater, excessively given to partaking of rich meats. He suffered many bouts of indigestion and from quinsy, from which he would recover after putting up with great discomfort. He was taken severely ill, afflicted with a serious quinsy, which killed him on 22 Jumādā II 564 [22 March 1169]. After him authority was entrusted to the sultan. His power base became firm and affairs prospered in excellent order. He bestowed money and distributed property. Temporal matters yielded to him and he took control, thanking God for His blessings. He renounced wine, gave up vain pastimes and donned the garments of seriousness and pious endeavour. He never retreated from that, but grew ever more serious until God gathered him to His mercy.

[41] I have heard him say, 'After God had enabled me to gain Egypt, I understood that He planned the conquest of the coast because he planted that idea in my mind.' From the time his position was well established he did not cease to launch raids on the Franks, against Kerak and Shawbak and their districts, and he overwhelmed people with such showers of benefits and gifts as have been recorded for no other period. All this was while he was a vizier subject to the palace establishment, but was strengthening the Sunni cause and planting in the local population pious learning, law, Sufi practice and [true] religion. People flocked to him from every direction and sought him out from every quarter, while he never disappointed a petitioner nor deprived a suppliant. [This was the situation] until the year 565 [1169-70]. However, when Nūr al-Dīn heard that the sultan had gained firm power in Egypt, he took Ḥims from the lieutenants of Asad al-Dīn. This was in Rajab 564 [April 1169].

Account of the Franks' attack on Damietta (may God protect it)

When the Franks learnt what the Muslims and their troops had done and how the sultan had succeeded in establishing his position in Egypt, they realised that he would take their lands, ruin their territories and remove all traces of them, because of the power and might he had acquired. The Franks and the Byzantines met together and planned to attack Egypt, to take control and rule there. They decided to target Damietta because an attack there would give control of land and sea and because they knew that, if it became theirs, they would gain a strong foothold and refuge. They took with them trebuchets, **[42]** testudos, crossbows and all sorts of siege engines. On hearing this, the Franks in Syria took heart and stole the fortress of 'Akkār[1] from the Muslims and took prisoner its lord, who was a mamluke of Nūr al-Dīn, called Khutlukh the standard-bearer. This was in Rabī'

---

1 A castle about half-way between Ḥimṣ and Tripoli (see description in Elisséef, *Nūr al-Dīn*, i, 239-240).

II of this year [565] [December 1169-January 1170], while in Rajab [March-April 1170] there died al-'Imādī, the companion of Nūr al-Dīn and his Emir Ḥājib. He had been the lord of Baalbek and Tadmur.

When Nūr al-Dīn saw the Franks were active and heard of their descent on Damietta, he purposed to distract their hearts, so he put Kerak **[43]** under siege in Sha'bān of this year [April-May 1170]. When the Franks on the coast moved against him, he raised the siege and marched to meet them but they did not stand to face him.

Then he was informed of the death of Majd al-Dīn Ibn al-Dāya[1] in Aleppo, which took place in the month of Ramaḍān of the year 565 [May-June 1170]. He was deeply distressed because Majd al-Dīn had been his leading supporter. He set out to return to Damascus and then he heard of the earthquake in Aleppo which ruined much of the region. It occurred on 12 Shawwāl [29 June], when he was at 'Ashtarā.[2] He set out to go to Aleppo, but news came to him of the death of Quṭb al-Dīn, his brother, in Mosul. That happened on 22 Dhū'l-Ḥijja in the same year [6 September 1170]. He heard the news when he was at Tell Bāshir and that very night he departed, making for the Mosul region.

When the sultan realised the seriousness of the enemy's plan to attack Damietta, he sent to the town and supplied it with sufficient men, champion horsemen, supplies and weapons of war to make him confident of its defence. He promised the garrison that he would supply them with troops and supplies and harrass the enemy if they beseiged it. He was extremely lavish with his gifts and presents and was a strong vizier, whose order was countermanded in nothing. On the date previously mentioned the Franks descended on the city and they carried out serious assaults and attacks. Meanwhile, the sultan harried them from without and his troops resisted from within. God aided the Muslims with His support[3] and His plan to give victory to God's religion by helping and aiding them was excellent. Eventually, it was clear to the Franks that they had lost and that true faith had conquered unbelief. They decided to save their own heads and escape with their lives, so they withdrew disappointed and beaten. Their trebuchets were burnt and their equipment plundered. A large number of them were slain and, by the grace and favour of God, the land was delivered from their attack, and by God's help their hostile edge was clearly blunted and the sultan's position firmly entrenched.

---

1 The Ibn al-Dāya brothers were an influential family who held many castles. Majd al-Dīn Abū Bakr was Nūr al-Dīn's foster-brother, hence the family name 'son of the wet-nurse'.

2 In the Ḥawrān, south of Nawā (Yāqūt, iii, p. 679).

3 Reading *yu'ayyidu-hum* instead of *yu'dhī-him*.

[44] How he sent for his father

The sultan then sent to ask for his father [to join him], to complete his happiness and crown his joy. The situation has a similarity with what happened to the Prophet Joseph[1] (may God's blessings and peace be upon him and all the other prophets). It was during Jumādā II 565 [February-March 1170] that his father Najm al-Dīn came to join him. Saladin received him with all his customary respect and deference, and invested him with all his authority but Najm al-Dīn refused to accept it, saying, 'My son, God selected you alone for this task since you are equal to it and it is not fitting that the designated recipient of felicity should be changed.' However, Saladin gave him a free hand in all his treasuries. He was generous, giving and never taking back. The sultan continued to be a firm vizier until al-'Āḍid Abū Muḥammad 'Abd Allāh died and with him the dynasty of the Egyptians came to an end.

Meanwhile, Nūr al-Dīn took Raqqa in Muḥarram 566 [September-October 1170] and from there marched to Nisibis which he took during the rest of that month, and in Rabī' II [December 1170-January 1171] he took Sinjār. He then made for Mosul, not planning any attack on it. He and his army crossed the ford at Balad, marched on and then camped facing Mosul on a hill called the Fort. He made contact with his nephew, Sayf al-Dīn Ghāzī, the lord of Mosul, informing him that his intentions were not hostile. They came to terms and he entered Mosul on 13 Jumādā I [22 January 1171]. He confirmed its ruler in possession and gave him his daughter in marriage. He gave Sinjār to [Sayf al-Dīn's] brother, 'Imād al-Dīn, and left Mosul to return to Syria, entering Aleppo in Sha'bān of this year [April-May].

[45] The death of al-'Āḍid

The caliph's death occurred on Monday 10 Muḥarram 567 [13 September 1171] and temporal power passed firmly to the sultan. He had made the khutbah in the name of the Abbasids towards the end of al-'Āḍid's reign, while he was still alive. The khutbah was first made in the name of al-Mustaḍī' bi-Amr Allāh and the formalities continued in proper form. Whenever the sultan gained possession of a treasury, he gave it away, and whenever he gained access to state stores, he let them be seized without reserving anything for himself. He began to make preparations for an expedition to attack the enemy's lands, to lay plans for this and to settle all arrangements.

Nūr al-Dīn also planned an expedition and summoned the lord of Mosul, his nephew, who came with his troops to serve with him. This was the campaign

---

[1] In Arabic: Yūsuf, also Saladin's personal name.

against 'Arqā,[1] which Nūr al-Dīn, accompanied by his nephew, took in Muḥarram 567 [September-October 1171].

The first expedition launched from Egypt

The sultan continued to bestow justice, extend his liberality and spread his bounty upon people until the year 568 [1172-3]. At that time he marched out with his troops against the territory of Kerak, which he began with because it was the nearest and because it was an obstacle on the route of anyone travelling to Egypt. No caravan was able to get through unless he went out in person to convey it through the enemy's lands. He wished to widen and improve the road so that the regions might be in contact one with another, and to make things easier for travellers. He took the field against Kerak during the year 568 and put it under siege. There were various engagements between him and the Franks, but he withdrew without any success against the place on this occasion, and yet he gained the reward for his intentions.

Nūr al-Dīn, on the other hand, conquered Mar'ash in Dhū'l-Qa'da of this year [June-July 1173] and then in Dhū'l-Ḥijja [July-August] he took Bahasnā.

[46] Account of the death of his father Najm al-Dīn

When the sultan returned from his expeditions he heard, before his arrival in Egypt, of the death of his father Najm al-Dīn. This pained him greatly since he was not present at his end. The cause of his death was a fall from his horse. He was a fierce rider, passionately fond of polo, so much so that anyone who saw him play would say, 'It is a fall from a horse that is certain to kill him.' He died in Cairo during the year 568 [1172-3].

Account of the conquest of Yemen

In the year 569 [1173-4] the sultan considered the might of his troops, the large number of his brothers and the strength of their valour. He had heard that in Yemen a man had taken control and seized the local fortresses and that he had had his own name, which was 'Abd al-Nabī ibn Mahdī,[2] proclaimed in the Friday khutbah. He was claiming that his rule would spread throughout the

---

1 A town and citadel north of Tripoli, a little way inland (Le Strange, *Palestine*, pp. 397-398, s.v. 'Arkah).

2 'Abd al-Nabī ibn 'Alī ibn Mahdī, the last of a short-lived dynasty in Zabīd, was executed in 571/1176 (*EI*[2], v, pp. 1244-1245).

whole earth and that his cause would prosper. The sultan decided to dispatch his eldest brother, Shams al-Dawla al-Malik al-Muʿaẓẓam Tūrānshāh, to Yemen. He was a noble and generous man of excellent character. I heard Saladin praise his nobility and the fine points of his character and rate him higher than himself.

Tūrānshāh set out for Yemen during the month of Rajab 569 [February-March 1174]. After his arrival, God made him His agent for its conquest. The rebel heretic was killed and Tūrānshāh, having taken control of most of the land, distributed it and enriched a great number of people.

[47] The death of Nūr al-Dīn Maḥmūd ibn Zankī

Nūr al-Dīn's death also occurred as the result of a quinsy which afflicted him. The doctors were unable to treat it and he died on Wednesday 11 Shawwāl 569 [15 May 1174] in the citadel of Damascus. He was succeeded by his son, al-Malik al-Ṣāliḥ Ismāʿīl.

The sultan related to me as follows: 'We had heard that Nūr al-Dīn would perhaps attack us in Egypt. Several of our comrades advised that he should be openly resisted and his authority rejected and that his army should be met in battle to repel it if his hostile move became a reality. I alone disagreed with them, urging that it was not right to say anything of that sort. Our difference of opinion lasted until news of his death arrived.'

The rebellion of Kanz al-Dawla in Aswān during the year 570 [1174-5]

Kanz al-Dawla, one of the generals of the Egyptians, had withdrawn to Aswān and based himself there, where he continued to govern independently and gather black [troops] around himself, allowing them to imagine that he would conquer the land and restore the Egyptian dynasty. In the hearts of the people there was such fondness for the Egyptians **[48]** that these undertakings were considered an easy matter. A large host flocked to him and a considerable number of blacks. He marched against Qūṣ and its dependencies.

News of this came to the sultan so he dispatched against him a large army bristling with weapons, made up of those who had tasted the sweetness of ruling the land of Egypt and feared to lose it. He put in command of them his brother, al-ʿĀdil Sayf al-Dīn, who led them forward until they came upon the enemy and met them in open battle, breaking them, killing a great number of them and thus removing their threat and suppressing their revolt. That was on 7 Ṣafar 570 [7

September 1174].[1] The basis of the regime was strengthened and its affairs prospered. To God be the praise and blessing!

Account of the Franks' attack on the port of Alexandria (may God protect it)

When the Franks (may God forsake them) learnt of the vicissitudes of Egypt and of the changes of the regime there, they were filled with ambition to take the land. They sent their forces by sea, which were in 600 ships, namely galleys, taridas,[2] [**49**] busses or others, and numbered 30,000 men, according to report. They put the port under siege on 7 Ṣafar 570 [7 September 1174]. The sultan strengthened the port with his royal troops and took energetic measures. God put such fear and terror in their hearts as did not allow them to show steadfastness. They withdrew, disappointed and downcast, after they had closely invested the port and carried out assaults for three days. They fought hard against the town, but God preserved it safe from them.

When they became aware that the sultan was moving towards them, it was not long before they abandoned their trebuchets and their equipment. The town's inhabitants emerged to plunder and burn them. This was one of God's greatest favours to the Muslims and a sign of all happy success. To God be thanks and blessing!

Nūr al-Dīn had left his son, al-Ṣāliḥ Ismā'īl, in Damascus, while the citadel of Aleppo was held by Shams al-Dīn 'Alī ibn al-Dāya and Shādhbakht. 'Alī had been tempted to hatch some plots, so al-Ṣāliḥ marched from Damascus to Aleppo, arriving outside on 2 Muḥarram [3 August 1174], accompanied by Sābiq al-Dīn. Badr al-Dīn Ḥasan went out to meet him, but Sābiq al-Dīn was arrested.[3] When al-Ṣāliḥ entered the citadel, he arrested Shams al-Dīn along with his brother Ḥasan and put all three in prison. The same day Abū'l-Faḍl ibn al-Khashshāb[4] was put to death for discord that he had caused in Aleppo. It is

1 Previously, in the summer of 1171, Kanz al-Dawla, an emir of the Arab tribe of Rabī'a, had cooperated with an Ayyubid force against Nubian invaders. During this revolt he was killed (Lyons and Jackson, *Saladin*, pp. 60-61, 77).

2 In Arabic *ṭarrāda*. There is a commoner form *ṭarīda* which is normally described as a transport ship (horses often being mentioned). In this form it was a term used by Europeans (see Pryor, 'Transportation of horses by sea', *passim*).

3 The surviving Ibn al-Dāya brothers were Shams al-Dīn 'Alī, Sābiq al-Dīn 'Uthmān and Badr al-Dīn Ḥasan, who hoped to take control of affairs after the death of Nūr al-Dīn. They were opposed by a Damascus faction around al-Ṣāliḥ, with whom Sābiq al-Dīn had gone to Damascus to negotiate. At this point the *Nawādir* text reads 'and Sābiq al-Dīn arrested him', but he would hardly have arrested his own brother. I prefer to read with *RHC Or*, p. 56, *'alā* rather than *'alayhi*, although I construe the sentence differently. For a discussion of these complicated events, see Lyons and Jackson, *Saladin*, pp. 78-80.

4 He was the *ra'īs* of Aleppo, the representative of local interests and chief of the militia.

related that his execution took place the day before the arrest of the Ibn al-Dāya brothers, because they were the ones who ordered it.

[50] Account of the sultan's march to Syria and his taking Damascus

When the sultan received confirmation of Nūr al-Dīn's death, aware that his son was a child unable to shoulder the burdens of kingship and incapable of taking on the defence of the lands against God's enemies, he made his preparations to march to Syria, since it is the cornerstone of Muslim territory. He set out with a large force of troops, leaving in Egypt some to assume its protection and defence and the ordering and governance of its affairs. He departed with some of his family and relatives, sending letters ahead to the inhabitants and emirs of Syria. The followers of al-Ṣāliḥ were not united and their policies were in disarray. They were fearful of one another and several of them had been arrested. This was the reason why the remainder were fearful of those who had taken that step and a reason for people's change of heart towards the youngster. The situation led Shams al-Dīn ibn al-Muqaddam to make contact with the sultan by letter. The sultan arrived in Syria demanding that he himself should take on al-Ṣāliḥ's guardianship, direct his affairs and set straight what had gone awry. The sultan reached Damascus, without having renounced allegiance, and entered the city after a peaceful hand-over on Tuesday, the last day of Rabīʿ II 570 [27 November 1174], and he took over the citadel.

He went straight to his father's house and people flocked to him rejoicing at his coming. That same day he distributed huge sums of money to the people and showed himself pleased and delighted with the Damascenes, as they did with him. He went up into the citadel and his hold on power was firmly established. He was not long in setting out for Aleppo. Ḥims was besieged and the town taken in Jumādā I of this year [December 1174], without bothering with the citadel. He came eventually to Aleppo, which he put under siege on Friday, the last day of the said month [27 December 1174]. This was the first occasion.

How Sayf al-Dīn sent his brother ʿIzz al-Dīn to confront him

After Sayf al-Dīn, the lord of Mosul, became aware of what had happened, he realised that this man Saladin's position had become a serious threat, that his power was now great and his influence increased. He feared that, if he neglected him, he would overwhelm the region, become firmly entrenched in power and his position impinge on his own. He therefore dispatched a considerable force of troops, putting his brother, ʿIzz al-Dīn Masʿūd, in command of them. They marched out with the intention of confronting the sultan, bringing him to battle and dislodging him from Syria. Hearing of this, the sultan withdrew from Aleppo on 1 Rajab 570 [26 January 1175], moving back to Ḥamā and from there on to Ḥims, where he busied himself with the successful taking of its citadel. 'Izz al-Dīn came to Aleppo, where he was joined by the local troops, and they took the field with a large host.

[**51**] Having learnt of their approach, the sultan set out and came upon them at the Horns of Ḥamā. There was an exchange of envoys and he strove to come to terms with them but they would not agree, thinking that perhaps they would achieve their greatest aim and fullest desire by battle, but destiny was dragging them to an outcome of which they had no perception.

Battle began between the two armies and God decreed that the enemy were broken. Many were taken prisoner, but Saladin was gracious and freed them. This took place at the Horns of Ḥamā on 19 Ramaḍān 570 [13 April 1175]. Following on their rout he proceeded to besiege Aleppo, which was the second occasion, and then they made peace on the basis that he took Ma'arrat al-Nu'mān, Kafarṭāb and Ba'rīn, this being towards the end of the year.

Sayf al-Dīn takes the field in person

When this battle took place, Sayf al-Dīn was at Sinjār besieging his brother, 'Imād al-Dīn, with the aim of taking it from him and having him accept his lordship. His brother had already declared his alliance with the sultan and held to that. Sayf al-Dīn intensified the siege and bombarded the place with trebuchets until many breaches had been made in the city wall. He was on the point of taking the town when he received news of that battle. He feared that his brother would hear of it too, and so take heart and stiffen his resolve. Therefore he established contact with him and made peace.

He immediately departed for Nisibis, where he busied himself with assembling troops and paying them. He then marched to the Euphrates and crossed at Bīra, making camp on the Syrian side of the river. He corresponded with Gumushtakīn[1] and al-Ṣāliḥ to establish a basis of agreement on which he could join them. Gumushtakīn came to him and long negotiations took place, during which he many times made up his mind to go back, but eventually his meeting with al-Ṣāliḥ was agreed and allowed. He travelled to Aleppo, where al-Ṣāliḥ came out in person to meet him. Sayf al-Dīn met him near the citadel. He embraced him, wept and told him to return to the citadel, which he did, while he

---

1 Sa'd al-Dīn Gumushtakīn, a eunuch emir, had been Nūr al-Dīn's governor in Mosul. He emerged as the chief man behind al-Ṣāliḥ after the arrest of the Ibn al-Dāya brothers.

himself made camp at 'Ayn al-Mubāraka.[1] He remained there for some time while the Aleppan troops came out daily to attend upon him.

With a small retinue he ascended the citadel, took bread there and then went down again. He marched out to Tell al-Sulṭān,[2] accompanied by the forces of Diyār Bakr and a large host. Meanwhile, the sultan had sent requesting troops from Egypt, whose arrival he was awaiting. They were delayed over their affairs and their preparations, not realising that in delay there was a consequence. Eventually, the army of Egypt arrived and the sultan marched out and came [**52**] to the Horns of Ḥamā. The enemy received a report that his army was near, so they posted pickets and despatched men to gather intelligence. They found that he had arrived without his baggage train at the Turkomans' Wells and that his army had scattered to find water. Had God willed their victory, they would have attacked him in that hour, but in order that God might fulfil his predestined plan, they held back until he and his troops had watered their horses, assembled and formed up for battle.

The morning of Thursday 10 Shawwāl 571 [22 April 1176] found the hosts in battle lines. The two armies met, collided and a fierce battle ensued. The sultan's left wing was broken by Muẓaffar al-Dīn ibn Zayn al-Dīn,[3] for he was on Sayf al-Dīn's right wing, but the sultan charged in person and the enemy broke. He captured a large number of senior emirs, including Fakhr al-Dīn 'Abd al-Masīḥ, whom he graciously allowed to go free. Sayf al-Dīn withdrew to Aleppo, from where he recovered his treasury, and then proceeded across the Euphrates to return to his own lands.

The sultan refrained from pursuing the enemy troops but camped for the remainder of that day in their tents. They had left their baggage just as it was and their kitchens with food prepared. The sultan distributed [the contents of] their stables and gave away their stores. Sayf al-Dīn's tent he gave to 'Izz al-Dīn Farrūkhshāh. Then he marched to Manbij and received its surrender during what remained of that month.

He then went to the castle of A'zāz[4] to put it under siege. This was on 4 Dhū'l-Qa'da 571 [15 May 1176] and while he was there, the Ismā'īlīs tried to assassinate him, but God delivered him from their plots and gave them into his hands. That did not blunt his resolve. He continued to besiege the place until he took it on 14 Dhū'l-Ḥijja [24 June 1176]. He then descended upon Aleppo on the 16th [26 June], remained for a while and then departed. They sent out to him a young daughter of Nūr al-Dīn who asked him for A'zāz and he gave it to her.

---

1 Literally, 'Blessed Spring', mentioned by Ibn al-Shiḥna as a place of recreation south of Aleppo where newly appointed viceroys in Mamluke times were met by local dignitaries (Ohta, *The History of Aleppo*, pp. 245, 247).

2 About 40 km south of Aleppo.

3 Muẓaffar al-Dīn Kūkbūrī ibn 'Alī ibn Baktakīn (born 549/1154, died 630/1232) was lord of Ḥarrān (Ibn Khallikān, *Wafāyāt*, iv, pp. 229-237).

4 Half-way between Antioch and Edessa.

During the remainder of the month his brother, Shams al-Dawla, came from Yemen to Damascus, where he took up residence for a while. Later, having returned to Egypt, he died in Alexandria on Thursday 1 Ṣafar 576 [26 June 1180].

The sultan returned to Egypt to investigate local conditions and to arrange its administration. He travelled there in Rabīʿ I 562 [September-October 1176], leaving his brother, Shams al-Dawla, as his deputy in Damascus. Saladin remained in Egypt, arranging its administration and making good its deficiencies.

The sultan rested his troops, then made preparations for campaigning. He marched out to the coastal plain, where he encountered the Franks at Ramla. That was early in Jumādā I 573 [late October 1177].

[53] Account of the defeat at Ramla

The commander of the Franks was Prince Reynald, who had recently been ransomed at Aleppo, for he had been a prisoner there from the time of Nūr al-Dīn. This day the Muslims suffered a setback, and the sultan told me how the defeat happened. The Muslims had drawn up for battle and when the enemy approached, some of our men decided that the right wing should cross to the left and the left cross towards the centre, in order that when battle was joined they might have at their backs a hill known as Ramla Land. While they were occupied in this manoeuvre, the Franks charged them and God decreed their defeat. They suffered a terrible reverse and they had no nearby fortress they could take refuge in. They set out for Egypt, got lost[1] on the way and were scattered. Many of them were taken prisoner, including the jurist ʿĪsā.[2] It was a major defeat which God mended with the famous battle of Ḥaṭṭīn (to God be the praise).

As for al-Ṣāliḥ, his affairs fell into disorder. He arrested Gumushtakīn, the leading man of his regime, and demanded that he surrender Ḥārim to him, but he would not, so he killed him. When the Franks heard that he had been killed, they descended on Ḥārim, ambitious to seize it. That was in Jumādā II 573 [November-December 1177] and al-Ṣāliḥ's troops confronted the Frankish forces. Seeing the danger from the Franks, the garrison of the citadel surrendered it to al-Ṣāliḥ during the last ten days of Ramaḍān of this year [mid-March 1177]. Having learnt this, the Franks departed from Ḥārim, making for their own lands. This was on 19 Ramaḍān [11 March 1177] and then al-Ṣāliḥ returned to the city of Aleppo. His men continued in dissension, some inclining towards the sultan, until he heard of the rebellion of Ghars al-Dīn Qilij[3] in Tell Khālid and sent his

---

1 Reading with B: *wa-ḍallū*.

2 Ḍiyā' al-Dīn ʿĪsā al-Faqīh (the jurist), an Hakkārī Kurd, who began as imam for Asad al-Dīn Shīrkūh and became a trusted warrior and advisor of Saladin. He died in 585/1189.

3 This emir, formerly in the service of Shīrkūh, joined Saladin.

troops against him on 10 Muḥarram 576 [5 June 1180]. [**54**] Subsequently he heard of the death of his uncle, Sayf al-Din Ghāzī, the lord of Mosul, who died on 3 Ṣafar of this year [28 June 1180]. His place was taken by his brother, 'Izz al-Dīn Mas'ūd. The date of the death of Shams al-Dawla (God have mercy on him) has already been mentioned.

The sultan's return to Syria

After the defeat the sultan returned to Egypt and stayed there until the troops had repaired their ravaged state. He then learnt of the disorder in Syria and determined to return there, which return was for warfare against the Franks. Envoys of Qilij[1] came to him, requesting a treaty with the sultan and asking him for aid against the Armenians. The sultan planned to move towards the territory of the son of Leon[2] to help Qilij Arslan against him. He camped at Qarā Ḥiṣār and took the troops of Aleppo under his command, because he made that condition when peace was made. They assembled at the Blue River[3] between Bahasnā and Manṣūr's Fort.[4] From there he crossed to the Black River[5] and raided the territory of the son of Leon, taking from the enemy a fort which he destroyed. They offered him [return of] prisoners and sued for peace, whereupon he withdrew.

Then Qilij Arslān made overtures concerning a general peace treaty for all the eastern princes. Peace was concluded and the sultan took an oath on 10 Jumādā I 576 [1 October 1180]. The peace treaty covered Qilij Arslān and the rulers of Mosul and Diyār Bakr. It was concluded on the river Sanja, which is a tributary of the Euphrates. The sultan then set out to return to Damascus.

[55] The death of al-Ṣāliḥ

After the beginning of Jumādā II 577 [mid-October 1181] al-Ṣāliḥ fell ill with colic. His illness began on 9 Rajab [18 November 1181] and on the 23rd of that month [2 December] the gate of the citadel was closed because of the severity of his illness. One by one he summoned the emirs and made them swear an oath [of loyalty] to 'Izz al-Dīn, the lord of Mosul. On the 25th [4 December] he died (God have mercy on him) and his death greatly affected the hearts of his people.

---

1 Qilij Arslān II, the Seljuq sultan of Rūm (Anatolia), ruled 1155-1192 (*EI*^{2}, v, p. 104).

2 This is the ruler of Lesser Armenia, Roupen III.

3 The Gök Su, sometimes called the Sanja (see below).

4 A small fortified town, north of the Blue River between Ṣumayṣāt and Malaṭya, now called Adiyaman (*EI*^{2}, i, pp. 199-200).

5 Otherwise known as Kara Su, flowing east of the Amanus Mts to a point Antioch.

Account of 'Izz al-Dīn's coming to Aleppo

After al-Ṣāliḥ's death they hastened to convey the news to 'Izz al-Dīn Mas'ūd ibn Quṭb al-Dīn and to inform him that al-Ṣāliḥ had named him in his will and made his people swear an oath to him. 'Izz al-Dīn made all speed to travel to Aleppo, fearing the sultan. The first of his emirs to arrive at Aleppo were Muẓaffar al-Dīn ibn Zayn al-Dīn and the lord of Sarūj. With them both came men to take an oath from all the emirs [of Aleppo]. They arrived on 3 Sha'bān of this year [12 December 1181].

On 20 Sha'bān [29 December] 'Izz al-Dīn came to Aleppo and went up into the citadel, whose stores and treasure he took possession of, and he married al-Ṣāliḥ's mother on 5 Shawwāl [11 February 1182].

Account of 'Izz al-Din's exchange of territory with his brother, 'Imād al-Dīn Zankī

'Izz al-Dīn remained in the citadel of Aleppo until 16 Shawwāl [22 February]. He realised that he was unable to hold Syria in addition to Mosul because of the need to stay on in Syria on account of the sultan. The emirs pressed him with demands for extra resources. They considered that they themselves had chosen him and his field of action was restricted. His chief minister Mujāhid al-Dīn Qaymāz, also a man of limited range, was unfamiliar with the obduracy **[56]** of the Syrian emirs. 'Izz al-Dīn departed the Aleppo citadel on 16 Shawwāl [22 February], making for Raqqa, and left his son and Muẓaffar al-Dīn ibn Zayn al-Dīn in charge. He arrived at Raqqa and was met by his brother, 'Imād al-Dīn, by prior agreement between them. An exchange of Aleppo for Sinjār was settled, confirmed by 'Izz al-Dīn's oath to his brother 'Imād al-Dīn on 21 Shawwāl [27 February]. On behalf of 'Imād al-Dīn some persons went to take over Aleppo, and others on behalf of 'Izz al-Dīn took over Sinjār. It was on 13 Muḥarram 578 [19 May 1182] that 'Imād al-Dīn made his entry into the citadel of Aleppo.

Account of the sultan's return from Egypt

After peace had been made through Qilij Arslān, the sultan proceeded to Egypt (God protect her), leaving his nephew, 'Izz al-Dīn Farrūkhshāh, in charge. However, having heard of the death of al-Ṣāliḥ, he determined to return to Syria, fearing a Frankish attack on those lands. He also heard of the death of Farrūkhshāh on Friday 1 Rajab 577 [10 November 1181 (Tuesday!)], so his determination was strengthened.

He arrived at Damascus on 17 Ṣafar 578 [22 June 1182]. He then initiated preparations for a raid on Beirut, for on his return from Egypt he had crossed Frankish territory in open defiance without a truce. He marched to Beirut and put it under siege, but achieved nothing. The Franks assembled their forces and obliged him to move away. He re-entered Damascus.

Information reached the sultan that envoys of Mosul had come to the Franks urging them to undertake hostilities against the Muslims. Understanding that they had broken their sworn undertakings, he decided to attack them to bring about the unity of the forces of Islam against the enemies of God. He began to make his preparations and 'Imād al-Dīn, hearing of this, sent to Mosul to make them aware of this fact and to urge their armies to action.

The sultan came to camp before Aleppo on 18 Jumādā I this year [19 September]. He remained for three days and then on 21 Jumādā I [22 September] marched away to the Euphrates. He arrived at an understanding with Muẓaffar al-Dīn, who was lord of Ḥarrān [57] and whose relations with Mosul were already strained. He feared Mujāhid al-Dīn [Qaymāz] and sought protection with the sultan, so he joined him, crossing over the Euphrates, and encouraged him to invade their lands, saying that they were an easy target. The sultan then crossed the Euphrates and took Edessa, Raqqa, Nisibis and Sarūj. Then he garrisoned Khābūr and gave it away as a fief.

Account of his siege of Mosul

On this occasion Saladin besieged the city on Thursday 11 Rajab 578 {12 November 1182}. At that time I was in Mosul, but a few days before he besieged it I was sent as an envoy to Baghdad. I travelled in haste down the Tigris and within two days and two hours I came to Baghdad to seek their aid. The only thing we got from them was that they sent to the Shaykh al-Shuyūkh,[1] who was already with the sultan as an envoy on their behalf, ordering him to speak with him and to settle the matter diplomatically. An envoy was also sent from Mosul to Pahlawān[2] asking for support, but all that resulted from that direction was a demand which, if accepted, would be more dangerous than war with the sultan.

For some days the sultan remained before Mosul. He realised that it was a great city against which nothing would be achieved by besieging it in that manner. He saw that the way to take it was to take its fortresses and the

1 Ṣadr al-Dīn Muḥammad (1148-1220), a member of the Ḥamawiya family, influential Sufis and legists of Iranian origin (see *EI²*, i, 765-6).

2 He was Shams al-Dīn Muḥammad ibn Ildekiz, who, as Atabeg of the last Seljuqs, ruled Azerbayjan and N.W. Persia until his death in 581/1186.

surrounding territory and to weaken it by the passage of time. So he moved away and descended on Sinjār on 16 Sha'bān 578 [15 December 1182].

Account of his taking Sinjār

Saladin maintained his siege of Sinjār, which was held by Sharaf al-Dīn[1] ibn Quṭb al-Dīn and a garrison, and pressed it vigorously until on 2 Ramaḍān [30 December] he took the place by assault. Sharaf al-Dīn and his men left for Mosul with full honours of war. The sultan gave the town to his nephew, Taqī al-Dīn, and departed for Nisibis.

[58] The incident with Shāh Arman, the lord of Khilāṭ

It was the case that the ruling men of Mosul had sent to Shāh Arman,[2] asking for his aid, and had thrown themselves on his mercy. He marched from Khilāṭ to help them, camped at Ḥarzam[3] and sent to 'Izz al-Dīn, lord of Mosul, to tell him. The latter set out on 15 Shawwāl 578 [21 February 1183] and joined forces with him and also the lord of Mardīn.[4] A detachment of the army of Aleppo also arrived, all this with the intention of confronting the sultan.

Shāh Arman sent Baktimur to the sultan to discuss peace through the mediation of the Shaykh al-Shuyūkh, but no settlement was arranged. The sultan marched towards Shāh Arman's army, and the latter, when he heard of the approach of the sultan, turned tail and returned to his own lands. 'Izz al-Dīn also returned home and all dispersed. Whereupon the sultan set out for Āmid and, having camped before it, he attacked and took it in eight days. That was early in Muḥarram 579 [late April 1183]. He gave the town to Nūr al-Dīn ibn Qarā Arslān and granted all the money and other things that it contained to Ibn Nīsān[5] and then he set out with Syria as his destination, to attack Aleppo.

During this period 'Imād al-Dīn marched out and destroyed the fortress of A'zāz on 9 Jumādā II 578 [10 October 1182] and he also demolished the castle of

---

1 According to *Kāmil*, xi, pp. 487-488, Sharaf al-Dīn Amīr Amīrān, the brother of the lord of Mosul, lost the city through the treachery of a Kurdish emir and his own lack of spirit.

2 Suqmān II (died 581/1185) was one of the dynasty of Turkoman rulers of Khilāṭ (or Akhlāṭ) who held this title, 'king of the Armenians' (see *EI*^{2}, ix, p. 193).

3 A town between Mardīn and Dunaysir, mostly populated by Armenians (Yāqūt, ii, p. 239).

4 Shāh Arman's nephew, Quṭb al-Dīn Īlghāzī ibn Alpī.

5 Power in Āmid had been usurped by a chief minister called Mu'ayyad al-Dīn Abū 'Alī ibn Nīsān, whose son, Bahā' al-Dīn Mas'ūd (this Ibn Nīsān), continued his harsh, unpopular rule. He was given three days to remove what he could (*Rawḍ*, ii, pp. 38-40, Ibn Wāṣil, *Mufarrij*, ii, pp. 134-136, *Kāmil*, xi, 493-494).

Kafarlāthā, having taken it from Bakmish, for he had joined the sultan on 12 Jumādā I of that year [13 December]. He also attacked Tell Bāshir, whose lord, Dildirim al-Yārūqī, had joined the sultan but he could effect nothing against it. There was a series of raids by the Franks on account of the disunity of the Muslim forces but God repelled them. 'Imād al-Dīn received the surrender of Karzayn,[1] then returned to Aleppo.

[59] Account of the sultan's return to Syria

After Saladin's return to Syria, he began with Tell Khālid, which he besieged and attacked, taking it on 22 Muḥarram 579 [17 May 1183]. He then made for Aleppo, which he put under siege on 26 Muḥarram [21 May]. His first position was in the Green Hippodrome.[2] He sent his troops into battle and they were skirmishing with the Aleppan army at Bānqūsā and the Gardens' Gate[3] morning and evening. On the day he began the siege his brother, Tāj al-Mulūk, was wounded.

Account of his capture of Aleppo

When Saladin descended upon Aleppo, he summoned troops from all quarters and a vast host assembled. He pressed the assault strongly and 'Imād al-Dīn realised that he did not have the strength to resist him. He had already become exasperated with the emirs' demands and recalcitrance. He suggested to Ḥusām al-Dīn Ṭumān that he should negotiate with the sultan for the restoration of his lands in return for the surrender of Aleppo. The basis for an agreement was established and no-one in the population or the army was aware of the business until it was over. The agreement was made and news of it spread abroad. The army asked for confirmation which he gave and allowed them to make their own arrangements. They sent on behalf of themselves and of the populace 'Izz al-Dīn Jurdīk al-Nūrī and Zayn al-Dīn Bilik al-Yārūqī, who sat with the sultan till night-time and sought his sworn word to protect the army and the citizens. That was on 17 Ṣafar [11 June].

The troops and the leading citizens of Aleppo went out to the Green Hippodrome to submit to Saladin. He bestowed robes of honour and eased their minds. 'Imād al-Dīn remained in the citadel to complete his affairs and shift his

---

1 Correct *Nawādir* here. Karzayn is six miles south of al-Bīra (Birejik).

2 Clearly not the grassed polo ground of the same name created by Nūr al-Dīn in the Aleppo citadel (see Elisséef, *Nūr al-Dīn*, iii, pp. 713 and 732).

3 Bānqūsā was a suburb of Aleppo and the city gate was one on the west side.

baggage and treasures, while the sultan stayed in the Green Hippodrome until Thursday 23 Ṣafar {16 June}.

[60] That day his brother, Tāj al-Mulūk[1], died from the wound he had received. His death grieved the sultan and he sat to receive condolences. Also on that day 'Imād al-Dīn came down to make obeisance and express sympathy for his loss. They went together to the Green Hippodrome. A settlement was reached between them and the sultan received him in his tent, giving him a splendid gift and some handsome horses. He gave robes of honour to several of his men. That day 'Imād al-Dīn travelled to Qarā Ḥiṣār en route for Sinjār. The sultan remained in his camp after 'Imād al-Dīn's departure, not bothered about the city nor over-concerned about its state until Monday 27 Ṣafar[2] {20 June}. Then, on that day, the sultan ascended into the citadel of Aleppo joyful and victorious, and Ḥusām al-Dīn Ṭumān prepared a splendid banquet for him, for he had remained behind to take the clothes and other things belonging to 'Imād al-Dīn that were still left.

Account of his taking of Ḥārim

Saladin had previously sent people to Ḥārim to take its surrender, but the governor delayed compliance. The garrison sent to secure the sultan's oath. Their message came to him on Tuesday 28 Ṣafar {21 June}, when he gave them his oath and immediately set out for Ḥārim. He arrived there on 29 Ṣafar [22 June] and took the place over. He remained there two nights and settled its affairs, putting Ibrāhīm ibn Shirwa[3] in charge. He then returned to Aleppo, which he entered on 3 Rabī' I of this year [26 June 1183]. He gave his troops leave and all returned to their own lands. He himself stayed to make arrangements for Aleppo and to organise its administration.

[61] Account of the raid on Goliath's Spring

Saladin only remained in Aleppo until Saturday 22 Rabī' II {13 August}. He decided to make a raid, so that day he moved out to al-Waḍīḥī[4] in the direction of Damascus and summoned the troops, who answered his call. On 24 Rabī' II {15 August} he departed for Ḥama, which he came to and left during that same day. He continued his stages without a break and eventually entered Damascus on 3

1 The youngest son of Najm al-Dīn Ayyūb, born 556/1161 (see *Rawḍ*, ii, 42 and 44).

2 *Nawādir* has '17th' in error.

3 This is Falak al-Dīn Abū Manṣūr Ibrāhīm ibn Shirwa ibn Jaldik, al-'Ādil Sayf al-Dīn's step-brother on his mother's side (see *Rawḍ*, ii, 239, line 12).

4 Ibn al-'Adīm, *Zubdat*, iii, 212, note 2, and 262, note 2: 'a village near Aleppo'.

Jumādā I [24 August]. There he stayed making his preparations until 27 Jumādā I [17 September], and on that day he marched out and camped at Wooden Bridge.[1] The troops followed him, equipped for an expedition, and he waited there for nine days. On 8 Jumādā II [28 September] he left and marched till he came to al-Fuwwār. He there disposed his troops in battle order and camped for the night at al-Quṣayr. In the morning he came to the ford and, having crossed, travelled on to Baysān. He found that the inhabitants had already deserted it and abandoned all their non-portable goods, provisions and possessions. The army plundered all as booty, burning what they could not take away. He then proceeded as far as Goliath's Spring, which is a flourishing village with a copious source of water. There he made camp.

'Izz al-Dīn Jurdīk, several of the mamlukes of Nūr al-Dīn and Jāwulī, Asad al-Dīn's mamluke, had already gone ahead to scout for news of the Franks. It happened that they fell in with the troops of Kerak and Shawbak who were marching to reinforce the main Frankish force. Our men attacked them, made great slaughter amongst them and took about a hundred of them prisoner. They returned having lost on the Muslim side only a single person, whose name was Bahrām **[62]** the herald. The sultan came up during what remained of the day of this engagement, which was Friday[2] 10 Jumādā II {30 September}. The Muslims took it as an omen of a great victory.

On Saturday 11 Jumādā II [1 October 1183] news reached him that the Franks had assembled at Ṣaffūriyya,[3] so he marched to al-Fūla, which is a well-known village. He planned a pitched battle, so when that intelligence came to him, he made his dispositions for an engagement and formed his squadrons into right wing, left wing and centre, and then marched to meet the enemy. The Franks also came on to confront the Muslims. Both sides came eye to eye. The sultan sent out the vanguard of 500 picked men. They engaged the Franks and a fierce fight ensued. Several of the enemy were killed and several wounded. They grouped close one to another, with the infantry protecting the cavalry. Not halting for a pitched battle, they continued their march until they reached the spring, where they made camp. The sultan camped around them, while their losses continued in dead and wounded, to force them to come to battle. However, they would not, fearing the Muslims, who were very numerous.

When he saw that they would not join battle, he decided to withdraw from them, to see whether they would then move and whether he could force them into an engagement. He moved towards al-Ṭūr.[4] That was on 17 Jumādā II [7

---

1 In Arabic: Jisr al-Khashab. According to Elisséef, *Nūr al-Dīn*, iii, p. 341: 'perhaps near Rabwa where the River Barada enters the plain of the Ghūṭa'.

2 'Thursday' in both *Nawādir* and B is incompatible with the following date.

3 Known to the Franks as Sepphoris, this was a frequent mustering place, north of Nazareth.

4 That is, Mt Tabor.

October]. He took station below the mountain, watching for their departure to seize any opportunity to attack.

[**63**] On 18 Jumādā II [8 October] the Franks moved, retracing their steps. The sultan moved to intercept them and many arrows were loosed and great efforts made to provoke them to a pitched battle, but they would not break their formation. The sultan continued to beset them until they made camp at al-Fūla, mentioned above, on the way back to their lands.

When the Muslims saw that, they gathered around the sultan and advised him to retire because their provisions were depleted and he had inflicted damaging losses on the enemy and demolished 'Afarbalā, the citadel of Baysān and Zar'īn, noted castles of theirs. He had also destroyed numerous villages. He returned victorious and happy, and came to camp at al-Fuwwār. He then gave the troops leave from their campaigning and he himself went on to Damascus, which he entered in joyful celebration on Thursday 24 Jumādā II {13 October}.

Consider this zeal, which the taking and acquisition of Aleppo did not distract from campaigning [against the Franks]. Indeed, his purpose was to gain aid from these territories for the Holy War. May God reward him well in the life to come, as He supported him in his approved deeds in this life.

Account of the expedition he mounted against Kerak

He remained in Damascus until 3 Rajab 579 [22 October 1183] and then set out on an expedition to Kerak. He had already sent to al-'Ādil, who was in Egypt, ordering him to rendezvous with him at Kerak. He heard the news of his departure from Egypt, so set out to meet him. He arrived at Kerak, where he was met by al-'Ādil, with whom a large multitude, merchants and non-merchants, had travelled. That was on 4 Sha'bān [22 November].

The Franks too (God damn them) had heard of his move and set out with their infantry and cavalry to Kerak to defend it. On receipt of this intelligence he dispatched al-Malik al-Muẓaffar Taqī al-Dīn to Egypt on 15 Sha'bān [3 December]. On the morning of the 16th [4 December] the Franks came to camp at Kerak and the sultan withdrew after some serious assaults on the town. Sharaf al-Dīn Buzghush al-Nūrī met a martyr's death during one of them on 22 Sha'bān[1] [10 December].

---

1 This is the date given in B.

[64] His gift of Aleppo to his brother, al-'Ādil

The sultan then departed for Damascus, taking his brother, al-'Ādil, with him, because he despaired of Kerak after the Franks' arrival. He came to Damascus on 24 Sha'bān [12 December] and, after staying there until 2 Ramaḍān [19 December], he presented his brother with Aleppo, who travelled there that same day. He arrived and went up into the citadel on Friday 12 Ramaḍān[1] [29 December]. The sultan's son, al-Ẓāhir, had been there, along with Sayf al-Dīn Yāzkūj, as manager of his affairs, while Ibn al-'Amīd[2] was in the town.

Al-Ẓāhir was the dearest of his sons to his heart, because of the bravery, intelligence, wisdom and upright behaviour and passion for kingship that God had especially bestowed upon him and which was plain to all. He was the most respectful and obedient of people towards his father. However, the sultan took Aleppo from him for some good purpose he saw. Al-Ẓāhir, accompanied by Yāzkūj, left Aleppo when al-'Ādil entered and went to wait upon the sultan. He arrived at Damascus on Monday 28 Shawwāl [13 February 1184] and remained at the service of his father, showing nothing but obedience and compliance, despite his inner disappointment which did not escape his father's notice.

During this month we came to the sultan as envoys from Mosul. We had contrived with the Caliph al-Nāṣir li-Dīn Allāh that the Shaykh al-Shuyūkh Ṣadr al-Dīn be sent as an envoy and intermediary to the sultan. He was sent with us from Baghdad, a person full of virtue and greatly respected at the caliphal court and in all lands. His standing with the sultan was such that he frequented his presence on most days.

[65] Account of our coming before him as envoys

The Shaykh, having reached Mosul as an envoy, travelled onwards after the Qāḍī Muḥyī al-Dīn ibn Kamāl al-Dīn[3] had joined his company. There was a friendship between them since childhood. I was one of the party. We arrived at Damascus, where the sultan came out some distance to meet the Shaykh with us in attendance on him. Our entry into Damascus took place on Saturday 11 Dhū'l-Qa'da 579 [25 February 1184] and we met from the sultan everything handsome in the way of a generous and respectful welcome. We stayed several days debating a solution to the situation, but on this occasion no peace was agreed.

---

1 Emending the given date 22 Ramaḍān, which would correspond to 8 January 1184, a Sunday.

2 This man from Damascus, whose name was Nāṣiḥ al-Dīn Ismā'īl, had been put in charge of the civilian administration in Aleppo (Ibn al-'Adīm, *Zubdat*, iii, p. 71).

3 Muḥyī al-Dīn Abū Ḥāmid Muḥammad ibn Muḥammad followed his father as a senior official of the Zengid state in Damascus, Aleppo and Mosul. He died in the last named in 586/1190 (Ibn Khallikān, *Wafāyāt*, iv, pp. 246-8).

We set out to return to Mosul and the sultan travelled as far as al-Quṣayr to see the Shaykh on his way. During that day he did his utmost to get some business concluded, but without success. The hold-up was on the part of Muḥyī al-Dīn, for the sultan stipulated that the lords of Irbil and Jazīrat [ibn 'Umar][1] should have the option of giving allegiance either to himself or to Mosul. Muḥyī al-Dīn said, 'Their position must be made clear in the text,' so the negotiations stalled.

We departed on Thursday[2] 7 Dhū'l-Ḥijja {22 March 1184}. On that occasion the sultan offered me, through the mouth of the Shaykh, the positions of Bahā' al-Dīn al-Dimashqī in Egypt. I made my excuses and declined for fear that the lack of progress might be put down to me. From that time a regard for me was firmly established in his noble heart, something I only learnt after I had begun to serve him.

While the sultan remained in Damascus, envoys arrived to see him from various quarters. The envoy of Sanjar Shāh, the lord of Jazīrat [ibn 'Umar] came and, asked to swear, gave him his allegiance, as did the envoy of Irbil. The sultan gave them his word and both left. His brother, al-'Ādil, came to him on Monday 4 Dhū'l-Ḥijja {19 March}. He stayed awhile until after the Feast[3] and then went back to Aleppo.

[66] Another expedition to Kerak

The sultan sent to summon his armies, and Nūr al-Dīn ibn Qarā Arslān responded by coming to Aleppo on Thursday 18 Ṣafar 580 [31 May 1184], where al-'Ādil received him with great honour, took him up into the citadel and treated him with open friendliness. He left with him for Damascus on the 26th [8 June]. The sultan had been ill for a few days but God cured him. Hearing of Ibn Qarā Arslān's arrival, he went out to meet him, for the sultan treated people very graciously. He met him at the crossing of the bridge in the Bekaa on 9 Rabī' I [20 June]. He then returned to Damascus, leaving Nūr al-Dīn to come on with al-'Ādil. He made his preparations for the expedition and marched out to Wooden Bridge in the middle of the month [26 June].

On the 24th [4 August] al-'Ādil, accompanied by Ibn Qarā Arslān, arrived at Damascus, where they stayed for a few days and then set out to join the sultan. On 2 Rabī' II [13 July] the sultan left Ra's al-'Ayn making for Kerak. For a few days he halted nearby to wait for al-Muẓaffar Taqī al-Dīn to arrive from Egypt, which he did on 19 Rabī' II [30 July] when he joined him and came under his

---

1 This is modern Cizre, a town on the Tigris, not to be confused with al-Jazīra in the sense of Mesopotamia.

2 'Thursday' is added in B.

3 The *'Īd al-aḍḥā* (the Feast of Sacrifices), held on 10 Dhū'l-Ḥijja to mark the end of Pilgrimage rites at Mecca.

command. He had al-'Ādil's household and treasure chest with him, which the sultan sent to al-'Ādil and ordered him and the rest of the armies to join him at Kerak. The troops came in a steady stream to his standard until they surrounded Kerak. That was on 14 Jumādā I [23 August]. He set up trebuchets to attack the place. The armies of Egypt and Syria and also those of al-Jazīra under Ibn Qarā Arslān had now met.

Having heard this, the Franks marched out with their infantry and cavalry to defend Kerak. The place caused great trouble to the Muslims, for it cut communications with Egypt, so that caravans were only able to move with sizeable military escorts. The sultan was very concerned about it, to make the route to Egypt passable (may God facilitate that, to Him be praise and gratitude).[1] Aware that the Franks were on the move, he made his dispositions for battle. He ordered the forces to move out beyond Kerak and sent his baggage train towards his own territory, so that the troops were left unencumbered. Then he marched to intercept the enemy.

[**67**] The Franks made camp at a place called al-Wāla,[2] whereas the sultan moved to Balqā' to stop at a village called Ḥusbān, opposite the line of march of the Franks. He shifted from there to a place called Spring Water, while the Franks remained at al-Wāla until 26 Jumādā I [4 September]. Then they set out for Kerak. Some of our forces came behind them and engaged them until the end of the day.

Seeing that the Franks were determined to procede to Kerak, the sultan ordered his forces to enter the coastal regions as it was devoid of troops. They attacked Nablus and plundered it, taking what it contained as booty. Only its two forts survived. They also took Jīnīn and then joined the sultan at Ra's al-Mā',[3] having plundered, taken captives, burned and destroyed. The sultan then entered Damascus on Saturday 7 Jumādā II 580 [15 September 1184] with al-'Ādil and Nūr al-Dīn ibn Qarā Arslān, delighted and well-pleased. He showed the latter much honour, respect and largess.

During this month the caliph's envoys came, bringing robes of honour which the sultan donned. He invested his brother, al-'Ādil, and Asad al-Dīn's son with robes of honour which had come for them. On 14 Jumādā II [22 September] the sultan invested Nūr al-Dīn ibn Qarā Arslān with the caliph's robe of honour and gave him and the armies leave to depart. Ibn Qarā Arslān left for his own lands on 19 Jumādā II [27 September].

1 This phrase in this full form is found in B only.

2 Identified in Lyons and Jackson, *Saladin*, p. 218, as 'Ayn Awaleh, some 6 miles (10 km) from Ḥusbān.

3 Situated in the Ḥawrān on the Ḥajj route, south-east of Nawā.

On this date envoys of [Muẓaffar al-Dīn] ibn Zayn al-Dīn arrived, seeking aid from the sultan and reporting that the army of Mosul and that of Qizil,[1] led by Mujāhid al-Dīn Qaymāz, had besieged Irbil and that they had plundered and burned, but he had defeated and broken them.

The sultan's expedition against Mosul for the second time

Apprised of this the sultan set out from Damascus for those lands and on his orders the armies followed him. He set out for Ḥarrān by way of al-Bīra, at which place he met with Muẓaffar al-Dīn on 12 Muḥarram 581 [15 April 1185]. [**68**] 'Izz al-Dīn ibn 'Abd al-Salām had come as an envoy to the sultan and met him at Ḥamā to apologise for what had happened. The sultan gave him leave to depart after receiving him graciously, but he left without achieving anything. Sayf al-Dīn al-Mashṭūb was commanded by the sultan to proceed with the vanguard of the army to Ra's al-'Ayn,[2] and the sultan himself reached Ḥarrān on 22 Ṣafar [25 May].

The arrest and release of Muẓaffar al-Dīn

On 26 Ṣafar 581[29 May 1185] the sultan arrested Muẓaffar al-Dīn for something he had done and some comments that his envoy passed on, which the sultan did not enquire into but which he censured. He took the citadels of Ḥarrān and Edessa from him and he remained in prison as a punishment until 1 Rabī' I [2 June]. Then the sultan gave him a robe of honour and reconciled his heart, restoring to him the citadel of Ḥarrān and its territories which he had held, and restoring him to his normal level of honour and respect. The only possession not regained was the citadel of Edessa, but the sultan held out promises of that.

The sultan left Ḥarrān on 2 Rabī' I [3 June] for Ra's al-'Ayn, and at that time the envoy of Qilij Arslān came to inform him that the princes of the East had all agreed that they would attack the sultan if he did not withdraw from Mosul and Mardīn and that they were determined to bring him to battle if he persisted in that. The sultan marched on to Dunaysir, where he was joined by 'Imād al-Dīn ibn Qarā Arslān and the army of Nūr al-Din, lord of Mardīn, on Saturday 8 Rabī' I {8 June 1185}. He received them with great respect and then left Dunaysir on Tuesday the 11th {11 June} in the direction of Mosul and marched until he camped at a place called al-'Ismā'īlāt near Mosul, from where a fresh detachment of his army could daily come to besiege Mosul. 'Imād al-Dīn ibn Qarā Arslān heard of the death of his brother, Nūr al-Dīn, and requested permission from the

1 That is, Qizil Arslān, who was to succeed his brother Pahlawān within a year.

2 Literally, 'Head of the Spring', in the Jazīra, about 85 km east of Ḥarrān.

sultan to leave, desirous of taking over his brother's rule. Permission was granted.

[69] The death of Shāh Arman

When Rabīʿ II 581 came [July 1185], Shāh Arman, the lord of Khilāṭ, died and was succeeded by a mamluke of his, called Baktimur, who was the person that had come as an envoy to the sultan at Sinjār. He ruled with justice and was considerate to the people of Khilāṭ, being by persuasion a Sufi, who had the obedience and affection of his subjects.

When he had taken over Khilāṭ, various greedy interests looked Baktimur's way, now that Shāh Arman was dead. Pahlawān ibn Ildekiz marched towards the town, and therefore, when Baktimur heard that, he sent the sultan men who would arrange his surrender of Khilāṭ and his own incorporation into the sultan's alliance, in return for the grant of something satisfactory. The sultan was eager to gain Khilāṭ, so he set out from Mosul in that direction, sending before him the jurist ʿĪsā and Ghars al-Dīn Qilij to agree and draw up the terms. These envoys arrived when Pahlawān had already approached very near. Baktimur threatened him with the sultan and made him understand that, if he attacked him, he would surrender the city to the sultan, so Pahlawān sought to make peace and gave him his daughter in marriage, recognised his authority there and restored the city to him. Baktimur made his excuses to the sultan's envoys, who returned 'without the cream'. Meanwhile the sultan had camped before Mayyāfāriqīn to besiege it.

Account of the taking of Mayyāfāriqīn

After his withdrawal from Mosul the sultan put Mayyāfāriqīn under siege and attacked it very fiercely, setting up trebuchets. It was held by a person called Asad al-Dīn,[1] who was far from slack in its defence, but the divine plans are not to be overcome and the sultan took it over on terms on 29 Jumādā I 581 [28 August 1185].

[70] The sultan's return to Mosul

Having given up any hope of Khilāṭ, he returned to Mosul, where he camped at some distance from it, this being the third time, at a place called Kafr Zammār. The weather was intensely hot, so he remained there for a while. Sanjar Shāh

1 According to ʿImād al-Din (quoted in *Rawḍ*, ii, p. 63), this was an emir called Asad al-Dīn Yarunqush.

came to him at this encampment from Jazīrat [Ibn Umar]. They had a meeting and then Saladin sent him back to his town. The sultan came down with a serious illness at Kafr Zammār, which he feared would be a disaster. He struck camp, making for Ḥarrān, though still ill. He showed great fortitude and did not ride in a litter. He arrived at Ḥarrān very sick and extremely weak. His life was despaired of and a rumour went around that he had died. He left Kafr Zammār on 1 Shawwāl [26 December 1185]. His brother, al-'Ādil, arrived from Aleppo bringing his doctors with him.

Account of his peace treaty with the Mosulis

The treaty came about because the Atabeg 'Izz al-Dīn, lord of Mosul, sent me to the caliph to seek his support, but no 'cream' was forthcoming from that direction, so he sent to the Persian princes, but again no benefit resulted. When I arrived back from Baghdad and delivered the reply to the mission, he despaired of any aid. However, hearing of the illness of the sultan, they decided that this was an opportunity, as they had learnt how readily tractable and soft-hearted he was at this time. They therefore commissioned me for this task, along with Bahā' al-Dīn al-Rabīb, and they entrusted me with the matter of the text to which he would swear. They said, 'Ratify whatever your joint efforts and abilities can manage.' We left and reached his camp when all were despairing of the sultan.

Our arrival was early in Dhū'l-Ḥijja [end of February 1186]. He gave us a respectful welcome and held a reception for us, the first he had held since his illness. He took his oath on the day of Arafat.[1] We received from him the land between the two rivers [Tigris and Euphrates], which he had taken from Sanjar Shāh and now gave to Mosul. I administered a comprehensive oath to him and also got his brother, al-'Ādil, to swear. The sultan, at his death, still held to that treaty, having never diverged from it.

[71] We left him at Ḥarrān, already convalescing. News came to him of the death of [Muḥammad] ibn Asad al-Dīn [Shīrkūh], the lord of Ḥimṣ. He had died on the day of Arafat when we were at his camp. Al-'Ādil sat to receive condolences.

During those days there was a battle between the Turkomans and the Kurds, a huge number being killed.

This month news was received of the demise of Pahlawān ibn Ildekiz, who died on the last day of Dhū'l-Ḥijja [23 March 1186].

---

1 The day on which, as part of the pilgrimage rituals, Mt Arafat near Mecca is visited, that is, 9 Dhū'l-Ḥijja, equivalent in this present year to 3 March 1186.

The sultan's return to Syria

When the sultan found some energy during his convalescence, he set out for Aleppo, where he arrived on Sunday 14 Muḥarram 582 [6 April 1186], a notable day because of the happiness of the people at his recovery and return. He remained for four days, then on the 18th [10 April] he went to Damascus. He was met by Asad al-Dīn Shīrkūh ibn Muḥammad [ibn] Shīrkūh and the latter's sister at Tell al-Sulṭān. He had brought a large gift and numerous offerings. The sultan bestowed Ḥimṣ on him and remained for several days assessing his father's estate, before proceeding to Damascus, which he entered on 12 Rabī' I [2 June 1186], a day of unparalleled joy and happiness.

During this month there occurred many battles between the Turkomans and the Kurds in the territory of Nisibis and elsewhere. On both sides a great many were killed. The sultan received information that Mu'īn al-Dīn ibn Mu'īn al-Dīn had rebelled in Rāwandān.[1] He sent instructions to the troops of Aleppo to besiege him, which they did during the first ten days [of Rabī' I] of the year 582 [22-31 May 1186]. The sultan granted him Burj al-Raṣāṣ[2] to get him to surrender the place in the remainder of the month.

On 8 Jumādā I [27 July] Mu'īn al-Dīn arrived from Rāwandān, having handed it over to 'Alam al-Dīn Sulaymān before he came to present himself before the sultan.

On 17 Jumādā I [5 August] al-Afḍal, who had not previously seen Syria, came to Aleppo.

[72] Account of al-'Ādil's journey to Egypt and al-Ẓāhir's return to Aleppo

The sultan decided that al-'Ādil should go to Egypt, for he was more familiar with conditions there than al-Muẓaffar and, while the sultan was ill at Ḥarrān, he had kept talking to him about it. Al-'Ādil had set his heart on this as he was very fond of Egypt.

After the sultan had returned to Damascus and God had bestowed health upon him, he sent for al-'Ādil to come to Damascus. The latter left Aleppo without heavy baggage on the eve of Saturday 24 Rabī' I [14 June 1186], and came to Damascus, where he remained in attendance on the sultan, while they held conversations and discussions on arrangements for an administrative settlement until Jumādā II [August-September 1186]. It was then settled that al-'Ādil

---

1 A castle two day's journey north-west of Aleppo

2 Literally, 'the Lead Tower', a castle between Aleppo and Antioch.

should return to Egypt and give up Aleppo. He dispatched Ṣanī'at al-Dīn[1] to fetch his family from Aleppo.

The return of al-Ẓāhir to Aleppo.

The two princes, al-Ẓāhir and al-'Azīz, were in Damascus in attendance on their father. When it was decided that al-'Ādil should return to Egypt, it was also decided that he should be the atabeg of al-'Azīz. His father would entrust his education to al-'Ādil and al-'Ādil would surrender Aleppo to al-Ẓāhir.

Al-'Ādil said to me, 'When this arrangement was settled, I had a meeting with the two princes, al-Ẓāhir and al-'Azīz, sat between them and I said to al-'Azīz, "Know well, my lord, that the sultan has commanded me to travel in your service [73] to Egypt. I realise that trouble-makers are legion and that in due course there will not be lacking people who will say unacceptable things about me and make you fear me. If you have any intention of listening, just tell me and I will not come." He replied, "I shall not listen. How could that be?" Then I turned to al-Ẓāhir and said, "I know that your brother may sometime listen to what trouble-makers have to say about me. I have only you. Whenever I am in trouble from him, I am content to receive Manbij from you." "Rest easy," he said and made me every fair promise.'

His father then sent al-Ẓāhir[2] to Aleppo and restored it to him. He was aware that Aleppo was the very root, foundation and source of power. That is why he had been so eager to gain it. Having gained it, he left all the lands of the East alone, satisfied with their allegiance and their aid in the Jihad. He gave his son Aleppo, knowing his aptitude, determination, learning, understanding[3] and high aspirations. Al-Ẓāhir came to 'Ayn al-Mubāraka on his journey, attended by Ḥusām al-Dīn Bishāra, who was sent as garrison commander, and by 'Īsā ibn Balāshū, designated as governor. He arrived at 'Ayn al-Mubāraka on the Friday and the people came out to welcome him on the morning of Saturday 9 Jumādā II 582.[4] He ascended into the citadel towards noon that day and the people rejoiced greatly to see him. He spread the wing of his justice over them and showered them with his copious bounty.

As for the princes al-'Azīz and al-'Ādil, the sultan settled their position and wrote to al-Muẓaffar to inform him that his son, al-'Azīz, accompanied by the latter's uncle, al-'Ādil, was coming and to order him to come to Syria. This

1 Ṣanī'at al-Dīn ibn al-Naḥḥāl, a converted Christian, was a leading member of al-'Ādil's secretariat (Ibn al-'Adīm, *Zubdat*, iii, p. 75).

2 In the original al-Ẓāhir is here referred to as 'the sultan', anticipating his independent role after Saladin's death.

3 These last two qualities reflect the reading of B: *adabi-hi wa-fiṭnati-hi*.

4 The direct equivalent would be 27 August 1186, but this was a Wednesday. Perhaps one should read 19th, which would correspond to Saturday 6 September.

distressed al-Muẓaffar, so much so that he made it obvious to people and he made up his mind [74] to go off to the west, to Cyrenaica. Several of the great men of state disapproved of his plan and they told him that his uncle, the sultan, would disown him immediately and God knows what would happen to him afterwards. God opened his eyes to perceive what was right and he answered with 'I hear and obey.' He gave up Egypt and set out to present himself at the service of the sultan, who came out to meet him. They met at Marj al-Ṣuffar and the sultan was very happy that he had come. This was on 23 Sha'bān[1] [8 November]. The sultan presented him with Ḥamā and he set out to go there.

A marriage had been arranged between al-Ẓāhir and one of the daughters of al-'Ādil. Everything was concluded and the marriage was consummated on Wednesday 26 Ramaḍān [10 December].[2] Al-Afḍal entered into union with his wife, the daughter of Nāṣir al-Dīn [Muḥammad] ibn Asad al-Dīn, during the month of Shawwāl this year [15 December-12 January 1187].

Account of an expedition mounted against Kerak

When Muḥarram of the year 583 came [March 1187], the sultan decided to attack Kerak and sent men to Aleppo to summon the troops. He marched from Damascus in the middle of Muḥarram [27 March] and moved to camp in the district of Qunayṭra[3] to await the concentration of the troops of Egypt and Syria. He ordered the various detachments as they came to join him to carry out raids on the coastal lands that lay on their route, which they did. He then remained in the territory of Kerak until the Syrian pilgrim caravan arrived in Syria and was safe from any enemy threat and the winter caravan from Egypt arrived, bringing with it the household of al-Muẓaffar and all that he had possessed in Egypt.

The troops of Aleppo were delayed because they were occupied with the Franks in the territory of Antioch and in the lands of the son of Leon. This is because he had died and had willed the kingdom to his brother's son (God curse him). Al-Muẓaffar was in Ḥamā and when the sultan heard the news, he ordered him to enter the enemy's lands and subdue his obduracy. He arrived at Aleppo on 17 Muḥarram [29 March] and lodged in the house of 'Afīf al-Dīn ibn

1 *Nawādir* gives '13th' but B has '23rd'. Cf. *Sanā'*, p. 281: 'news that [al-Muẓaffar] had arrived during the last ten days of Sha'bān ... he entered Damascus at the end of Sha'bān'.

2 *Sic* B, while *Nawādir* has '16th'.

3 *Nawādir* has 'Nayṭra', which is deleted in the list of corrections, leaving the text to read 'in a district', which is also all that B has. Wilson, *Saladin*, p. 108, gives 'Ḳuneiṭera', which, as the main centre of the Golan, would tally with 'Imād al-Dīn's information (in *Sanā'*, p. 291) that Saladin first camped at Ra's al-Mā' (about 7 km north of Sheikh Miskin) and then moved to Bosra.

Zurayq,[1] remaining there until 3 Ṣafar [14th April], when he moved to the house of Ṭumān.[2]

[75] On 9 Ṣafar [20 April] al-Muẓaffar marched with the troops of Aleppo to Ḥārim, where he remained to let the enemy know that this region was not neglected. Meanwhile the sultan returned to Damascus, arriving there on 15 Rabī' I [25 May]. On Thursday 17th of that month [27 May] he came to 'Ashtarā[3] where he was met by his son, al-Afḍal, Muẓaffar al-Dīn ibn Zayn al-Dīn and all the armies. He had ordered al-Muẓaffar to arrange a truce with the Franks on the Aleppan front, in order that his mind might be easy as regards the enemy in one direction. Al-Muẓaffar made a truce during the last ten days of Rabī' I [30 May-9 June] and then went to Ḥamā to put himself at the service of the sultan for the expedition planned by the latter. He and the eastern armies under his command, that is to say, the army of Mosul, led by Mas'ūd ibn al-Za'farānī, and the army of Mardin, finally came to 'Ashtarā during the middle period of Rabī' II [approx. 19-23 June], to be met by the sultan with respect and honour.

Midway through this month [24 June] the sultan reviewed the army for his planned expedition on a hill known as the Tell Tasīl.[4] He commanded the men on the right and left wings to maintain their positions, and the centre likewise. How eager he was for the victory of Islam!

Account of the Battle of Ḥaṭṭīn, a blessing for the Muslims

It took place on Saturday 24 Rabī' II 583 {4 July 1187}. The sultan perceived that his gratitude for God's favour towards him, evidenced by his strong grasp on sovereignty, his God-given control over the lands and the people's willing obedience, could only be demonstrated by his endeavouring to exert himself to the utmost and to strive to fulfil the precept of Jihad. He sent to summon all his forces, which gathered on the date given at 'Ashtarā. He reviewed them and made his dispositions, then set forth into the God-forsaken enemy's lands at midday on Friday 17 Rabī' II [26 June]. He always sought out Fridays for his battles, especially the times of Friday prayer, to gain the blessing of the preachers' prayers on the pulpits, for they were perhaps more likely to be answered.

---

1 He was Abū 'Abd Allāh Muḥammad ibn Zurayq al-Tanūkhī, recorded as the builder of a mosque and a bath-house in Aleppo (Ibn Shaddād, *La Description d'Alep*, pp. 65, 146).

2 Ḥusām al-Dīn Ṭumān's house, situated outside the city proper in the suburb of al-Ḥāḍir, became the property of the historian Ibn al-'Adīm (*Zubdat*, pp. 50, 66, 91).

3 Situated in the Ḥawrān.

4 According to Lyons and Jackson, *Saladin*, p. 255, 'some 6 miles (10 km) north of 'Ashtarā'.

As he marched out at that time in battle array, he heard that the enemy, when they learnt that he had concentrated his armies, gathered in full on the plain of Ṣaffūriyya in the territory of Acre and intended to come to battle. The same day, the sultan camped at Lake Tiberias near a village called **[76]** Ṣannabra. He then moved and camped west of Tiberias on the top of the mountain, in battle formation and expecting that the Franks, when they heard that, would come against him. However, they did not move from their encampment. He took up this position on Wednesday 21 Rabīʿ II [1 July], and having seen that they were not moving, he descended upon Tiberias with a light force, leaving the main divisions in position facing the direction in which the enemy were. He attacked Tiberias and took it within one hour after a direct assault. Eager hands then turned to plundering, taking captives, burning and killing. The citadel alone held out.

Learning what had happened to Tiberias, the enemy could not bear not to give into their impulsive zeal, but set out at once and marched to defend Tiberias. The Muslim scouts told the emirs that the Franks were on the move, and they sent people to inform the sultan. He left men in Tiberias to watch the citadel and then he and his force joined the main army. The two armies encountered one another on the slopes of the mountain of Tiberias, to the west of the town, late on Thursday 22 Rabīʿ II [2 July].

Nightfall separated the two sides and both spent the night at battle stations, bristling with weapons, until the morning of Friday 23rd [3 July]. Both armies mounted and clashed together. The vanguard was in operation, then the main divisions moved forward and battle was joined, and became very intense. This was around a village called Lūbiyā. They were closely beset as in a noose, while still marching on as though being driven to a death that they could see before them, convinced of their doom and destruction and themselves aware that the following day they would be visiting their graves.

The conflict continued at close quarters, each horseman clashing with his opponent, until victory [for the Muslims] and for the infidels the onset of disaster were imminent, but night and its darkness intervened. That day there occurred mighty deeds and momentous doings, such as have not been related of past generations. Each party spent the night in arms, expecting his adversary at every moment, though too weak through tiredness to stand up and unable through fatigue to crawl, let alone run.

Eventually, there came the Saturday morning, on which the blessing was vouchsafed. Both sides sought their positions and each realised that whichever was broken would be driven off and eliminated. The Muslims were well aware that behind them was the Jordan and before them enemy territory and that there was nothing to save them but God Almighty.

[77] God had already ordained and prepared the believers' victory, and he duly brought it about according to what he had predestined. The Muslim divisions

charged on the wings and in the centre. They let out a shout as one man, at which God cast terror into the hearts of the unbelievers. 'It was right for Us to give aid to the believers.'[1]

The Count [Raymond] was a clever and shrewd leader of theirs. He saw that the signs of defeat were already upon his co-religionists and no notion of aiding his fellows stopped him thinking of himself, so he fled at the beginning of the engagement before it grew fierce and made his way towards Tyre, pursued by a group of Muslims. He alone was saved, but Islam became safe from his wiles.[2]

The forces of Islam surrounded the forces of unbelief and impiety on all sides, loosed volleys of arrows at them and engaged them hand to hand. One group fled and was pursued by our Muslim heroes. Not one of them survived. Another group took refuge on a hill called the Hill of Ḥaṭṭīn, the latter being a village near which is the tomb of Shu'ayb (on him and on the rest of the prophets be blessings and peace). The Muslims pressed hard upon them on that hill and lit fires around them. Their thirst was killing and their situation became very difficult, so that they began to give themselves up as prisoners for fear of being slain. Their commanders were taken captive but the rest were either killed or taken prisoner, and among those who lived were their leader, King Guy,[3] Prince Reynald, the brother of the king, the prince who was lord of Shawbak, the son of Humfrey, the son of the Lady of Tiberias, the Master of the Templars, the lord of Jubayl and the Master of the Hospitallers. The rest of the commanders were killed, and the lowly soldiers were divided up, either to be slain or made captive. Everyone not killed was made prisoner. Some nobles amongst them willingly surrendered in fear for their lives. Someone I trust told me that in the Ḥawrān he met a single person holding a tent-rope with which all by himself he was pulling along thirty odd prisoners because of the desperate defeat that had befallen them.

As for their leaders that survived, we shall recount their fate. The count who fled arrived at Tripoli and was taken ill with pleurisy, and thus God brought about his death. As for the officers of the Hospitallers and the Templars, the sultan chose to put them to death and killed them all without exception. **[78]** The sultan had vowed to kill Prince Reynald if he got him in his power. This was because a caravan from Egypt had passed through his land at Shawbak during the state of truce. They halted there under safe conduct, but he treacherously killed them. The sultan heard of this and religion and his zeal encouraged him to swear that, if he seized his person, he would kill him. After God had bestowed the great victory on him, the sultan sat in the entrance lobby of his tent, for it had not been fully erected, while people were offering him prisoners and any commanders they had found. The [main] tent was then erected and he sat there in

---

1 Koran xxx, 47.

2 Through his death soon afterwards (see below).

3 *Nawādir* has *Jafrī*, i.e. Godfrey. Cf. *Fatḥ*, p. 27: 'King Guy (*Kī*) and his brother Godfrey.'

great delight, expressing his gratitude for the favour that God had shown him. Then he summoned King Guy, his brother and Prince Reynald. He handed the king a drink of iced julep, from which he drank, being dreadfully thirsty, and he then passed some of it to Prince Reynald. The sultan said to the interpreter, 'Tell the King, "You are the one giving him a drink. I have not given him any drink."' According to the fine custom of the Arabs and their noble ways, if a prisoner took food or a drink of water from whoever had captured him, his life was safe. His intention was to follow these noble ways.

He ordered them to proceed to a place assigned for their lodging. They did so and ate something. Then the sultan summoned them again, now having with him none but a few servants. He gave the king a seat in the vestibule and, having summoned Prince Reynald, confronted him as he had said. He said to him, 'Here I am having asked for victory through Muhammad, and God has given me victory over you.'[1] He offered him Islam but he refused. **[79]** The sultan then drew his scimitar and struck him, severing his arm at his shoulder. Those present finished him off and God speedily sent his soul to Hell-fire. His body was taken and thrown down at the door of the tent. The king, when he saw him brought out in this manner, was convinced that he would be next. The sultan called him in and reassured him, saying, 'It has not been customary for princes to kill princes, but this man transgressed his limits, so he has suffered what he suffered.' That night was spent by our people in the most complete joy and perfect delight, raising their voices in praise of God and gratitude towards him, with cries of 'God is great' and 'There is no god but God', until daybreak on Sunday.

The taking of the citadel of Tiberias

On Sunday 25 Rabīʿ II {5 July} the sultan camped at Tiberias and during the remainder of that day received the surrender of the citadel. He remained there until the Tuesday [7 July].

Account of the taking of Acre

Saladin then departed for Acre, where he arrived on Wednesday, the last day of Rabīʿ II [8 July]. He attacked on the morning of Thursday 1 Jumādā I [9 July] and took the city, delivering the Muslim prisoners there, who were about 4,000 souls. He seized the money, stores, goods and commodities it contained, for it was renowned as a trading emporium. The troops dispersed throughout the coastal lands, taking forts, castles and fortified places. They took Nablus, Haifa,

---

1 Following B: *hā ana istanṣartu bi-Muḥammad fa-naṣara-nī Allāh ʿalaykum.*

Caesarea, Ṣaffūriya and Nazareth. That was because they were empty of men, who had been either killed or captured. When the administration of Acre had been settled and those due booty had received their share of wealth and captives, the sultan set out for Tibnīn.

[80] The taking of Tibnīn

Tibnīn, a strong fortress, was besieged on Sunday 11 Jumādā I [19 July]. The sultan set up trebuchets and pressed hard with assaults and a blockade. It was held by courageous men, strong in their religion. The Muslims required an extreme effort, but God gave Saladin the victory and he took the place by assault on Sunday the 18th [26 July] and made prisoners of those who had escaped death. He moved away to the city of Sidon, which he attacked and took control of after one day, that is, on Wednesday 21 Jumādā I[1] [29 July].

His taking of Beirut

The sultan remained at Sidon long enough to arrange its administration and then he marched to Beirut. He attacked it on Thursday 22 Jumādā I [30 July], carried out assaults and pressed hard on the city, eventually taking it on Thursday 29 Jumādā I [6 August]. While he was attacking Beirut, his men gained possession of Jubayl.[2]

When his mind was easy concerning these parts, he decided to go to Ascalon as, after he had camped before Tyre and made a trial assault at this time, he determined not to occupy himself with it because his troops had scattered throughout the coast. Every man had gone to take something for himself, tired of fighting and constant campaigning. Every Frankish survivor on the coast had flocked to Tyre. Thus he decided to attack Ascalon because it was an easier objective.

The capture of Ascalon

Saladin came to camp before the city on Sunday 16 Jumādā II [23 August], having taken many places on his way there, such as Ramla, Yubnā[3] and Dārūm.

---

1 The text has 'Wednesday 20th', but note that *Fatḥ*, p. 37, gives the correct date, Wednesday 21 Jumādā I.

2 According to *Fatḥ*, p. 41, Jubayl surrendered on Tuesday 27 Jumādā I/ 4 August.

3 Known to the Crusaders as Ibelin, situated 11 km south-west of Ramla and 21 km south of Jaffa.

He set up trebuchets and made fierce attacks. The city fell to him on Saturday 29 Jumādā II [5 September], and he remained there while his men took over Gaza, Bayt Jibrīn and Latrun without meeting any resistance.

[81] Between the recovery of Ascalon and the Franks' taking it from the Muslims thirty-five years had passed, for the enemy gained control of it on 27 Jumādā II 548 [19 September 1153].

The conquest of Jerusalem the Blessed, the Noble

Having gained Ascalon and the places surrounding Jerusalem, the sultan buckled down to the task and supreme effort of attacking the latter place. The forces which had scattered throughout the coast rejoined him after satisfying their desire for plunder and pillage. He then marched towards it, relying on God and entrusting his cause to Him, to take the opportunity to open the door to success which one is urged to grasp when it opens, in the words of Muḥammad (upon him be peace), 'If a door to some advantage is opened for anyone, then let him grasp it, for he knows not when it may be closed against him.'[1]

He descended on the city on Sunday 15 Rajab 583 [20 September 1187]. He took up position on the western side. It was crammed with fighting men, both mounted and foot soldiers. Experienced sources estimated the number of soldiers who were there at more than 60,000, apart from women and children. Then, because of an advantage he saw, he transferred to the north side, which move took place on Friday 20 Rajab [25 September]. He set up trebuchets and pressed hard on the city with assaults and a hail of missiles. Eventually, he undermined the city wall on the side next to the Valley of Gehenna in the northern angle.[2] The enemy saw the indefensible position they had fallen into and the signs were clear to them that our true religion would overcome the false. Their hearts were downcast on account of the killing and imprisonment that had befallen their knights and men-at-arms and the fall and conquest of their fortresses. They realised that their lot was ineluctable and that they would be killed by the sword that had killed their brethren. Humbled, they inclined towards seeking terms. An agreement was reached through an exchange of messages between the two sides.

[82] The sultan received the surrender on Friday 27 Rajab [2 October]. The eve had been the [date of the] Prophetic Ascension which is written about in the Noble Koran. Observe this remarkable coincidence, how God facilitated its restoration to Muslim hands on the anniversary of their Prophet's Night-Journey. This is a sign that God had accepted this proffered obedience. It was a great victory, witnessed by a vast crowd of men of religion, Sufis and mystics. The

---

1 Not traced in the canonical collections.

2 This last phrase is based on the reading of B, fol. 59a: *fī'l-qurna al-shimāliyya*. The *Nawādir* text has *fī qarya shimāliyya*, 'in a northern village'.

reason for this was that, when people heard of the conquest of the coastal lands that God had effected at Saladin's hand and his intention to move against Jerusalem became widely known, the ulema from Egypt and Syria made their way to him, so much so that no-one of any note failed to be present. Voices were raised in shouts and prayers, with cries of 'There is no god but God' and 'God is great'. On the Friday of the conquest the khutbah was delivered and Friday prayers held in Jerusalem. The cross of vast size, which was over the Dome of the Rock, was lowered. God gave victory to Islam by His might and strength.

The basic provision in the treaty was that they would pay ransoms, for every man ten Tyrian dinars, for every woman five dinars and for every child, male or female, a dinar. All who produced the ransom would secure their freedom, otherwise they would be made captive. God freed those Muslims who were prisoners, a large multitude of about 3,000 souls.

The sultan remained there, collecting money and distributing it to the emirs and the ulema, and also conveying all who payed their ransom to their place of safety, namely Tyre. I have heard that the sultan departed from Jerusalem without keeping any of that money, which amounted to 220,000 dinars. He left on Friday 25 Sha'bān 583 [30 October 1187].

[83] His attack on Tyre (may God facilitate its capture)

When Jerusalem was firmly in the sultan's control, his heart was fixed on attacking Tyre. He understood that, if he delayed the task, it would perhaps grow more difficult. He marched to Acre, where he made camp and looked into its affairs. He then set out for Tyre on Friday 9 Ramaḍān {13 November}.[1] He came in sight of the town and took a position nearby to await the arrival of his siege engines.

The arrival of his son, al-Ẓāhir

Once his determination to attack Tyre was settled, Saladin sent to summon his son, al-Ẓāhir. He had left him at Aleppo to block off that region, because he himself was busy with the lower littoral. Al-Ẓāhir came to him at this present camp on 18 Ramaḍān [21 November] and his arrival caused much rejoicing.

---

[1] The text has Friday 5 Ramaḍān, which corresponds to 8 November 1187, but that was a Sunday. *Fatḥ*, p. 74, gives the date of the *arrival* as Friday 9 Ramaḍān.

Account of his siege of Tyre

When his engines of war, trebuchets, siege towers and screens and so forth were all complete, the sultan began the siege on 22 Ramaḍān [25 November] and pressed hard with fierce assaults on the city. He called on the Egyptian fleet, which began to blockade from the sea, while the troops did so by land. He had left his brother, al-ʻĀdil, in Jerusalem to arrange its affairs. He now summoned him and he arrived on 5 Shawwāl [8 December]. The sultan sent troops to besiege Ḥūnīn, which surrendered on terms on 23 Shawwāl 583 [26 December 1187].

[84] Account of the sinking of the fleet

The sultan had given command of the fleet to a person called Fāris al-Dīn Badrān, who was an energetic and valiant seaman. The admiral ʻAbd al-Muḥsin had strongly urged him to be cautious and watchful in order to give no opportunity to the enemy. The crews disobeyed him and kept no watch at night. The infidels' fleet sailed from Tyre and took them by surprise, capturing their captains and five of their ships and killing a multitude of men in the Egyptian fleet. That was on 27 Shawwāl [30 December].

When he learnt what had happened to the Muslims, the sultan was extremely vexed. With the onset of winter the rains were constant. The troops refused to fight because of the heavy rain. He assembled the emirs and consulted them about what to do. They counselled withdrawal to allow the army some rest and make fresh preparations for this task. He thought this the best plan, so withdrew after having dismantled the trebuchets and dispatched them or burnt what could not be transported.

He raised the siege on Sunday 2 Dhū'l-Qaʻda 583 [3 January 1188], disbanded the armies and gave them leave to depart. Each force returned home, while he, with a group of his elite forces, remained in Acre until the beginning of 584 [early March 1188].

His siege of Kawkab

At the beginning of this year Saladin decided to occupy himself with the fortresses still remaining in Frankish hands, something that would weaken the morale of those in Tyre and bring its resistance to an end. So he turned his attention to that and invested Kawkab at the beginning of Muḥarram of this year [early March 1188]. The reason why he began with Kawkab was that he had already stationed some men around it to watch it so that no force or body could enter it. The Franks made a sally at night and took them unawares, surprising them at 'Afarbalā, killing their commander, one of the emirs called Sayf al-Dīn, the brother of al-Jāwulī, and also seizing their weapons.

The sultan left Acre and besieged Kawkab with those of his elite forces who had remained with him at Acre. He had **[85]** given the armies leave to depart and his brother, al-'Ādil, had returned to Egypt and his son, al-Ẓāhir, to Aleppo, the latter being met en route by severe snow and cold. Nevertheless, the sultan's enthusiasm encouraged him to put Kawkab under siege, where he remained for a while carrying out attacks.

It was while he was at camp there that I arrived to join his service. I had been on the pilgrimage in the year 583 [1188] when the Ibn al-Muqaddam incident occurred. He was wounded on Arafat Day at Mt Arafat because of a dispute that arose between him and the Emir of the Hajj Tashtakīn[1] over the beating of cymbals and drums. The Emir of the Hajj forbade him to do so, but Ibn al-Muqaddam took no notice.[2] He was one of the senior emirs of Syria and was very charitable and a great Jihad warrior. God decreed that he was wounded on Arafat Day at Mt Arafat and he was carried in that state to his residence and died at Minā on Thursday, the day of the Great Feast {11 February 1188}. Prayers were said over him in the mosque of al-Khayf during the remainder of that day and he was buried at al-Ma'lā,[3] one of the most perfect blessings. The news, when he heard it, grieved the sultan.

It came about that I returned from the Hajj via Syria to visit Jerusalem and its sites, and to unite a visit to the Prophet with a visit to his ancestor Abraham.[4] I came to Damascus and then left for Jerusalem. News of my arrival came to the ears of the sultan, who imagined that I had come from Mosul with some message. He summoned me to him and went to great lengths to show me honour and respect. When I took my leave to depart for Jerusalem, one of his retinue came out to me and delivered his command that I should return and present myself at his service upon my return from Jerusalem. I thought that he would charge me with some important business with Mosul. I returned to Jerusalem on the day he raised the siege of Kawkab, which he did because he realised that this castle could only be taken by a concentration of forces. It was a strong castle, garrisoned by doughty men, veterans of battles, and well-provisioned. The sultan marched to Damascus, which he entered on 6 Rabī' I [5 May].

That was the day I chanced to enter Damascus on my way back from Jerusalem. He remained there for five days, having been absent for sixteen

---

1 *Nawādir* (see corrigenda) reads Gumushtakīn, but B and *Fatḥ*, p. 101, have Tashtakīn. Ibn al-Athīr, *al-Kāmil*, xi, p. 559, names him as Mujīr al-Dīn Tashtakīn.

2 The Emir of the Hajj was the leader of the Iraqi pilgrim caravan and the representative of the Abbasid caliph. This dispute over precedence reflected a certain strain in relations.

3 The cemetery of al-Ma'lā is in the north of Mecca. The mosque of al-Khayf is at Minā.

4 That is, to the tomb at al-Khalīl (Hebron).

months. On the last day of his stay he heard news of the Franks, that they had attacked Jubayl and done great damage there. Very disturbed, he left the moment he heard the news, having [**86**] sent to summon the armies from all quarters. He set out for Jubayl and, when the Franks learnt that he had done so, they gave up their operations. The arrival of ‘Imād al-Dīn with the army of Mosul and of Muẓaffar al-Dīn ibn Zayn al-Dīn at Aleppo came to the sultan’s ears. They were coming to serve in the Jihad. He moved towards Ḥiṣn al-Akrād, making for the upper coastal regions.

His entry into the Upper Coast and his capture of Lattakia, Jabala and other places

At the beginning of Rabī‘ II [30 May] the sultan camped on a hill opposite Ḥiṣn al-Akrād and then sent to al-Ẓāhir and al-Muẓaffar with instructions to join forces and position themselves at Tīzīn opposite Antioch to cover that front. At this time they proceeded to Tīzīn, while all the forces of the East mustered under the command of the sultan where he was then camped, and I, too, joined him there. He had sent to Damascus, saying, ‘Catch up with me towards Ḥimṣ.’ I set out fully intending and prepared to travel to Mosul. I joined him in obedience to his command, and when I was with him, he expressed his delight at my arrival and behaved very hospitably.

During my stay in Damascus I had composed a book for him on the Jihad, comprising its precepts and its practices. I presented it to him and he was pleased with it. He used to read it continually. I was ever asking him for leave to depart, while he was always putting me off and inviting me at every moment to stay in his service. I would hear from the mouth of those who had been present to hear him, how he praised me and spoke fair of me. He spent the whole of Rabī‘ II [June] in his camp, during which time he climbed up to Ḥiṣn al-Akrād and besieged it for a day to probe the place. He decided it was not the time to take on a full siege.

The armies gathered from all sides and, during this month, he twice raided the territory of Tripoli. He invaded to cause damage, to find out what forces it had and to strengthen his troops with booty. At the end of the month he proclaimed, ‘We are going into the coastal region. It is short of provisions and the enemy will be surrounding us on all sides in his own lands, so carry provisions for a month.’

[**87**] He then sent to me by the jurist ‘Īsā and revealed to me that it was his intention not to allow me to return home. God had already planted love for him in my heart since I saw how he loved the Jihad, so I agreed and entered his service on 1 Jumādā I 584 [28 June 1188], which was the day he entered the Coast. All that I have related before this date is just my narrative of what I have heard from eye-witnesses I trust. From this date on I shall only record what I

witnessed or what I was told by people I trust, which is tantamount to eye-witness. God is the One who gives success.

Account of his expedition into the Coastal Lands

On Friday 4 Jumādā I[1] [1 July] the sultan marched out to meet the enemy and drew up his battle divisions. The left wing went first, commanded by 'Imād al-Dīn Zankī. The centre went next and lastly the right wing, led by Muẓaffar al-Dīn ibn Zayn al-Dīn. The baggage moved in the middle of the army until camp was reached, which that night was in enemy territory. On Saturday morning [2 July] he went on and camped before al-'Urayma but made no attack on it or any hostile move. For the rest of Saturday he remained there and moved on during Sunday [3 July].

Account of the conquest of Anṭarṭūs

Saladin arrived at Anṭarṭūs at midday on Sunday 6 Jumādā I [3 July] and halted opposite the place to inspect it. It was his plan to pass by, for he had business at Jabala, but he decided it was an easy target, so determined to attack. He sent people to recall the right wing and ordered it to camp beside the sea, while ordering the left wing to camp by the sea on the other side. He took up position where he was. The armies thus encompassed it from sea shore to sea shore. It is a city built by the sea and it has twin towers like two strong castles. The leader of the left wing was 'Imād al-Dīn, lord of Sinjār, and of the right Muẓaffar al-Dīn ibn Zayn al-Dīn. The sultan mounted and, drawing near to the city, he ordered the troops **[88]** to begin the assault.

They put on their armour and the battle and the assault grew fierce. He pressed the enemy hard and caught them unprepared. Hardly was the erection of his tent completed before our troops had scaled the wall and taken the city by the sword. They seized all that it contained, men and goods, as booty. Our men came out with their hands full of prisoners and money. The servants abandoned the putting up of his tent and busied themselves with pillage and looting. The sultan's word proved true because he had been offered lunch, but had replied, 'God willing, we shall lunch in Anṭarṭūs.'

He returned to his tent happy and delighted, and we came to him to congratulate him on events. Food was provided and people came and took their regular meal. He organised the siege of the two remaining towers. One he entrusted to Muẓaffar al-Dīn who continued to press it hard until he demolished it

---

1 *Nawādir* has '14th', which must be an error.

and took the defenders. The sultan ordered the city wall to be destroyed and allotted various parts to the emirs, who started on the demolition, while he turned to attacking the other tower. It was strong and defensible, built of dressed stone and encircled by a moat filled with water. The remaining knights and foot-soldiers had gathered there. Many crossbows within were causing casualties to our forces at some distance, while no Muslim had the means of doing any damage. The sultan decided to postpone its fate and to concentrate on what was more important. He pressed on with the demolition of the city wall until it was all done, and then he demolished the church, an important one in their eyes and the object of pilgrimage from all over their lands. He ordered the city to be torched and everything was burnt. Fire roared through the palaces and houses, while our voices were raised in cries of 'There is no god but God' and 'God is great'. He stayed there, carrying out this destruction, until 14 Jumādā I [11 July], then he left for Jabala. During his march to Jabala his son, al-Ẓāhir, fell in with him, for he had sent for him, ordering him to come with all the troops that were at Tīzīn, which he duly did.

[89] The taking of Jabala

The sultan arrived there on Friday 18 Jumādā I [15 July] and hardly had the army completed their dispositions before the city was taken. There were resident Muslims and a *qāḍī* to settle their disputes. He had taken over authority in the town, but surrendered it peacably. The citadel was left holding out. The army camped all around the town after Muslim troops had entered. Attention focused on the citadel and an assault was made which provided the garrison with sufficient justification to surrender on terms on Saturday 19 Jumādā I [16 July]. The sultan remained there until the 23rd of the month [20 July] and then moved off towards Lattakia.

The taking of Lattakia

We came down on the town, which is pleasant and delightful, unprotected [by any wall] but possessed of a celebrated harbour, on Thursday 24 Jumādā I [21 July]. There are two adjacent forts on a mound overlooking the city. The sultan camped all around the city and the troops took up their positions encircling the two forts from all sides except on the city side. The engagement was fierce and heavy assaults were made. Loud were the cries and mighty the clamour until the end of the day. The city fell, but not the forts, and our men took much booty for it was a commercial city. The onset of night separated the combatants.

Friday morning [22 July] found Saladin attacking, and attempting to mine, the forts. During the day mines were dug on their north side and the mining operations were well under way, their length reaching, as I was told by someone who measured them, sixty cubits and their breadth four. The assault intensified and troops climbed the hill and approached the wall. Fighting was non-stop. They were even hurling stones at one another by hand. When the enemy saw the humiliation and ruin that had come upon them, they sought refuge in seeking terms the evening of Friday 25 Jumādā I [22 July]. They requested the *qāḍī* of Jabala to enter to arrange their terms of surrender, which was granted. **[90]** Whenever terms were asked for, the sultan was not niggardly in granting them. The troops returned to their tents, exhausted, and slept until Saturday morning [23 July], when the *qāḍī* of Jabala went to the defenders and reached an agreement with them, that they were to be set free with their children, wives and personal belongings, other than corn, stores, weapons and mounts, although he allowed them mounts to ride to their place of refuge. This was granted and the victorious banner of Islam rose over the place during the continuation of Saturday. We remained there until Sunday 27 Jumādā I [24 July].

The taking of Ṣahyūn

The sultan left Lattakia at midday on the Sunday to go to Ṣahyūn, where he arrived on Tuesday 29 Jumādā I [26 July]. Early on the Wednesday [27 July] the army encompassed the place on all sides and erected six trebuchets. It is a well-fortified and strong castle on the spur of a hill. Awful, wide and deep valleys serve as its moats and on one side only does it have an excavated moat, which is sixty cubits deep, unassailable for it is dug out of the rock. It has three walls, a wall around its bailey, a wall around the castle and the wall of the keep. Over the keep flew a long standard. At the time of the Muslim army's approach, I saw that it fell. Our troops took that as a good omen and knew that it meant victory and a successful attack. From all sides the assault was fierce and the trebuchet of his son, al-Ẓāhir, the lord of Aleppo, hurled its missiles against the castle. He had joined the sultan a little before Jabala with his full forces and was present at its fall. He set up a trebuchet to attack Ṣahyūn opposite an angle of its wall across the valley. The stones were on target and he kept up the blows until he had demolished a large section of the wall, through which it was possible for those scaling the wall to gain access.

[91] On Friday morning, 2 Jumādā II [29 July], the sultan decided on a general assault. He mounted up, advanced and ordered the trebuchets to maintain a constant hail of missiles. Loud rose the cries and great was the clamour of 'God is great' and 'There is no god but God'. Within an hour the Muslims had scaled the walls of the bailey. The fight was hard, the struggle great and the Muslims broke into the bailey.

I was watching our men seize the cooking pots, in which food had just been prepared, and eat while battling against the castle. The defenders of the bailey joined those in the castle and took whatever property they could carry. The rest was plundered. Our soldiers surrounded the castle walls and the enemy, when they stared destruction in the face, sought relief by asking for terms. Hearing this, the sultan offered them terms and graciously allowed them their lives and their property, except that ten dinars should be taken from each man, five from each woman and two from every child. Thus the castle was surrendered (praise be to God) and the sultan stayed there until he had taken several forts, such as al-'Īdhū[1] and Balāṭunus among others. His lieutenants took them over. They were satellites of Ṣahyūn.

The taking of Bakās

The sultan moved on and we came on 6 Jumādā II [2 August] to Bakās, a strong castle beside the Orontes, which has a stream issuing from beneath it. We made camp there on the bank of the Orontes and the sultan, leaving the baggage train, climbed up to the castle, which is on a mountain looking down on the Orontes. He surrounded it and attacked strongly with trebuchets and closely pressed assaults until Friday 9 Jumādā II [5 August] when God brought about its fall to our arms. The garrison was taken into captivity, apart from those that had been killed in battle, and all that the place contained was seized as booty.

There was a twin castle next to it, called al-Shughr, to which one could cross by a bridge. It was defensible in the highest degree because there was no other access to it. Our trebuchets assailed it from all sides and the defenders saw that they had no hope of outside help, so they asked for quarter on Tuesday 13 Jumādā II [9 August]. They requested a delay of three days to seek permission from Antioch, which was granted. The castle finally fell and the sultan's banner raised aloft over the keep on Friday 16th [12 August].

[**92**] The sultan returned to the baggage-train and on Saturday the 17th [13 August] sent his son, al-Ẓāhir, to the castle of Sarmāniyya, which he attacked fiercely and beset very closely, receiving its surrender on Friday 23rd [19 August]. These conquests on the Coast from Jabala to Sarmāniyya took place on Fridays, a sign of the acceptance of the Muslim preachers' prayers and of the blessed good-fortune of the sultan, in that God enabled him to achieve these

1 Spelt thus in Yāqūt, iii, p. 751. In a treaty of Baybars with the Hospitallers in 669/1271 it appears as 'Aydūb (al-Qalqashandī, *Ṣubḥ*, xiv, p. 49), emended to Īdhūn in Holt, *Early Mamluk Diplomacy*, p. 55.

victories on the day during which the reward of good deeds is multiplied. These are rare victories on successive Fridays, unparalleled in history.

The taking of Burzey

The sultan then detached a light force to go to the castle of Burzey, an impregnable castle of the utmost strength and inaccessibility on the point of a precipitous mountain, which was a by-word in all the lands of the Franks and the Muslims. It was surrounded by ravines on all sides and was 570 odd cubits high. After viewing it he renewed his determination to besiege it. He summoned the baggage-train, which along with the rest of the army arrived on Saturday 24 Jumādā II [20 August] and camped below the mountain.

On the morning of Sunday the 25th [21 August] the sultan, with his troops, the trebuchets and siege engines but without the main baggage-train, climbed the mountain and invested the castle on all sides. The assault was mounted from every direction. The trebuchets battered the walls incessantly day and night and the attack continued until Tuesday 27th [23 August]. He divided the army into three parts and organised each part to carry on the fight for a portion of the day, then rest and allow another to continue the attack so that there was no respite at all for the defenders. The commander of the first shift was 'Imād al-Dīn, lord of Sinjār. He fought hard until his shift was completed and his troops, well tried in battle, retired. The second shift the sultan took on in person. He spurred forward several paces, loudly urging on the troops. They attacked as one man and shouted as one man and made for the wall from all sides. Within less than an hour they had scaled the walls and entered the castle, which fell to their arms. The Franks pleaded for quarter when they were already in our hands. [**93**] 'Their faith benefited them not, when they saw our might.'[1] Everything there was taken as plunder and all the defenders were taken prisoner. A large number of people had taken refuge there, as it was one of their renowned fortresses. It was a wonderful day.

Our troops returned to their tents with their plunder (thanks be to God) and the sultan regained the baggage-train in joy and delight. The lord of the castle was brought before him, one of their nobles. He and the members of his family who had been taken numbered seventeen souls. The sultan showed pity and dispatched them to the lord of Antioch, to win his good will, for they were connected with him and of his family.[2]

---

1 Koran xl, 85.

2 According to *Kāmil*, xii, p. 17, this was in recognition of the intelligence that he had been receiving from the lord of Burzey's sister-in-law, that is, Sybilla, the wife of Bohemond III of Antioch.

The conquest of Darbsāk

The sultan then proceeded to Iron Bridge where he remained for several days. From there he went to Darbsāk, arriving on Friday 8 Rajab [2 September]. This is a strong fortress near Antioch (may God facilitate its conquest). He made a strong attack on it with trebuchets and a tight blockade. Beneath one of its towers a mine was prepared and then sprung so that the tower collapsed. They defended it with their fighting men, who stood in the breach to hold it against those who tried to climb through it. I saw them myself. Whenever one was killed, another took his place. They stood like a replacement wall, with no cover. The battle became hot and, eventually, they asked for terms, stipulating that they should consult Antioch. The terms agreed were that they could depart with their lives, the clothes on their backs and nothing else. The banner of Islam was hoisted on Friday again, 22 Rajab [16 September]. The sultan gave Darbsāk to ʻAlam al-Dīn Sulaymān ibn Jandar and departed on Saturday morning 23 Rajab [17 September].

The conquest of Baghrās

This is a strong fortress, nearer to Antioch than Darbsāk, which was well-supplied and garrisoned. The sultan camped in the local plain and the troops, lightly equipped, encircled the fortress, although we needed a screening force, camped where we were, to keep watch on the Antioch direction, to prevent a force from there surprising our army. Such a Muslim force was planted at the gates of Antioch, and so placed that no-one could leave the city undetected. For some days I was with that detached body to view the city and to visit the tomb of Ḥabīb the Carpenter, who is buried there.[1] The sultan continued his fierce attacks on Baghrās until **[94]** they asked for terms subject to permission from Antioch. The sultan's banner was hoisted over it on 2 Shaʻbān 584 [26 September 1188].

During the remainder of that day the sultan returned to his great tent and received a communication from Antioch seeking peace. He made a truce with them due to his troops' exhaustion and the extreme anxiety of ʻImād al-Dīn, the lord of Sinjār, to seek leave to depart. A truce was signed between us and Antioch, alone of Frankish lands, on condition that they release all their Muslim prisoners. It was for seven months, and unless any help came, they would surrender the city to the sultan.

The sultan set out for Damascus, but was asked by his son al-Ẓāhir, lord of Aleppo, to pay him a visit. He agreed and came to Aleppo on 11 Shaʻbān [5

---

1 The legendary Ḥabīb al-Najjār, buried in a tomb below Mt. Silpius, is identified with the unnamed martyr referred to in Koran xxxvi, 20 (see *EI*^{2}, iii, pp. 12-13).

October]. He remained in the citadel for three days, while his son provided all the hospitality that was due. There was not a single person in the army who did not receive a gift from his bounty. Indeed, he did so much that his father was anxious for him.

He left Aleppo on 14 Sha'bān [8 October], making for Damascus. His nephew, al-Muẓaffar Taqī al-Dīn, intercepted him and took him up to the citadel of Ḥamā and spread a handsome banquet for him. He also invited him to a religious recital of the sufis. The sultan spent one night there and bestowed Jabala and Lattakia on al-Muẓaffar.

He took the Baalbek road and having arrived stayed for a day in the plain there, visiting its bath-house. He travelled on to Damascus, arriving a few days before the beginning of Ramaḍān. He stayed until the start of the month [24 October] but he was thinking that, as far as he was able, he ought not waste his time away from the Jihad. He still had to deal with Ṣafad and Kawkab, castles near the Ḥawrān, which he feared presented a danger to it. He decided that he should be busy with taking these two places while keeping the fast.

[95] Account of the conquest of Ṣafad

Early in Ramaḍān [began 28 July] Saladin left Damascus to go to Ṣafad, unconcerned at parting from his household, his children and his home town in this month, when people, wherever they may be, travel to be united with their families. 'O God, he bore that out of a desire for Your good pleasure, so give him a great reward.'[1]

He came to Ṣafad during the blessed month of Ramaḍān. It is a strong fortress, which is surrounded on all sides by abrupt ravines. The army invested the place and set up trebuchets. It was during this same month that Kerak was surrendered by the lieutenants of its lord, in return for which he was released from captivity. He had been taken prisoner at the blessed battle of Ḥaṭṭīn.

The rains were heavy and the mud copious, but this did not prevent the sultan's great efforts. I was in attendance on him one night when he specified the positions of five trebuchets to be set up, and said that night, 'We do not sleep until the five are in place.' He entrusted each trebuchet to a group and his messengers were going to and fro with reports for him and instructions for what they should do, until dawn rose over us and we were still attending him. The trebuchets were finished and only the fitting of their 'sows'[2] remained to be done. I recited to him the *ḥadīth* well-known in the genuine collections and commented on the resultant happy augury for him. This was the saying of the Prophet,

---

1 This is not an exact Koranic quotation but closely echoes Koran iv, 114

2 See above, p. 32, note 1.

'There are two eyes Hell-fire will never touch, an eye that has been watchful all night on Jihad, and an eye that has wept from fear of God.'[1]

The assault on Ṣafad continued unremittingly in shifts despite the period of fasting and, eventually, it surrendered on terms on 14 Shawwāl this year [6 December 1188].[2]

[96] Account of the conquest of Kawkab

Saladin then set out for Kawkab and came to camp on the mountain plateau. He formed the army into separate detachments and surrounded the fortress, pressing hard upon it so totally that he himself took a position which was within bow shot of the enemy and built a wall of stones and mud to shelter behind while the arrows flew past. No-one could stand at the door of his tent unless wearing armour. The rains were continuous and the fields of mud vast, so that movement on foot or on horseback was only possible with great difficulty and appalling hardships were endured owing to the strong winds and incessant rains and the fact that the enemy dominated them because of the height of his position. Several of our men were killed and wounded, but the sultan continued on his course of diligent striving until the castle wall was successfully mined.

When the doomed enemy became aware that the mine had been successfully dug under the wall, they knew that all was lost and sued for terms. The sultan agreed, granted them terms and received the surrender in the middle of Dhū'l-Qa'da [5 January 1189]. He descended into the Jordan valley to his baggage-train, which had previously moved down because of the mud and wind on the summit. He spent the rest of the month in discussion with his brother, al-'Ādil, about affairs that concerned him until the new moon of Dhū'l-Ḥijja was sighted [20 January], when he gave the troops leave to depart. With his brother, al-'Ādil, he went to pay a visit to Jerusalem and there say farewell to his brother, for he was returning to Egypt. They arrived on Friday 8 Dhū'l-Ḥijja {27 January} and performed the Friday prayer in the Dome of the Rock. They also celebrated the Great Feast there on the Sunday {29 January}. He returned to his camp and remained[3] there for the rest of the day.

On Monday 11 Dhū'l-Ḥijja {30 January} he set out for Ascalon to inspect its affairs and to convey his brother on his way. He remained there for some days, restoring its shattered fabric and putting its affairs to right. Then he bade his brother farewell, giving him Kerak and taking Ascalon from him. Following the coastal route he made for Acre, inspecting the towns which he passed by and

---

1 According to Wensinck, *Concordance*, this *ḥadīth* is only in al-Tirmidhī's *Ṣaḥīḥ*, in the 'Excellencies of Jihad' chapter, section 12, i, p. 308, the latter two phrases being reversed.

2 *Fatḥ*, pp. 163 and 165, says that Ṣafad was taken on 8 Shawwāl [30 November].

3 Reading with B: *wa-aqāma*.

leaving garrisons and supplies. Having arrived at Acre he spent most of Muḥarram 585 [February-March 1189] there and appointed Bahā' al-Dīn Qarāqūsh[1] as governor, whom he ordered to repair the city wall and be very thorough over it, along with Ḥusām al-Dīn Bishāra. He departed for Damascus after the arrival of a detachment of troops from Egypt, whom he stationed in Acre as a garrison, and arrived at Damascus on 1 Ṣafar [21 March].

[97] His march to Shaqīf Arnūn, the expedition that is followed by the Acre affair

Saladin remained in Damascus until the month of Rabī' I 585 [began 19 April 1189]. During this month the envoy of the Caliph al-Nāṣir li-Dīn Allāh[2] came to him, ordering him to make the khutbah in the name of the caliph's son and heir apparent, which was duly done.

The sultan expressed his determination to attack Shaqīf Arnūn, a fortified place close to Bānyās. He marched forth after Friday prayers on 3 Rabī' I [21 April] and made camp on the Marj al-Fulūs. The morning of Saturday found him on the move. He came to the Marj al- Barghūth, where he halted, waiting for his armies. He remained until the 11th [29 April], while successive detachments arrived. He then moved to Bānyās and from there to Marj 'Uyūn on the 17th [5 May], where he camped. It was close enough to Shaqīf Arnūn for him to ride each day to inspect the place and return, while his troops were assembling and making their way to him from every hill and dale. For several days we continued to view the place daily, while the armies of Islam were every day increasing in numbers and equipment and what the lord of al-Shaqīf[3] could observe was convincing him that his security was at an end. He saw that improving his relationship with the sultan offered a way to be rescued, so he came down in person and the next thing we knew he was standing at the entrance to the sultan's tent. He was allowed to come in and was received with honour and respect. He was one of the Frankish nobles and one of their wise heads who knew Arabic and had some familiarity with histories and Ḥadīth collections. I heard that he kept a Muslim who read to him and explained things. He was a man of cautious deliberation.

He came before the sultan and ate a meal with him. Closeted together, he remarked that he was the sultan's mamluke, subject to his orders, and that he would surrender the place to him without trouble, stipulating that he be given a

---

1 Originally a mamluke of Shīrkūh, Saladin entrusted to him building work on the citadel and walls of Cairo. He later served Saladin's successors and died in 597/1201 (see *EI*², iv, pp. 613-614).

2 Abbasid caliph in Baghdad, reigned 575-622/1180-1225 (*EI*², vii, pp. 996-1003).

3 The lord of the castle of Beaufort was Reginald of Sidon.

place to live in at Damascus, for he could not subsequently live amongst the Franks, and also a fief in Damascus to support him and his family and that he be allowed to remain where he was, coming to and fro to attend upon the sultan, for three months from that day's date, so that he could safely retrieve his family and retainers from Tyre, and that he should receive the present year's revenue. Agreement was given [**98**] to all this. All the time he continued to frequent the sultan's presence, disputing with us about his religion while we argued for its falsity. He was an excellent conversationalist and cultured in his talk. During the month of Rabīʿ I news came of the surrender of Shawbak. The sultan had stationed a large force there, besieging it for a year. Their provisions were exhausted and they yielded the place on terms.

Account of the Franks' gathering to attack Acre

At the time of the surrender of Ascalon the sultan had undertaken that he would free the king if he ordered the garrison to hand over the city. The king did so and they obeyed, at which the king demanded his release and the sultan duly released him to be true to his word, while we were at Ḥiṣn al-Akrād. He was released from Anṭarṭūs. The sultan stipulated that the king should not draw a sword against him ever again and that he would be his servant, mamluke and freedman for ever. He broke faith (God curse him) and gathered troops together, then came to Tyre, seeking entry there. He camped at the gates, negotiating with the marquis who held the place. The marquis[1] (the accursed one), who was in Tyre, was a great and politic man, mighty in valour for his religion and very severe. He said, 'I am the lieutenant of the kings across the sea and they have not given me permission to hand it over to you.' The discussions lasted long and the agreement finally reached was that they should all cooperate against the Muslims, and that the forces in Tyre and other Frankish troops should unite to confront the Muslims. They made camp before the gate of Tyre.

Account of the battle in which Aybak al-Akhrash[2] met a martyr's death

On Monday 17 Jumādā I [3 July], the sultan was informed via the advanced pickets that the Franks had crossed the bridge that divides the territory of Tyre from that of Sidon, where we were. The sultan mounted up and the heralds aroused our men with their cries. The army rode off towards the pickets, but the

1 This is Conrad of Montferrat, who arrived to hold Tyre against Saladin after the battle of Ḥaṭṭīn and was to be briefly the elected king of Jerusalem.

2 *Nawādir* (see corrigenda) emends to al-Akhras, but *Fatḥ*, p. 181, has al-Akhrash in a passage where the rhyming prose demands the 'sh'.

sultan arrived when the battle was already over, for a body of the Franks had crossed the bridge in force and large numbers, and had been met by the Muslim pickets who fought them fiercely, killed a large number and wounded many more than they killed. Several were thrown into the river and drowned. Thus God gave victory to Islam [**99**] and its adherents. On the Muslim side only a mamluke of the sultan, called Aybak al-Akhrash, was killed. That day he met a martyr's death. He was a brave and valiant mounted warrior, well-experienced in warfare, but his horse unseated him and he sought the protection of a rock. He engaged the enemy with his arrows, until they were exhausted, and then with his sword, killing several, but they overwhelmed and slew him. The sultan grieved for him as he had been so brave and withdrew from the battle to some tents that had been pitched for him nearby without the full baggage-train.

Account of a second battle in which some Muslim infantry died as martyrs

The sultan remained in those tents until Wednesday 19 Jumādā I [5 July], when he rode out to reconnoitre the enemy, as was his custom. He was followed by a vast host of foot soldiers, voluntary warriors for the faith and common folk. He urged them to withdraw, but they would not. He even ordered his men to beat them, but still they would not. He feared for them, as the site was confined and there was no escape for men on foot. The foot soldiers charged the bridge and engaged the enemy in a skirmish. Several crossed over towards them and a fierce fight ensued. A large number of Franks assembled to oppose them, though they were not aware of that. After scouting the situation to learn that there was no ambush in wait behind them, the Franks charged as one man, taking the sultan by surprise, for he was some way away and had no main force with him. He had not gone out in any state of battle readiness, but had only ridden to view the situation as was his daily custom.

When it was clear what was happening and he could see the dust of battle, he sent the men he had with him to make the Muslims withdraw, but they found the situation already out of hand. The Franks were so superior in numbers that the squadron of cavalry sent by the sultan was itself in fear. The Franks overwhelmed the foot soldiers totally and a fierce engagement followed between them and the squadron. Many of the foot were taken prisoner or killed. The martyrs numbered 180 souls. On the Frankish side, too, a great number were killed and several also were drowned. One of those killed was the commander of the Germans, who was an important and respected man amongst them. Of men of note on the Muslim side, Ibn al-Biṣār[1] won martyrdom. He was a handsome, brave youth, whose death his father accepted with resignation for the sake of the

1 This person is named by *Fatḥ*, p. 182, as the Emir Ghāzī ibn Sa'd al-Dawla Mas'ūd ibn al-Baṣārū (*sic*).

Jihad [**100**] and shed not one tear for him, according to the testimony of several who were close to him. The Franks never had such a victory in all the battles that I was present at and witnessed, nor did they inflict such numerous losses on the Muslims as at this time.

The reason for his going to Acre with a flying column

When the sultan saw what had befallen the Muslims in this unusual battle, he gathered his staff and consulted them. He decided with them to attack the Franks, to cross the bridge and engage them to extirpate them utterly. The Franks had already moved from Tyre and had camped near the bridge at a distance of somewhat more than a league[1] from Tyre. Having confirmed his intention to do this, he set about it and rode away on the morning of Thursday 27 Jumādā I [13 July], followed by his staff, guards and the various troops. When the rear detachments had caught up with the leading ones, they found the screening force returning and their tents already dismantled. Asked why, they said that the Franks had withdrawn towards Tyre to seek the protection of its wall and be secure in its vicinity, and that they themselves, when they heard that, retired disappointed. The advanced screen was now not needed, so they drew back. Seeing this, the sultan decided to go to Acre to view how much of the wall had been built, to urge the remainder's completion and then to return. He travelled via Tibnīn and did not return to Marj 'Uyūn. He came to Acre and organised its affairs, ordering the completion of the construction of the city wall and that it should be done strongly and solidly. He also ordered them to be well-prepared and vigilant and then returned to his camp at Marj 'Uyūn, to await [the expiry of] the lord of al-Shaqīf's time-limit (God curse him).

Account of another battle

On Saturday 6 Jumādā II [22 July] the sultan heard that a group of the enemy's infantry were incautiously going as far as the Mount of Tibnīn to collect firewood. He still felt sore at heart for the Muslim foot soldiers and what had happened to them. He decided to make a plan and set an ambush to catch the enemy, having also heard that cavalry came behind these men to protect them. He laid an ambush suitable to confront all of them and sent to the troops of Tibnīn, ordering them to come out with a small force to harrass those foot soldiers and that, when the enemy's cavalry pursued them, they should flee [**101**] in a direction which he specified and that this should take place on the morning of

1 Used as equivalent for *farsakh* (parasang), about three to three and a half miles.

Monday 8 Jumādā II [24 July]. He also sent to the garrison of Acre, ordering them to position themselves behind the enemy's army, so that, if they made a move to aid their comrades, their tents would be attacked.

The sultan and his army moved out at dawn on the Monday, bristling with weapons, but with no baggage-train (they had not a single tent), towards the place specified for the [planned] retreat of Tibnīn's force. He passed beyond Tibnīn and organised his troops into eight divisions, from each of which he drew twenty brave and excellently mounted troopers. He ordered them to make themselves clearly visible to the enemy, to engage them and give way before them back to the ambush. This they undertook and were confronted by most of the Frankish army, led by the king (God curse him), for they had received some information and drawn up their battle formations. A sharp fight developed between the Franks and this small squadron, but the latter prolonged the encounter, too proud to retreat and induced by their zeal to disobey the sultan and to meet a numerous enemy with such a little band. The conflict continued till late on the Monday and nobody returned to the main army to tell them what had happened.

The sultan finally received information towards the end of the affair, when night had already fallen. He sent many detachments forward when he realised that there was little or no time left for a pitched battle and his plan would fail. When the Franks observed the first reinforcements that had joined the squadron they withdrew in retreat after much bloodshed on both sides. The dead on the Frankish side, according to the report of those present, for I was not a witness of the battle, numbered about ten, and on the Muslim side six, two from the advance guard and four Bedouin, one of whom was the Emir Zāmil, a fine, handsome youth, the chief of his clan. He died because his horse fell, his cousin gave up his own horse for him but this horse also was brought down. He and three relatives were taken. When the Franks saw that reinforcements had come, they killed them, fearing that they might be rescued. On both sides very many men and many horses were wounded.

A curious incident in this battle was as follows. One of the sultan's mamlukes, called Aybak, was severely wounded and fell among the corpses with his wounds gushing blood. He passed the whole night in that state until the Tuesday morning [25 July]. His comrades searched for him but could not find him, so informed the sultan that he was missing. The latter sent people to find out what had happened to him, who discovered him among the corpses as previously described. They took him up and carried him to the camp in that state and God restored him to full health. The sultan returned to his camp triumphant and rejoicing on Wednesday 10 Jumādā II [26 July].

[102] The arrest of the lord of al-Shaqīf and the reason why

It became widely understood that the lord of al-Shaqīf had set his proposed time limit deceitfully and was not dealing truthfully. Procrastination was his only aim. Many indications of that became obvious, such as his eagerness to gather provisions, his strengthening the gates and other matters. The sultan decided to climb to the top of the mountain to be near the place, in sight of it indeed, and to prevent the entry of any reinforcements or provisions. He put it out that the reason for this was the current extreme heat and the need to escape the unhealthy valley bottom. The move to the plateau was made on the eve of Friday 12 Jumādā II [28 July], when a quarter of the night had past. The next morning the lord of al-Shaqīf found the sultan's tent already pitched there. Some of the army remained as they were in the valley. When the lord of al-Shaqīf saw how close the sultan now was and he realised that of his period of grace only the remaining days of Jumādā II were left, he was tempted to go down to wait upon the sultan and to wheedle him into granting an extension of the time-limit. He imagined from what he had seen of the sultan's character and kindness that that could be managed, so he went to him and reviewed the situation, saying, 'Only a little of the period is left. What difference is there between handing it over today or tomorrow? It is best for the sultan to send people to take the place over.' He pretended, however, that he still had several family members in Tyre and that they were about to leave during the next few days.

He spent the day with the sultan until nightfall, when he climbed back to the castle. The sultan had revealed nothing to him and kept him to his agreement and the stipulated time-limit. After some days he came down again, when the end and expiry of the period was imminent, and asked for a private audience with the sultan at which he asked him to grant him an extension of nine months to complete the year. The sultan scented treachery but he led him a dance without killing all his hopes and said, 'We will think about that. We will call a council and ask their opinion. Whatever comes out of that we will let you know.' He pitched a tent for him near his own and set a watch over him without his realising it. All the while he was treated with extreme honour and respect and the discussions and consultations between them were kept up in that vein, until time ran out and the demand for the place's surrender was made. Saladin charged him directly, saying 'You have plotted treachery, completed new construction in the place and brought in stores.' He denied this. It was agreed that he should send his trusted representative and the sultan should send his to carry out the hand-over and to see whether there had been any fresh construction or not. They went to the castle, but his garrison within ignored orders. It was found that he had built a gate in the wall that had not been there before. A close guard was put on him, which was now done openly, and he was prevented from entering into **[103]** the sultan's presence. He was told, 'Time has run out. You must surrender the place,' but he gave specious reasons for not doing so and delaying a response. A second time he sent to the garrison ordering them to surrender, but they made their disobedience quite clear and said, 'We are lieutenants of the Messiah, not yours.' The fortress was closely blockaded and pickets were put in place around it to stop any entry or egress.

When it was Sunday 28 Jumādā II[1] in the year 585 [13 August 1189], he himself acknowledged the expiration of the time-limit, for he had previously repudiated it, and said, 'I shall go and hand over the place.' He was given a mule to ride and with him went a large body of emirs and troops. They came to al-Shaqīf and he ordered his men to give up but they refused. He asked for a priest with whom, when he appeared, he conversed in his language. The priest went back in and after his return their resistance grew stronger. It was thought that he had strongly urged the priest to hold out. All that day he continued negotiating, but they took no notice, so he was taken back to the sultan's camp. That night he was dispatched to Bānyās and put under guard in its castle. Our troops surrounded al-Shaqīf, maintaining a siege and making assaults. The lord of al-Shaqīf remained in Bānyās until 6 Rajab [20 August]. The sultan was furious with him because he and his army had lost three months in which nothing had been achieved. He was summoned to the camp and threatened with terrible things the night he arrived but to no effect.

On the morning of Wednesday 8 Rajab [22 August] the sultan moved up to the summit of the mountain with his tents to a position which overlooked al-Shaqīf more than where he first had been and which was further from the unhealthy air of the plain. His constitution had already begun to suffer. Subsequently, we heard that the Franks in Tyre and those who were with the king had set out towards al-Nawāqīr,[2] making for Acre and that some of them had come to Iskandarūna where a skirmish took place between them and Muslim infantry. The Muslims killed a small number of them, but the Franks held their place there.

The conflict at Acre (may God facilitate its conquest) and its cause

The sultan was appalled when he heard that the Franks had moved in that direction, but he decided not to be hasty for fear that their intention might be to force him to move from al-Shaqīf and not really to attack Acre. He therefore

---

1 *Nawādir* has Sunday 18th, which would correspond to 3 August 1189 but that was a Thursday. The editor of *Fatḥ*, p. 179, accepts '28th', which is required for the elapse of three months.

2 This plural form (also found in Yāqūt, iv, p. 816: 'a gap in the mountains between Acre and Tyre on the coast') is normally replaced by al-Nāqūra. There was a narrow and difficult passage around the Ra's al-Nāqūra (the Ladder of Tyre), see Dussaud, *Topographie historique*, p. 20.

remained to await reports on the situation until Sunday 12 Rajab [27 August]. Then a courier arrived [**104**] with information that the Franks during the remainder of that day had moved and camped at 'Ayn Baṣṣa, while their advanced units had arrived at al-Zīb.[1] Worried by this, the sultan wrote to all the rulers of regions [under his dominion], ordering the armies of Islam to come to his camp. Again he renewed his letters of urgent encouragement and ordered the baggage-train to move that night.

The morning of Monday 13 Rajab [28 August] found him on the road to Acre via Tiberias since that was the only route able to accommodate his army. He sent a detachment by the Tibnīn route to keep watch on the enemy and to keep him regularly informed of their movements. Our march brought us to al-Ḥūla at midday, where we rested for a while. Then off again and he marched the whole night long until he came to a place called al-Minya on Tuesday morning 14 Rajab [29 August]. There we heard that the Franks had reached Acre on Monday 13th [28 August]. The sultan sent the lord of al-Shaqīf to Damascus after abusing him severely for his double dealing.

From al-Minya the sultan travelled without heavy baggage to link up at Marj Ṣaffūriyya with those troops that he had sent by the Tibnīn route. He had appointed a rendezvous with them there and also ordered the baggage train to join him later at Marj Ṣaffūriyya. He moved forward until he was in sight of the enemy from al-Kharrūba and he sent some troops, undetected by the Franks, into Acre as reinforcements for the garrison. He continued to send detachment after detachment until there was a large force within and plentiful supplies. He formed his army into left and right wing and centre, and moved from al-Kharrūba, where he had camped on Wednesday 15 Rajab [30 August], and proceeded to take up position at Tell Kaysān where the Acre plain begins. He ordered his men to remain in battle readiness. The extremity of the left wing rested on the Sweet River and that of the right wing was in the vicinity of the Tell al-'Ayyāḍiyya. Thus the Muslim army encompassed the God-forsaken enemy and blocked all their escape routes. The forces of Islam mustered progressively and the sultan stationed a permanent screening force and advance guard to be daily in contact with the enemy, who were so confined to their camp on all sides that nobody could leave it without being wounded or killed.

The enemy's camp was around a half of Acre and their king's tent was on Tell al-Muṣallabīn[2] near the gate [**105**] of the city. Their mounted soldiers numbered 2,000 and their foot 30,000. I have not seen anyone who made them less than that but I have seen others who estimated them to be more numerous. Their reinforcement by sea did not cease and a series of major skirmishes occurred between them and our forward detachment. The Muslims were eagerly calling

---

1 Called Castel Imbert by the Crusaders, it is on the coast north of Acre.

2 Thus *Nawādir*, meaning 'Hill of the Crucified'. Wilson, *Saladin*, p. 156, read *al-muṣallīn*, 'Hill of those who pray', according to him also known as Tell al-Fukhkhār.

for a confrontation, but the sultan held them back until his chosen moment, for the various Muslim expeditionary forces were arriving one after another as were the princes and emirs of the various regions. The first to arrive was the great and noble emir Muẓaffar al-Dīn ibn Zayn al-Dīn, who was followed by al-Muẓaffar Taqī al-Dīn, the lord of Ḥamā, with his army. The armies of Islam came in a steady stream.

At this juncture Ḥusām al-Dīn Sunqur al-Akhlāṭī died as a result of severe diarrhoea. The Muslims greatly grieved for him, for he was a brave and pious man (may God have mercy on him). This was on Monday 27 Rajab [1 September] at a hill on the Acre plain overlooking al-'Ayāḍiyya.

The Franks, having grown very numerous and their position now being very strong, so completely encompassed Acre as to prevent all entry and egress. That was on Thursday the last day of Rajab [14 September]. Seeing this, the sultan was very distressed and disturbed. His lofty zeal burned to open up a way into Acre to maintain a route for supplies and reliefs and such like. He summoned his emirs and councillors of state and consulted them about how to bring pressure on the enemy. It was concluded that he should press them hard to inflict a comprehensive defeat and open a route into Acre. Therefore early in the morning of Friday 1 Sha'bān [15 September] he attacked with his army, organised as right wing, left wing and centre, and pressed the enemy very hard.

The attack was launched after the Friday prayer to benefit from the prayers of the Muslim preachers in their pulpits. Mighty assaults and many charges were made. The enemy's army spread out and gained control of the hills. The left wing of their force reached to the Sweet River towards the sea, while their right was opposite the middle fort of Acre. The fighting continued until nightfall separated the two sides. In both camps men passed the night under arms, each side watchful of the other until the morning of Saturday 2 Sha'bān [16 September] dawned.

[106] The successful opening of a route into Acre

The fighting began on the morning of the Saturday. The sultan sent a body of our brave troops to the sea to the north of Acre. The enemy had no tents there, but their troops without any baggage-train had extended north of Acre as far as the sea. Our picked band attacked the Frankish troops positioned to the north of Acre, who were soundly defeated, many of them being killed. Their survivors turned back to their tents, while the Muslims pursued them to where their tents began. The Muslim advanced guard took position to prevent their troops either coming out or going in, and so a route to Acre was opened, from the gate of the fort known as the King's Gate as far as the Gate of Qarāqūsh, a new one he had built. The route became a frequented highway, along which traders with their commodities passed as did individual men and women, while the advanced guard protected the route from the enemy.

That same day the sultan entered Acre and climbed on to the wall to view the enemy's camp below. The Muslims rejoiced at their God-given victory. The troops within Acre made a sortie led by the sultan and the whole force of Islam surrounded the Frankish army, encompassing it from every side.

With this settled, our men relaxed their martial efforts - it was after the noonday prayer - to water their horses and to take some rest. The break was on the understanding that, if they enjoyed a little rest, they would resume the battle to engage the enemy comprehensively because of the confidence they felt to deal with them. But that day there was little time left and our men were seized with discontent and tiredness, so they did not return to the fight that day. They passed the night expecting to go into battle on the Sunday morning, hoping for a decisive encounter. The enemy, however, skulked[1] in their tents, not one of them making an appearance.

The morning of Sunday 3 Sha'bān [17 September] our men were drawn up in battle formation and surrounded the enemy, intending a general attack, with the emirs and most of the army dismounting and engaging the enemy in their tents. When all preparations had been made, some of the emirs proposed that there should be a postponement **[107]** until Tuesday morning 4 Sha'bān [18 September] and that all the infantry should enter Acre and attack the rear of the enemy through the city gates along with the troops garrisoning the city, while the forces of Islam outside the city charged from all sides, making the attack a concerted one. The sultan was personally seeing to these matters and dealing with them[2] himself, present at every crisis point like a bereft mother in his great anxiety and abundant care. One of his doctors told me that from Friday till this Sunday he took no nourishment except for something very light, so great was his concern. They carried out the plan but the enemy resisted strongly, protecting themselves amongst their tents. Until Friday 8 Sha'bān [22 September] the battlefield remained a lively market where lives were sold for precious gains[3] and the storm of war rained down the heads of captains old and young.

Our forces withdraw to Tell al-'Ayyāḍiyya

On Friday 8 Sha'bān the enemy determined to march out with all their forces. Both foot and horse came forth and spread over the hills. They marched steadily, not exhausting themselves, keeping within the infantry who were like a solid wall

---

1 B also reads *iḥtawā*, which perhaps has the meaning of the Vth form, *taḥawwā*, 'to coil (like a snake)'. *RHC Or*, p. 136, reads *ikhtafā*, 'to hide'.

2 Taking the alternative reading *yukāfiḥu-hā*.

3 That is, for entry into Paradise as a martyr.

around them, all following one another, until they drew near to the tents of the advanced guard. When the Muslims saw this and how boldly the enemy came against them, our brave soldiers shouted to one another and our warriors singled out their opponents. The sultan cried aloud to the troops of Islam, 'Huzzah for Islam!' All our men mounted up. Horse and foot, young and old, all were of one accord. As one man, they attacked the wretched enemy who retired in a rout, while the sword was at work on them. Those who escaped did so with a wound and the doomed ones were thrown down. Frantic in retreat, their wounded trampled their dead, none of them having any care for their fellows, until the survivors gained their tents. They refrained from battle for several days, their furthest ambition being to preserve their lives and keep their heads. **[108]** The route to Acre remained open and the Muslims continued to go back and forth. I was one of those who went in, climbed on the city wall and shot at the enemy from on top of the wall with whatever came to hand.

Fighting between the two sides continued unbroken day and night until 11 Sha'bān [25 September]. The sultan decided to enlarge the circle that enclosed them, in the hope that they might venture out and meet their doom. He therefore transferred the baggage-train to Tell al-'Ayyāḍiyya, which is a hill opposite Tell al-Muṣallabīn that looked out over Acre and the enemy's tents. At this locality there died Ḥusām al-Dīn Ṭumān, one of the Muslims' champions. He was buried on the flat top of this hill. Along with a group of jurists I said prayers over him on the eve of mid-Sha'bān [29 September][1] when some part of the night had passed.

Account of a Bedouin clash with the enemy

This came about because we heard that a group of the enemy was going to gather what grew on the river bank as fodder. The sultan placed some of the Bedouin there to ambush them. He selected the Bedouin because of their fleetness on horseback and his confidence in them. The enemy left their camp, knowing nothing of the Arabs who charged the Franks, killing a large number of them and taking some prisoner. They brought several heads before the sultan, who rewarded them with robes and largess. That was on Saturday 16 Sha'bān [30 September].

The evening of that day a major battle took place between the enemy and our people in the city, in which a great number were killed on both sides. Similar conflicts went on for a long time and not a day passed without wounding, killing, capturing and plundering. They got to know one another, in that both sides would converse and leave off fighting. At times some people would sing and

1 According to *Fatḥ*, p. 195, Ṭumān died on the afternoon of Wednesday 13 Sha'bān/ 27 September.

others dance, so familiar had they become over time, and then after a while they would revert to fighting.

A strange occurrence during these encounters

One day the men on both sides were tired of fighting and said, 'How much longer will the older men go on fighting, while the young have no share? We want two young men to contend, one of ours and one of yours.' **[109]** Two youths were brought out of the city to meet two from the Franks. They fought fiercely together and one of the Muslim youths leapt on one of the infidel youths, clasped him in his arms and threw him to the ground and took him prisoner, tying him fast to take him away. A Frankish man ransomed him for two dinars. They said, 'He really is your prisoner,' so he took the two dinars and released him. This is a strange incident of war.

A ship arrived for the Franks, bringing horses. One of the horses bolted and fell into the sea. It kept swimming, while they were all around it, trying to recover it, until it entered Acre harbour and was seized by the Muslims.

Account of the great pitched battle before Acre (may God facilitate its conquest)

On Wednesday 21 Sha'bān [4 October] the Franks manoeuvred in a way that they had not normally done before, horse and foot, great and small, and they took up their battle formations beyond their tents as centre, right wing and left wing. In the centre was the king with the Gospel carried before him, covered by a cloth of satin. Four persons held the four corners as they walked before the king. The right wing deployed to face the left wing of the Muslim army across its whole length and the enemy's left wing deployed opposite our right wing, right to its limit. They seized the tops of the hills with their extreme right reaching the river, while their extreme left reached the sea. On the Muslim side, when the sultan observed the enemy's movements, he ordered the herald to proclaim, 'Huzzah for Islam and the troops of the true faith!' Our men mounted up, ready to sell their lives for Paradise. Our right stretched to the sea, with each detachment mounted and in position before their tents, and our left rested on the river, in similar readiness.

[110] The sultan had organised our men in the placement of their tents as right and left wings and centre, in battle formation, so that, when there was any alarm, they would not need re-positioning. He himself was in the centre and to the right of the centre was his son al-Afḍal, then his son al-Ẓāhir, then the troops of Mosul led by Ẓahīr al-Dīn Ibn al-Balankarī, then the troops of Diyār Bakr in the service of Quṭb al-Dīn ibn Nūr al-Dīn, the lord of Ḥiṣn Kayfā, then Ḥusām al-Dīn ibn Lājīn, the lord of Nablus, then the *Ṭawāshī*[1] Qaymāz al-Najmī, and large groups reaching to the extremity of the right wing. In this extreme position was al-Muẓaffar Taqī al-Dīn with his levies and standing troop, overlooking the sea. As for the near left wing, next to the centre was Sayf al-Dīn 'Alī ibn Aḥmad al-Mashṭūb, one of the leading notables and chiefs of the Kurds, and the Emir Mujallī with the bands of the Mihrānī and Hakkārī Kurds, and Mujāhid al-Dīn Yarunqush, commander of the Sinjār troops, then a detachment of mamlukes, then Muẓaffar al-Dīn ibn Zayn al-Dīn with his levies and standing troop. On the far left wing were the great mamlukes of Asad al-Dīn, such as Sayf al-Dīn Yāzkuj and Ruslān Bughā, and the Asadiyya company whose bravery was proverbial. In the advance guard of the centre was the jurist 'Īsā and his following. The sultan meanwhile was personally going the rounds of the divisions, encouraging them for the fight, urging them to stand firm before the enemy and motivating them to bring victory to God's religion.

The enemy kept moving forward, as did the Muslims, until four hours had passed and the day was well advanced. Thereupon the enemy's left moved against the Muslim right. Al-Muẓaffar sent the skirmishers out to meet them and there were many encounters between them. The enemy outnumbered al-Muẓaffar, who was at the far right next the sea, so he withdrew a little to encourage them in the hope they might advance too far from their comrades, thus enabling him to gain some success over them. When the sultan saw that he had retired, he thought he was in trouble, so reinforced him with several divisions from the centre which made his wing very strong. The enemy left withdrew and gathered on a hill overlooking the sea.

[111] When the Franks facing the centre saw that the centre had been weakened by the transfer of those divisions, their hopes soared and they moved against the right of the centre, attacking as one man, horse and foot. I saw the infantry keep pace with the cavalry, who, advancing at a walk, did not get ahead of them. As God willed it, the attack fell on the Diyār Bakr troops, who were inexperienced in warfare. They gave way before the enemy and were broken and routed. The panic spread so that most of the right wing fled the field and the enemy pursued those in flight as far al-'Ayāḍiyya. They surrounded the hill there and a group of the enemy climbed to the sultan's tents and slew one of the wardrobe staff who was there. Also on that day Ismā'īl al-Mukabbis and Ibn Rawāḥa[2] met a martyr's death.

---

1 Here it is not clear whether this term means 'eunuch' or 'trooper of higher grade'. Qaymāz was clearly of some seniority and the term could be applied to a leading emir (see Gibb, 'The Armies of Saladin', p. 87, note 31.

2 In *Fatḥ*, p. 206, Ismā'īl is qualified as 'the Sufi from Urmiya' and the other, Abū 'Alī ibn Rawāḥa, a jurist (*al-faqīh*) and poet, is said to be a descendant of 'Abd Allāh ibn Rawāḥa, a Companion of the Prophet, although this is denied by Abū Shāma in *Rawḍ*, ii, p. 147.

The left wing, however, stood firm because the charge had not affected them. The sultan began making the rounds of the divisions to raise their spirits, making them fair promises and encouraging them to wage the Jihad. He was shouting, 'On, on for Islam!' Only five persons remained with him as he did the rounds and traversed the ranks. He retired to a position below the hill on which his tents were. Meanwhile, the routed elements of the army went in their flight as far as al-Qaḥwāna, across the Tiberias bridge.[1] Some of them made their way to Damascus. The Frankish pursuers chased them as far as al-'Ayyāḍiyya. When they saw they had climbed the hill, they turned away and went back towards their army, where they were met by a crowd of pages, muleteers[2] and grooms as they were fleeing on the transport mules. They killed some of these and then came to the beginning of the market where they killed several persons, but themselves lost several dead because there was a vast crowd of people in the market and they had arms.[3]

Those who climbed to the sultan's tents did not loot anything at all, except that they killed those we have mentioned, three persons in all. Then they saw the Muslim left wing standing firm and realised that their victory was not complete. Back down the hill they went, looking for their army.

[112] The sultan kept his position beneath the hill, accompanied by a small contingent, rallying our men for a counter-attack on the enemy. When they were seen descending from the hill, our men wanted to engage them, but the sultan ordered them to wait until they had turned their backs and were eagerly seeking their comrades. Then he gave the signal and the troops charged and unseated several. Our men were eager to finish them and pursued them in overwhelming numbers until they reached their comrades with men hot on their heels. When their comrades saw the Franks in flight, pursued by the Muslims in great numbers, they thought that those who had attacked had been killed and that only this small band had survived and that they had suffered a defeat. They fled in a wild rout and our left wing moved on them.

Al-Muẓaffar returned with his company from the right wing and our men cheered and encouraged one another. From every direction they reassembled. God gave the lie to the Devil and brought victory to the Faith. On and on went the killing, the overthrowing, striking and wounding until the fugitives that survived reached the enemy camp. The Muslims stormed their tents, but fresh companies that they had prepared, fearing such an outcome, emerged and drove the Muslims back. Tiredness had taken its toll of our men. Fear and their

---

1 Al-Qaḥwāna (otherwise al-Uqḥuwāna as in Yāqūt, i, p. 334) is the area immediately south-east of Lake Tiberias.

2 Correct *Nawādir*'s text to *al-kharbandiyya*, as in B.

3 The sentence is based on B: *fa-qatalū minhum jamā'atan thumma jā'ū ilā ra's al-sūq fa-qatalū jamā'tan wa-qutila minhum jamā'atun fa-inna etc*. Cf. the quotation in *Rawḍ*, ii, p. 145.

sweating bodies curbed them, so they withdrew after the time for afternoon prayer, wading through the blood of the dead back to their tents, happy and delighted.

That day the sultan also returned happy and delighted to his tent. The clerks sat there recording the losses. Amongst the grooms and people of no standing those lost numbered 150, while from amongst men of mark a martyr's death that day was gained by Ẓahīr al-Dīn, the jurist 'Īsā's brother. I saw the latter sitting and laughing, while people were offering their condolences, but he reproved them and said, 'This is a day for congratulation, not a day for condolence.' He himself had fallen from his horse and been helped back into the saddle. Several of his relatives were killed protecting him. Also on that day the Emir Mujallī was killed. These were the Muslim losses. The enemy's dead were estimated to be 7,000. However, I saw them when they had been carried to the river bank to be thrown in and I estimated them to be less than that.

When the Muslims were first routed, the grooms saw that the camp was devoid of anyone to control them, for the army was split **[113]** into two, those fleeing or those fighting, and there was nobody left in the tents. They saw that a reverse had occurred and they believed it would become a comprehensive defeat and that the enemy would plunder everything in the tents. Therefore they helped themselves and carried off all that was there. People lost vast sums. This was more disastrous than the rout itself.

When the sultan returned to the camp and saw what had happened, the plunder of property and the flight, he hastened to send letters and messengers to bring back those that had fled and round up any deserters. To this end a succession of messengers went out even as far as the defile of Fīq.[1] They rallied our men, telling them of the Muslim successes. He ordered that the belongings should be collected from the servants' hands and brought to his tent, even the horse blankets and baskets. He took his seat with us around him and ordered 'Let it be given him' for anyone who recognised anything and swore that it was his. He met these disasters with a firm heart, a generous spirit, a cheerful face, a sound not a distraught mind, a resigned trust in God and a strong determination that God's religion would triumph.

The enemy returned to their tents, having had their champions killed and their commanders and princes overthrown and lost. The sultan ordered a cart to go from Acre to carry the Frankish dead to the bank of the river and throw them in. One of the persons who looked after this business of the cart told me that he took a thread and every time he loaded a corpse he made a knot. The number of the dead from the left wing reached 4,100 and a few extra. There still remained the dead from the right wing and the centre, whom he did not count, for others dealt with those. After this some of the enemy sought their own survival and stayed in

1 This leads up from Lake Tiberias to the town of Fīq (Aphek) about 7 km east of the lake on the route to Damascus (see Yāqūt, iii, pp. 932-933).

their camp, unconcerned with the Muslim troops, and a large number of the Muslim forces deserted because of the rout. Only men of known standing, fearing retribution, returned. The rest fled wherever they chose.

The sultan set about gathering the plundered property and restoring it to its owners. He organised proclamations throughout the army and backed up the announcements with dire threats. He personally supervised the distribution. **[114]** So vast an amount of goods was assembled in his tent that someone sitting on one side could not see anyone sitting on the other. A call was made for anyone who had lost anything. Crowds came and anyone who recognised his baggage and could give its detailed description, if he swore to it, took it away, things such as a horse covering and basket to a belt and jewel. This gave the sultan much trouble, but he looked upon it merely as a blessing from God for which one should be grateful and to which one should eagerly stretch an accepting hand. I was present the day the goods were distributed to their owners and I saw a market for justice in action, greater than which this world has never seen. That was on Friday 23 Sha'bān [6 October].

When this business was finished and the tumult had died down, the sultan ordered the withdrawal of the baggage-train to a place called al-Kharrūba, fearing the smells from the corpses and the unhealthy effects of the battlefield on the troops. It was near the battle site, but a little further away than where he had been camped. A tent was pitched for him by the baggage-train. He ordered the advance guard to stay where he had been camped. That was on Thursday 29 Sha'bān [12 October].

At the end of the month [13 October] he summoned the emirs and his councillors and bade them listen well to what he said. I was one of those present. He said, 'In the name of God. Praise be to God and blessing and peace be upon His Prophet. Know that this enemy of God's and our enemy has come down on our land and trampled the land of Islam. God willing, signs that we shall defeat him have appeared. He is left in small numbers and we must exert ourselves to root him out. God has made that our duty. You know that behind these forces of ours are no reserves that we may look for, apart for al-'Ādil, who is coming. If this enemy survives and lasts until the sea is open, he will receive vast reinforcements. Decidedly the right thing to do in my opinion is to engage them closely. Will each one of you tell us what his opinion is on this.' This was on the 13th of the solar month of Tishrīn [13 October]. People's opinions were in ferment and the views expressed see-sawed back and forth. In the end their opinion was that the best course was to withdraw the army to al-Kharrūba and that the troops should wait some days to rest from bearing arms and to recover themselves, for exhaustion had taken its toll and they were mentally worn out. To expect them to tackle a task other than one they were capable of bearing risked being a disaster. The troops had been fifty days under arms and on horseback. The horses, too, were upset and tired of the chafing of their bridles. With a chance to take a little rest their spirits would return. Al-'Ādil would come and share in our council and action. We could get the deserters back and assemble our foot-soldiers to be in position facing the [enemy] foot-soldiers. The sultan's constitution was disordered, for he had been affected by all that his mind had had to bear and the tiredness that had afflicted him from being in arms and full of cares at this time. What they said had weight with him and he thought it was for the best. Thus the army moved back to the baggage-train on Monday 3 Ramaḍān {16 October}. **[115]** The sultan moved that night and there he remained, improving his state of health, assembling the troops and waiting for his brother, al-'Ādil, until Monday 10 Ramaḍān {23 October}.

The arrival of news of the German emperor (God curse him)

As Ramaḍān of the year 585 began {14 October 1189} from Aleppo came letters from his son, al-Ẓāhir, reporting that he had confirmed that the German emperor[1] had set out for Constantinople in a great host, said to be 200,000 or 260,000, intending to come to the lands of Islam. This greatly troubled the sultan and caused him anxiety. He decided to rouse the population for the Jihad and to tell the current caliph of this development. He gave me this commission and commanded me to go to the lord of Sinjār, the lord of Jazīrat [Ibn 'Umar], the lord of Mosul and the lord of Irbil and to summon them personally to the Jihad with their troops. He also ordered me to travel to Baghdad to inform the caliph of the day of this and to urge him to provide help. The caliph at the time was al-Nāṣir li-Dīn Allāh Abū'l-'Abbās Aḥmad ibn al-Mustaḍī' bi-Amr Allāh. I set out on this mission on 11 Ramaḍān {24 October} and God helped me to reach these princes and deliver my message to them, to which they responded. 'Imād al-Dīn Zankī, lord of Sinjār, set out this year with his standing troops and his levies, as did his nephew Sanjar Shāh, lord of Jazīrat [Ibn 'Umar], leading his troops. The lord of Mosul, 'Izz al-Dīn, sent his son, 'Alā' al-Dīn Khurramshāh, with most of his troops. The lord of Irbil marched in person with his army.

I came to the August Divan at Baghdad and conveyed an account of the situation as instructed. Every fine promise was made and I returned to the sultan's presence, arriving on Thursday 5 Rabī' I 586 [12 April 1190]. I came earlier than the troops, but could tell him that the princes had responded with 'To hear is to obey' and that they were making their expedition plans. He was pleased and delighted at that.

[1] The Holy Roman Emperor Frederick I Barbarossa (1152-1190).

[116] Account of the battle of the dunes beside the river at Acre

When Ṣafar of this year came [March-April 1190], the sultan went out hunting, feeling secure because of the distance of his camp from the enemy. The chase led him far off. When the enemy heard of this, they took our forces by surprise and made a massed sortie to attack the Muslim army. Al-ʿĀdil, realising what they were about, roused our men. The troops mounted up and charged them. A great battle ensued, in which a multitude were killed and a large number wounded, but amongst men of note on the Muslim side the only fatality was a mamluke of the sultan, called Arghush,[1] a good man (God have mercy on him), who met a martyr's death that day.

Hearing the news, the sultan returned in great anxiety. He found the battle already concluded and every detachment back with their comrades. The enemy retired, frustrated losers (praise and thanks be to God). This is a battle that I did not witness because I was away on my travels. Of earlier battles I observed what a person of my sort is able to observe, but I gained a knowledge of the rest comparable to that of a participant.

The death of the jurist ʿĪsā

This is something I heard of, since I was not present when it happened. ʿĪsā fell ill with an illness that used to visit him when he was depressed. He then suffered diarrhoea which weakened him, but he did not miss his prayers nor did he lose his mind before he died, according to what people who attended him told me. He was a generous and brave man, well-intentioned and very eager to satisfy the needs of his fellow Muslims. He died at daybreak, Tuesday 9 Dhū'l-Qaʿda 585 [19 December 1189].

[117] A strange event

A strange event in this battle was as follows. A mamluke of the sultan's, called Sarāsunqur, a valiant man, had killed a great many of God's enemies and done much destruction amongst them. Their hearts were sore at the damage he was doing them, so they devised a plan. They assembled in ambush, from which several emerged and caught his attention. He charged them and was soon amongst them. From all sides they then leapt on him and laid hold of him. One seized his hair and another struck at his neck with his sword, for Sarāsunqur had killed a relative of his. The blow fell on the hand of the person who was holding

1 *Fatḥ*, p. 238, names the Ḥājib, Aydughmush al-Majdī.

his hair and cut it off, thus releasing his hair. The mamluke fled with all speed back to his comrades with the enemy running after him in hot pursuit, but nobody caught him and he returned safe and sound (God be praised) and 'God turned back the unbelievers in their wrath. They gained no benefit.'[1]

The surrender of al-Shaqīf in 586 [1190]

When it was Sunday 15 Rabī' I [22 April], the Franks holding al-Shaqīf realised that there was no-one to save them from what God had in store and, if they were taken by force, they would lose their heads, so they asked for terms. Many negotiations followed on the terms of surrender. They had learnt concerning the state of their lord that he had been severely tortured. It was finally settled that al-Shaqīf should be given up, that the lord and all the Franks in the place should be set free, but that all money and stores within should be left behind. On the date given above, the surrender took place. Talks had been held many times before the decision was reached on the aforementioned date. The lord of Sidon and the Franks who had been in al-Shaqīf withdrew to Tyre.

When the sultan saw how much importance the Franks who had come from their homelands attached to Acre and how it was the target at which all their determined plans were directed, he benefited from the winter closure of navigation and poured into Acre sufficient provisions, supplies, equipment and men to make him feel confident that it was secure, subject to God's foreordained plan. He ordered his deputies in Egypt to construct a large fleet to carry many men, which sailed **[118]** and entered Acre, outwitting the enemy despite their efforts. He gave the troops leave to depart for the duration of the winter, to recuperate and rest. He himself remained face to face with the enemy with a small troop. The two armies had become separated by areas of deep mud and thus it was impossible for either side to reach the other.

A curious piece of information

When the sultan heard the news that the enemy were moving against Acre, he gathered his emirs and councillors at Marj 'Uyūn and consulted them about what he should do. In his opinion, as he put it, 'The best course is for us to engage them closely and prevent them from investing the city. Otherwise, if they mount a siege, they will make their infantry a protective wall and dig a ditch, so it will be difficult for us to get to them. It is to be feared that the city will be lost.' The advice of most of the others was 'When they start a siege and our troops are all

---

1 Koran xxxiii, 25.

gathered, in one day we shall dislodge them.' It came about as the sultan said. By God, I heard him say those words and I witnessed what he said come true. This fits what the Prophet meant when he said, 'In my community there are those with insight who speak out, and 'Umar is one of them.'[1]

The sultan kept up his efforts to send provisions, equipment, weapons and men into Acre until winter passed and the sea was open again. The campaigning season came around and he wrote to summon the troops from the outlying lands. When the initial detachments came one after another and the forces of Islam had grown strong, the sultan moved towards the enemy and camped at Tell Kaysān. That was on 18 Rabīʿ I 586 [25 April 1190]. He formed the troops into centre, left and right wings. On the far right was his son, al-Afḍal. Reinforcements came with constant fresh waves of troops. The caliph's envoy also arrived.

Arrival of the caliph's envoy

On Monday 16 Rabīʿ I [23 April] the envoy of the caliph, a young man of noble descent from the Prophet, arrived, accompanied by two loads of Greek fire and a number of specialist artificers. He also brought a money order from the August Caliphal Divan (may God exalt it), containing authorisation for the sultan to borrow 20,000 dinars **[119]** from merchants to spend on the Jihad and for the debt repayment to be transferred to the Caliphal Divan. The sultan accepted everything that the envoy brought, but begged to decline the money order and the burden it imposed (God bless him).

On that day the sultan was informed that the Franks had made an assault on the city and pressed it hard, so he rode out to engage them and take the pressure off the city. He fought them hard until night separated the two parties and each returned to their comrades. The sultan considered the strength of the Islamic forces and considered how distant his position was from the enemy. He feared that the city might be attacked and its fate settled, so he decided to move with the whole army and baggage-train to Tell al-ʿAjūl.[2] This change of position took place on 25 Rabīʿ I [2 May]. The morning of that day a swimmer arrived from the city bringing letters with news that the enemy had filled in part of the moat and that they were strongly determined to intensify the seige. The sultan sent out fresh letters urging his armies to come. He disposed his forces in battle order and attacked the enemy to distract them from their purpose.

---

1 Two versions of this are in al-Bukhārī, *al-Jāmiʿ al-ṣaḥīḥ*, ii, p. 427, in 'Excellencies of the Companions', section 6: 'Among peoples before you were men with insight (*muḥaddathūn*). If there is one in my community it is 'Umar', and 'Among the Israelites before you were men who spoke out (*yukallimūn*) without being prophets. If there is one in my community it is 'Umar', i.e., 'Umar ibn al-Khaṭṭāb, the second caliph.

2 Not, of course, to be confused with the place on the coast south of Gaza.

The arrival of his son, al-Ẓāhir

At daybreak on Friday 27 Rabīʿ I [4 May] his son, al-Ẓāhir Ghiyāth al-Dīn Ghāzī, lord of Aleppo, arrived with a small retinue to pay his respects to the sultan, having left his troop at their camp. He waited on his father and satisfied his desire to see him. At dawn on Saturday 28th of the month [5 May] he returned to his troop and that same day brought them to Acre along with his levies. He put on a show of finery. They donned breastplates, unfurled flags and standards, beat drums and blew trumpets. They passed in review before the sultan, who had ridden out to meet them on the plain, and were led to take their positions opposite the enemy, who saw in these soldiers of God such as to cause them alarm **[120]** and anxiety.

Towards the end of that day Muẓaffar al-Dīn ibn Zayn al-Dīn arrived, also with a small retinue, hastening to the sultan's presence. He then returned to his troops, with whom he returned on the Sunday [6 May] in full battle array. The sultan reviewed them and led them to their positions before the enemy. They then withdrew to their camp. Every troop that came the sultan reviewed, paraded them before the enemy, received them at his tent and provided them with a meal, giving them gifts to win their hearts, if they were strangers. Then their tents would be pitched where he commanded and they would take up their quarters well satisfied with their reception.

A curious incident indicating the good fortune of his son, al-Ẓāhir

The enemy had constructed three towers of wood and iron, which they covered with skins soaked in vinegar, as it was reported, so that fires would have no effect on them. These towers seemed like mountains. We could see them from our positions, dominating the city walls. They were mounted on wheels and each one could accommodate more than 500 men, as it was claimed. Their flat tops were large enough for a trebuchet to be set up there. This worked on the minds of the Muslims and filled them with fear for the city, more than can be expressed. Everyone totally despaired for the city and the spirits of the defending fighting men were broken. The towers' construction was complete and all that remained was to drag them close to the walls. The sultan exercised his mind to find a way of burning and destroying them. He gathered artificers and Greek fire specialists and discussed with them all possible ways of setting them on fire. He promised them large sums of money and splendid gifts as a reward, but nothing they contrived was successful. One of those present was a young metal-worker from Damascus, who mentioned in the presence of the sultan that he had the skill to set fire to them and that, if he could be got into Acre and if he could acquire the ingredients that he knew, he would burn them. He did acquire all that he asked for, entered Acre and concocted the ingredients he had gathered with some naphtha in copper vats, until the whole mixture was like a burning coal.

The day that the sultan's son, al-Ẓāhir, arrived - or perhaps it was after his arrival - one of the towers was hit by an earthenware projectile. Hardly had it hit the target before it immediately burst into flames and the whole became like a huge mountain of fire, whose tongues of flame rose high into the sky. In relief the Muslims **[121]** broke into cries of 'There is no god but God' and 'God is great', so overwhelmed with joy that they were nearly out of their minds. As the people looked on in amazement, the second tower was hit by another projectile, which burst into flames the moment it hit the target, like the first one. The tumult on both sides was immense and the clamour of voices reached the sky. Hardly a moment later the third was struck and fire broke out. Our people were seized with such joy and delight that staid and stern men were as excited as flighty girls.

It was towards the end of the day, but the sultan and the troops, left and right wings and centre, rode out until they came up to the enemy's camp. He expected that they would come forth to allow him to engage them, following the saying of the Prophet, 'If a door to some advantage is opened for anyone, then let him grasp it.'[1] The enemy, however, did not appear outside their tents and, when night intervened between the two sides, each party returned to its comrades. People considered this to have been a blessing of the arrival of his son al-Ẓāhir. His father rejoiced to see him prominent and knew that this resulted from his righteousness of heart.

Every day the sultan continued to ride out against the enemy and to seek to bring them to battle, but they would not leave their tents. All the while, the forces of Islam were progressively gathering.

Account of the arrival of 'Imād al-Dīn Zankī, the lord of Sinjār

'Imād al-Dīn Zankī ibn Mawdūd ibn Zankī, the lord of Sinjār, arrived with his troops in train on Tuesday 22 Rabī' II [29 May]. He came in great style with a fully-equipped force. The sultan received him with all respect and honour, drawing up his troops to meet him. The first to greet him from the royal camp were the sultan's judges and secretaries, then his sons. The sultan then welcomed him and took him to give him a view of the enemy, before returning with him to his tent, where he welcomed him with a feast that he had had prepared, suitable for the occasion. The sultan and all his men attended and he presented him with gifts and favours that nobody but he was capable of. He honoured him to the extent that he placed a separate cushion for him next to his own and he had

1 A fuller version of this saying has been given above, p. 77.

brocade cloth spread before him when he entered. A tent for him was pitched on the far right wing beside the river.

The arrival of Mu'izz al-Dīn Sanjar Shāh, lord of Jazīrat [Ibn 'Umar]

On Wednesday 7 Jumādā I {13 June} there arrived the lord of al-Jazīra, Mu'izz al-Dīn Sanjar Shāh, son of Sayf al-Dīn Ghāzī ibn Mawdūd ibn Zankī. He came with a fine troop, exemplarily kitted out. The sultan met him **[122]** with all respect and honour and gave him hospitality in his tent. He gave orders that a tent should be erected for him alongside his uncle 'Imād al-Dīn's.

The arrival of 'Alā' al-Dīn, the son of the lord of Mosul

His arrival took place on 9 Jumādā I {15 June}. He - in full, 'Alā' al-Dīn Khurramshāh ibn Mas'ūd ibn Mawdūd ibn Zankī - came as the deputy of his father, 'Izz al-Dīn Mas'ūd, the lord of Mosul, and as commander of his army. The sultan was greatly delighted at his arrival and, along with members of his family, went some way to meet him. He found him a polite and noble youth and he gave him a very generous and hospitable welcome in his tent, offering him handsome gifts. He ordered that his tent should be pitched between [those of] his own sons, al-Afḍal and al-Ẓāhir. There was not a member of the sultan's family who did not willingly entertain him with unalloyed generous hospitality.

The arrival of the fleet and its entry into Acre

At noon this same day, that is the day of 'Alā' al-Dīn's arrival, many sails were visible out at sea. In the sultan's view it was the arrival of the fleet from Egypt, for he had ordered it to be built and to sail here. He then learnt that it was indeed the fleet, so he, with all his men at his command, rode out and they formed up in battle formation. His plan was to press the enemy hard to hinder their attacks on the fleet. Learning of the arrival of our fleet, the enemy made their preparations, manning a fleet to engage it and stop it from sailing into Acre. The enemy fleet put to sea, while the sultan fought the Franks fiercely from without. Our men went to the sea shore to support the fleet and to encourage its men. The two fleets met at sea, while the two armies met on land. The flames of battle flared and blazed, as those on either side gave their lives to purchase the next world's peace and valued this world's existence as nothing beside eternal life. A fierce battle raged between the two fleets, which was resolved by the victory of the Muslim fleet over the enemies of God (to God be the praise). An enemy galley was taken, all on board were killed and its cargo seized. Another ship that had sailed from Constantinople was captured from the enemy. The victorious fleet, which other ships from the Levant coast, carrying provisions and stores, had accompanied, then entered Acre.

The people in Acre were delighted at this and greatly relieved, for the difficult situation [**123**] had taken its toll on them. Fighting continued between the two armies outside the city until nightfall separated them. Both sides returned to their tents. On the enemy's side great numbers had been killed or wounded that day. There had been fighting on three fronts. The city garrison had fought them hard to prevent them from engaging the fleet, the two fleets had battled together and our army had fought them from the landward side. In all places on this day victory went to the Muslims by God's grace.

The arrival of Zayn al-Dīn, lord of Irbil

Zayn al-Dīn Yusūf ibn Zayn al-Dīn 'Alī ibn Baktakīn, lord of Irbil, arrived during the last ten days of Jumādā I [26 June-5 July]. He came with a fine army, handsomely equipped. The sultan received him with respect and honour, entertained him with very great hospitality in his tent and ordered that a tent for him be pitched close to his brother, Muẓaffar al-Dīn.

News of the German emperor

Constant reports came in that the German emperor had reached the lands of Qilij Arslān and that a large gathering of Turkomans had risen up to confront him and aimed to prevent him from crossing the river. However, this had been beyond them because of his vast multitude and because they lacked a leader to unite them. Qilij Arslān was making a show of hostility to the emperor, but the truth of the matter was that he had reached a secret understanding with him. Once the emperor had crossed the river into Qilij Arslān's lands, he revealed what he had kept hidden. He came to an agreement with the emperor and gave him hostages as a guarantee that he would send people to lead them to the lands of the son of Leon. He sent guides with him to show them the way. On the road they were stricken by great hunger. Provisions ran out and they had few pack animals, so that they threw away some of their baggage. I have heard (and God knows best) that they gathered together much equipment, chain-mail, helmets and weapons that they were unable to carry and made one heap of it. They set fire to it to destroy it so that nobody else could benefit from it. Afterwards a mound of iron was left. In this manner they marched on until they reached a town called Ṭarsūs. They halted at a river to make the crossing. Their accursed emperor had the notion to swim there. The water was very **[124]** cold and this was after he had suffered tiredness, fatigue, hardship and alarms. For this reason he caught a serious illness, which worsened until it killed him. When he had realised the state that he had come to, he made his testament in favour of his son, who was accompanying him. After his death, by common agreement, they boiled him in vinegar and collected his bones in a bag to convey him to Jerusalem and bury him there. His son took over his position despite the opposition of his men, for the eldest son had been left in charge in his own lands and a number of his men inclined towards him. However, his son who was on the spot firmly established himself in command of the army. When the son of Leon became aware of the problems that had come their way and the hunger, death, alarms and weakness that had befallen them by reason of their emperor's demise, he decided not to cast himself amongst them, for he did not know what might be forthcoming, since they were Franks and he was Armenian. He therefore took refuge in one of his impregnable castles.

The letter from the Armenian Catholicos

A letter came to the sultan from the Catholicos, the leader of the Armenians and lord of Qal'at al-Rūm on the banks of the Euphrates. The translation of the text is as follows:

> From the Catholicos with sincere prayers.
> Among the matters that I will bring to the attention of our lord and ruler, the Sultan al-Nāṣir, uniter of Islam, standard bearer of justice and fairness, Ṣalāḥ al-Dunyā wa'l-Dīn, sultan of Islam and the Muslims (may God perpetuate his good fortune, multiply his glory, preserve his life and perfection and make him attain his ultimate hopes through His might and splendour), concerning the fate of the German emperor and what befell him when he came on the scene is the fact that, when he first marched out from his lands and entered by force into the lands of the Hungarians, he forced the king of Hungary to submit and become obedient to him. He took such of his money and men as he wished. He then entered the land of the ruler of the Greeks, which he conquered and plundered. After his stay there he left it empty. He compelled the Greek ruler to obey him and took hostages from him, his son, his brother and forty of his close courtiers. He also took fifty *qinṭārs*[1] of gold, fifty of silver and a large amount of satin textiles. He seized ships and on them crossed to this side, accompanied by **[125]** the hostages, finally entering the lands of Qilij Arslān and returning the hostages.
>
> For three days he marched on, while Uwaj Turkomans met him with sheep, cows, horses and other goods. Then, prompted by greed, they gathered forces from the whole country. A battle between him and the

[1] A *qinṭār* of gold was 10,000 dinars in weight, or 42.33 kg (see Hinz, *Islamische Masse und Gewichte*, p. 24).

Turkomans followed. For thirty-three days they pressed him hard, as he continued his march. When he approached Konya, Quṭb al-Dīn, the son of Qilij Arslān, having assembled his forces, attacked him and brought him to a great pitched battle. The German emperor was victorious and inflicted a great defeat on him. As he came in sight of Konya, great crowds of Muslims came out against him but he repelled them in rout. He forced his way into Konya by the sword and killed great multitudes of Muslims and Persians. He remained there five days. Qilij Arslān asked for terms, which the emperor granted. An agreement was reached between the sides and the emperor took hostages, twenty great men of state. Qilij Arslān advised the emperor to travel via Tarsūs and al-Maṣīṣa, which he did.

Before he came to our lands, he sent a letter with an envoy, detailing his position, his destination and his experiences en route and stating that, come what may, he had to cross through these lands. The situation demanded the sending of the mamluke Ḥātim, taking what was asked for, and accompanied by a group of leading men to meet the emperor in response to his letter. They were charged with diverting him into the lands of Qilij Arslān, if at all possible. When they met with the great emperor and gave him the response, informing him of the situation, he refused to be diverted. His troops and massed followers gathered in their great numbers and he camped on the bank of a certain river. He ate bread and slept for a while. On awaking he had a desire to bathe in the cold water. He did so, came out and God decreed that he became seriously ill from the cold water.[1] After lingering for a few days he died.

Leon was travelling to meet the emperor, but when this event happened, the envoys fled from the army, came to him and told what had happened. He then entered one of his castles and sought security there.

The emperor's son, who accompanied him, had been set up by his father in his place since setting out for these regions and the son's position was well established.[2] He heard of the flight of the envoys of Leon's son and, sending after them, persuaded them to come back. He said, 'My father was an old man. He came to these regions only for the sake of making his pilgrimage to Jerusalem. I have acted as emperor and dealt with the difficulties of this march. If anyone does not obey me, I shall start by attacking his lands.' He persuaded Leon's son too, whom circumstances convinced of the necessity of meeting him. To put it briefly, the Germans were in great numbers.

[**126**] He reviewed his army, which consisted of 42,000 mailed men and foot-soldiers beyond numbering. They are of varied races and strange ways. Their cause is a great one and they are serious in their enterprise and of prodigious discipline, so much so that, if one of them commits a crime, the only penalty is to have his throat cut like a sheep. I was informed about one of their nobles, that he did wrong to a page of his and beat him beyond the limit. The priests gathered to give judgement and the case by general decision demanded that his throat be cut. Many petitioned the emperor on his behalf, but he paid no attention and had his throat cut. They have forbidden themselves pleasures even to the extent that, if they hear that

1 This sentence, given in a footnote in *Nawādir*, is in B and clearly belongs.

2 His successor in command was Frederick, duke of Swabia.

> anyone has allowed himself any pleasure, they treat him as an outcast and chastise him. All this is because of grief for Jerusalem.
>
> It is true that some of them renounced clothes for a long period, banned them and did not wear anything but iron [mail]. Eventually, their leaders disapproved of that. They are to an extraordinary degree capable of enduring hardship, humiliation and fatigue.
>
> Your humble servant reports these matters and, God willing, will report subsequent developments.

This is the letter of the Catholicos, which title is equivalent to caliph. His name was Lord Krikor,[1] son of Basil.

Account of the troops' move to the frontier on the German emperor's line of march

When the sultan had confirmed that the German emperor had arrived in the territory of Leon and that he was close to the lands of Islam, he assembled his emirs and councillors and consulted them about what was to be done. It was agreed that part of the army should proceed to the areas adjacent to the route of the approaching enemy and that he himself should remain besieging the Franks with the remainder of the army. The first to leave was the lord of Manbij, namely Nāṣir al-Dīn ibn Taqī al-Dīn, and 'Izz al-Dīn ibn al-Muqaddam, the lord of Kafarṭāb, Ba'rīn and other places. There followed Majd al-Dīn, the lord of Baalbek, then Ṣābiq al-Dīn, the lord of Shayzar, then the Yārūqiyya [Turkomans], part of the troops of Aleppo, then the standing troops of Ḥama. The sultan's son, al-Afḍal, left because of an illness he had caught, as did Badr al-Dīn, the military prefect of Damascus, also because of an illness. After him the sultan's son, al-Ẓāhir, went to Aleppo to discover their routes, to scout for news and to guard the lands he controlled. He was followed by al-Muẓaffar to guard his lands and to keep an eye on the enemy as they passed. He was the last to depart on the eve of Saturday **[127]** 9 Jumādā [II] 586 [14 July 1190]. After the departure of these troops, the right wing was weak, for most who left were from there. The sultan ordered al-'Ādil to transfer to al-Muẓaffar's position on the far right. On the far left was 'Imād al-Dīn Zankī.

The army was afflicted with much illness. Muẓaffar al-Dīn ibn Zayn al-Dīn, the lord of Ḥarrān, fell sick but recovered, as did the sultan's son, al-Malik al-Ẓāfir, who had also fallen ill. A great many of the leading men and others also became ill, although (praise be to God) the illness was mild. That amongst the enemy was greater in quantity and in seriousness and was linked with much

---

[1] This is the Catholicos Gregory IV (1174-1193). Correct the reading of *Nawādir*: B.r.k.rī Kūr. Read T.r. initially, followed by the name ('Ter' in Armenian is a high ecclesiastical title).

mortality. The sultan, however, remained in the field opposing the enemy and enduring all this.

Completion of the report concerning the German emperor

The son whom the emperor had made his successor fell seriously ill and therefore remained in a place called al-Mīnāt in the lands of the son of Leon. Twenty-five knights and forty Templars stayed with him. He sent his army on towards Antioch to finish their journey. They were so many that he divided them into three bodies. The first body, led by a great count of theirs, passed beneath the castle of Baghrās. The local garrison, despite its small size, seized by force 200 of them and wrote to report that the enemy was very weak and ill, short of horses, pack animals, provisions and military equipment.

When this news reached the sultan's deputies in Syria they sent a force to gather information. This force came upon a large number who had gone foraging. They attacked them fiercely, causing losses and taking prisoners. The number taken, according to what informants wrote in despatches, was about 500 souls.

I was present when a second envoy from the Catholicos delivered a letter to the sultan, and spoke of them as follows, 'They are very numerous, but they are weak, short of horses and equipment. Most of them have their baggage on donkeys and weak horses.' He continued, 'I halted at a bridge they were crossing to observe them. A great crowd of them passed over, but I did not discover that any of them, except very few, had any shield or spear. I asked them about that, and they replied, **[128]** "We stayed for several days on an unhealthy plain and provisions and firewood ran short. We burnt most of our equipment and very many of our number died. We needed to slaughter and eat our horses and we burnt our spears and equipment for lack of firewood." The count, who came to Antioch (God facilitate its conquest) with the vanguard of the army, died.'

He also related that when the son of Leon realised their weakness, he became eager to exploit it. He planned to seize the emperor's money because he was ill and weak and attended by very few men who had stayed behind with him. The prince, lord of Antioch, when he became aware of this, travelled to the German emperor to remove him to Antioch, eager that he should die in his control, so that he could take his money. Frequent reports of their weakness and sickness continued to arrive until the time when al-'Ādil's battle on the sea shore took place.

[129] Account of al-'Ādil's battle

On Wednesday 20 Jumādā II [25 July] the enemy learnt that our armies had become disorganised on the extreme wings and that our right wing was undermanned because it had contained most of those who had departed on account of their lands being close to the route taken by the German enemy. Thus they decided unanimously to make a sudden sortie and a surprise attack on our far right wing. They were beguiled by their hopes which God showed to be false. They came forth at noon on the Wednesday, deployed to form right and left wings and centre, and spread over the area in great numbers. Our right wing, at the extreme end of which was al-'Ādil's encampment, was thought by them to be an easy target.

When our men saw that the enemy had come out in battle array, the herald cried aloud and they came from their tents like lions from their lairs. The sultan mounted up and his herald cried, 'On, on for Islam!' Our troops mounted and formed their divisions with the sultan being the first to horse. I saw him already riding from his tent, surrounded by a small band of his special retinue, when the troops were not yet fully mounted and ready, as solicitous as a mother losing her only son. He struck his drum which was answered by the emirs' drums from their positions. Then the troops mounted. The Franks (God curse them) had hastened to attack our right wing and reached al-'Ādil's encampment before our troops were fully deployed. They entered his camp and laid their hands on what was in the market and the recesses of the tents, plundering and despoiling. It is said that they got as far as his personal tent and took things from his buttery.

Learning of this, al-'Ādil had mounted and left his tent. He urged his neighbours on the right wing, such as Qaymāz al-Najmī and his like amongst the lions of Islam, to get to horse. Then he halted craftily until the Franks' eagerness would bring them deep into his encampment and they would be preoccupied with their plundering. What he expected happened. They rummaged wildly amongst the tents, clothing, fruits and food stuffs and when he knew that they were busy with that, he charged in person, while his grown-up son, Shams al-Dīn, went before him. Those next to him on the right wing, such as the *Ṭawāshī* Qaymāz and others, charged along with him. The action spread all along the right wing and eventually the cry reached the Mosul troop. They charged the enemy like lions upon their prey. God gave them the upper hand and a rout followed. The Franks recoiled on their heels in precipitous flight back towards their tents, while the sword of God was gleaning spirits from persons, detaching heads from [**130**] bodies and separating souls from their human frames.

When the sultan saw the dust-cloud of war rise up near his brother's tents, a burning solicitude was kindled in his heart and its warmth stirred his fraternal feelings. His desire to aid God's religion and fear for its champions roused his determination. His herald proclaimed 'On, on for Islam and the heroes of the true unitarians! See, the enemies of God are now in His power, now that they have been forward enough to descend on your tents.' Among those who hurried to answer his call were a group of his mamlukes, personal troops and his guard, secondly the troops of Mosul, led by 'Alā' al-Dīn, son of 'Izz al-Dīn, and thirdly the Egyptian troops, led by Sunqur al-Ḥalabī. Our forces arrived progressively and our champions severally responded. The sultan himself stood in the centre, fearing that the enemy, finding it weak on account of the troops that he had sent from it, might take some advantage. As the forces gathered, the clash of arms was continuous and the battle grew hot. Only a short time passed before I saw the enemy 'laid low as though they were stumps of fallen palms'.[1] Their corpses reached where they lay from al-'Ādil's tents back to their own, starting with the Muslim camp and finishing in the enemy's, laid low on hillocks and in hollows. Our swords had drunk of their blood till they were slaked and the lions of battle had victoriously gorged themselves till they were sated. God manifested His word and activated His aid for His servants.

The distance over which the corpses were spread between the two camps was a league, or perhaps more than that. Only the odd few of the enemy escaped. I waded into the carnage there on my mount and strove to count them, but they were so many and so heaped up that I was unable to. I caught sight of two dead women amongst them. An eyewitness told me that he saw four women taking part in the battle. Two of them were taken prisoner. On this day very few of their men were taken. The sultan had ordered his troops not to spare anyone. All of this took place on the right wing and in part of the centre.

On the left wing the call to arms reached them only when the business was over and the decision had gone against the enemy, because of the distance between the extremities of the line. This engagement took place during noon and evening, for the enemy emerged at noon and the fighting was concluded after the evening prayer. When the enemy were routed, it is said that a detachment of Muslims entered their camp behind them. The sultan ordered them to withdraw when the nature of the great gain made became clear to him, seeing that so many of this great horde had been slain and on the Muslim side this day only ten souls of the common folk had been lost. When God's troops in Acre became aware of the battle between the Muslims and God's enemies - for they watched it from the tops of the city wall - they made a sortie into the enemy camp. Another battle ensued and the victory went to the Muslims (praise be to God), since they charged the enemy's tents and seized several women and some goods, even cooking pots with food within. A letter came from the city with this news. It was a hard day for the infidels.

There was a dispute about the number of their slain. Some said 8,000, others 7,000, but nobody made an estimate less than 5,000. [**131**] I witnessed five rows

---

1 Koran lxix, v. 7.

of them, the first at al-'Ādil's tents and the last at the enemy's tents. I met an intelligent soldier making his way between the rows of the dead and counting them. I asked him, 'How many have you counted?' He replied, 'Up to here 4,060 odd.' He was in the third row, having counted two, but the rows that he had done were more numerous than those left. This Wednesday produced the best possible result for Islam.

When it was Thursday 21 Jumādā II [26 July], in the evening there arrived a courier on a dromedary, having taken five days from Aleppo, whose despatch contained news that a large number of the enemy to the north had gone on a plundering expedition into Muslim territory, that the troops of Aleppo had intercepted them and blocked their route. None escaped but those whom God wished to do so. Coming just after this other victory, this news had a great affect. Drums were beaten in celebration and no day dawned sweeter than this one. Very early in the morning that day, Qaymāz al-Ḥarrānī came from the advanced posts and reported that the enemy had asked who on the sultan's behalf would come to discuss with them the question of peace because they had been weakened. From then on the wings of the enemy remained clipped and his spirit crushed until the arrival of a count of theirs, called Count Henry.[1]

The arrival of Count Henry

This person, one of their rich princes, arrived by sea with several ships, bringing a great amount of possessions, treasure, weapons and men. By his coming their courage was strengthened and their spirits raised high. They were tempted to make a surprise night attack on the Muslim forces. There was much talk of this from deserters to our side and from spies. The sultan gathered the emirs and councillors, and consulted them about what to do. In the end they advised widening the encircling cordon and withdrawing from the enemy, in the hope that they would emerge and leave their tents far behind, so that God would deliver them into our hands. The sultan agreed with their plan and gave it full approval. He therefore moved from the hill of al-Kharrūba with all his troops on Wednesday 27 Jumādā II [1 August], leaving only a small remnant in that position as an advance guard, amounting to 1,000 horse, to mount guard in shifts. Meanwhile, there was a stream of letters coming from Acre and going from us to Acre by pigeon post or carried by swimmers and small vessels, which set out at night and sneaked in past the enemy.

[132] To return to the progress of the German emperor, news of the enemy approaching from the north, his shortage of horses and small numbers continued to arrive. They were badly hit by disease and mortality, but they had assembled

---

[1] In Arabic: Kundharī, i.e., Henry of Troyes, Count of Champagne.

at Antioch and were distributing money to the foot-soldiers. Our men, the troops of Aleppo, were snatching their foragers, commissaries and any who strayed.

Account of a letter that came from Constantinople

There was diplomatic contact and correspondance between the sultan and the emperor of Constantinople. An envoy from the latter came to the sultan at Marj 'Uyūn during Rajab 585 [August - September 1189] in reply to an envoy that the sultan had sent to him after the conclusion of a mutual understanding and an agreement to institute Muslim prayers in the mosque of Constantinople. This envoy had gone there and established the khutbah, being met with great respect and much honour. The sultan had sent with him, in the one ship, the preacher, the minbar and a number of muezzins and Koran reciters. The day they entered Constantinople was one of the great days of Islam, witnessed by a large gathering of merchants. The preacher mounted the minbar and all the resident Muslims and the merchants gathered around, as he delivered the khutbah for the Abbasid caliph. Our envoy then came home, accompanied by theirs, to inform us that all had gone well. Their envoy stayed a while and I saw him deliver his mission. He had a dragoman to translate for him and was the finest example of an old man that one could expect to see. He was dressed in the fashion that is peculiar to them and brought a letter and a memorandum. The letter was sealed with gold. After he died, news of his decease reached the emperor, who sent this latest envoy to complete the business. He arrived with a letter of reply. Here is a description of the letter and its contents. It was in the form of a wide scroll, less wide than Baghdad paper and headed on the verso and the recto in two lines, between which was a space where the seal was put. The seal was stamped in gold, as is done in wax, with the image of the emperor. The gold weighed fifteen dinars and the content of the two lines of writing was as follows:

> From Isaac the Emperor, believer in the divine Messiah, crowned by God, victorious, ever exalted, Augustus, God's governor, invincible conqueror, the master of Rūm, Angelus, to his brother, the Sultan of Egypt Saladin ...

This is the wording of the rubric on the verso and the recto. As for the main text of the letter, it was as follows:

> Love and friendship. The letter of your Excellency which you sent to our realm has arrived. [133] We have read it and learnt that our envoy has died. We are sad that he died in a foreign land and was not enabled to finish what our Majesty ordered him to do. We ordered him to talk with your Excellency and to say in your presence that you must take care to send an envoy to us in order that he may inform us of the matter concerning which I communicated with you by our deceased envoy. The belongings which he

> left and which were found after his death please send to our Majesty that we may give them to his children and relatives. I do not imagine that he brought bad news to your Excellency's ears. The Germans have crossed our territory and it is not a surprise that our enemies spread lying rumours to suit their own aims. If you wish to hear the truth, they suffered and were inconvenienced more than the peasants of my lands suffered. They lost much money, many horses, baggage and pack animals. Many of them died or were killed. With difficulty they escaped from the hands of my troops. They have been so weakened that they will hardly reach your lands. If they do arrive, they will be weak, having suffered much and will be no benefit to their kindred and no harm to your Excellency. After all this it is surprising how you have forgotten what is between us and how you have not recognised any of the good intentions and efforts of our Majesty. We have no profit from your love other than the enmity of the Franks and their kin. Your Excellency, as you wrote in your letter which you sent us, must send an envoy to inform us of all the matters about which we have corresponded with you in the past. Let that be done as quickly as possible and do not be cast down by the coming of the enemy that you have heard of, for their failure will be as great as their aims and plans. Written during the year 1501.[1]

The sultan read this translation and gave the envoy, who was a fine looking and impressive old man, with a knowledge of Arabic, Greek and Frankish, an honourable welcome.

The Franks (may God curse them) intensified their siege and the pressure on the city, because of the access of strength through Count Henry's arrival. According to reports (and God knows best) he had provided financially for 10,000 fighting men. Then further reinforcements arrived by sea, which strengthened their hearts. They kept up their attacks on the city.

[134] The burning of the enemy's trebuchets

When the enemy felt themselves strong, because of the constant arrival of reinforcements, they became more ambitious and brought trebuchets to bear on the city from all directions. They operated them in shifts so that the bombardment never ceased day or night. This was so during Rajab 586 [August 1190]. Those in the city, seeing the pressure the enemy put them under and how confident they were, were moved by zeal for Islam. Their leaders at the time were, as governor of the city and its protector, the great emir, Bahā' al-Dīn Qarāqūsh, and, as commander of the army, the great emir, Ḥusām al-Dīn Abū'l-Hayjā', who was a man of honour, bravery, leadership among his clansmen and decisiveness in his plans. They agreed to make a sortie, with both horse and foot, to catch the enemy

1 Dated according to the Alexandrian era, equivalent to 1189 A.D.

unawares. The gates were opened and as one they charged out at all points. Before the enemy realised it, the sword was executing fair judgement on them and the arrow of God's power and decree was potent amongst them. Islam assailed Unbelief in its camp and seized the forelocks of its defenders and the heads of its champions.

When the Muslims penetrated the enemy's camp, the latter were too startled to guard and protect the trebuchets. The blazing meteors of the Greek fire specialists hit their targets and God's accustomed practice to aid His religion was manifest. After only a short moment they were consumed in flames and what the enemy had constructed over a long period was burnt in the shortest possible time. On that day seventy of the enemy's knights were killed and many people were taken prisoner. Amongst the prisoners was a man of note, who had been taken by one of our common people who did not know his rank. After the battle was over the Franks asked whether he was alive or not. From their questioning the man who held him realised that he was a great man and feared that he might be forcibly taken from him and given back in some mutual deal or for some reason or other, so he quickly killed him. The Franks offered large sums of money and continued their efforts to ask after him very eagerly until his corpse was thrown to them. Thereupon they cast themselves to the ground and smeared earth on their faces, being greatly disheartened by this. They concealed his status and did not reveal who it was.

After this the Muslims had less respect for them and the Bedouin raided them from all directions, stealing, killing and taking prisoners until the eve of Sha'bān [began 3 September]. According to the reports of spies and deserters, Count Henry had spent 1,500 dinars on a trebuchet of huge dimensions and had prepared it to be brought up to the city. Its being far from the city and not yet brought forward saved it being burnt this day. However, on this eve the Greek fire specialists and other soldiers went forward, with God watching over and guarding them, [**135**] and under God's protection they came to that trebuchet and set fire to it. It was consumed in a short time. Great cries went up from both sides. The enemy were taken aback for it was far from the city and they feared that they might have been overwhelmed from all sides. This was a victory from God. From its blaze a small trebuchet alongside also caught fire and burnt.

The ruse to enable a buss to get into the city from Beirut

The sultan had prepared and equipped a buss in Beirut, which he loaded with 400 *ghirāras*[1] of wheat and also cheese, corn, onions, sheep and other provisions. The Franks had surrounded Acre with their ships to guard against any Muslim

1 Literally, 'sacks'. A *ghirāra* at Damascus weighed about 200 kg, in cubic measure 265 litres (see Hinz, *Islamische Masse und Gewichte*, pp. 37-38).

ship entering the harbour. The garrison was by now in serious need of food and supplies. A number of Muslims boarded the buss in Beirut and dressed up as Franks, even shaving their beards. They also placed pigs on the deck, so that they could be seen from a distance, and flew crosses. They arrived making course for the city and were soon amongst the ships of the enemy, who had come out to meet them in their galleys. They said, 'We see that you are making for the city,' believing that they were Franks. Our men replied, 'Have you not taken the city?' 'No', they said, 'we have not taken the city yet.' The Muslims said, 'We shall tack to go to the camp. There is another buss behind us on our tack. Warn them not to enter the harbour.' Behind them was a Frankish buss, which they had fallen in with at sea making for the camp. The Franks saw it and sailed to warn it. The Muslim buss, meanwhile, set more sail and with the wind in the right quarter entered the harbour and so was safe, praise be to God. There was great rejoicing as the inhabitants were already in need. This incident took place during the last ten days of Rajab [24 August-2 September].

The tale of the swimmer 'Īsā

One of the most unusual and admirable things about this whole siege is that there was a Muslim swimmer, called 'Īsā, who used to get into the city at night without the knowledge of the enemy with letters and cash tied around his waist. He used to dive and emerge on the far side of the enemy's ships.

[136] One night he tied three purses around his waist containing 1,000 dinars and letters for the army. He swam out to sea, but something[1] fatal happened to him. We did not immediately hear any news. Normally, when he got into the city, a pigeon would be released to report his arrival. The pigeon was delayed, however, and people feared that he had been killed. Several days later some people by the shore in the city suddenly caught sight of a drowned man that the sea had cast up. They investigated and found that it was 'Īsā, the swimmer. Around his waist they found the gold and the wax seals of the letters. The gold was pay for the soldiers. This man is the only one seen to have fulfilled his duty during his life and also to have performed it after his death. This was also in the last ten days of Rajab [24 August-2 September].

The burning of the trebuchets

The enemy had erected against the city dreadful trebuchets that dominated the wall. They released a rain of stones which made a visible impression on the city

1 Reading *amr* as in B, instead of *man*.

wall. The resulting damage was greatly feared. Two arrows of a large ballista were taken, their tips set alight so that they were like a flame of fire and then they were shot at one of the trebuchets. They stuck fast while the enemy strove to extinguish the fire, but were unable to do so. Then a strong wind blew up and a great conflagration followed. The flames spread to the other and set fire to it. Both fires were so intense that nobody could get anywhere near them to attempt to put them out. It was a great day which gave much joy to the Muslims, but had a bad outcome for the infidels.

Completion of the account of the German

After the German had established himself in Antioch (may God facilitate its conquest) he took it from its ruler and took control there. Its lord was subject to him and carried out his orders, as he had taken it deceitfully and by guile. He deposited his treasure there, then left on Wednesday 25 Rajab {29 August} to march towards Acre with his troops and bands by way of Lattakia. He arrived at Tripoli (may God facilitate its conquest), where the marquis, lord of Tyre, had already gone, leaving the Frankish camp, to meet him. The marquis was one of their most cunning and brave leaders. He was the main person who motivated the bands from overseas.

The plan employed by the marquis to mobilise the Franks from overseas

The marquis produced a picture of Jerusalem on a large sheet of paper, depicting the Sepulchre to which they come on pilgrimage and which they revere. The tomb of the Messiah is there, where he was buried after his crucifixion, as they assert. This tomb is the centre of their pilgrimage and is the one on which they believe the Fire descends **[137]** each year at one of their festivals. He pictured the tomb and added a Muslim cavalryman on horseback trampling on the Messiah's tomb, upon which the horse had staled. This picture he publicised overseas in the markets and assemblies, as the priests, bareheaded and dressed in sackcloth, paraded it, crying doom and destruction. Images effect their hearts, for they are essential to their religion. Therefore multitudes of people, whom God alone could number, were roused up. Amongst them was the German emperor with his troops.

The marquis went to meet him as he was the original motivator of their being called to this entreprise. Having joined him, he encouraged him, gave him an understanding of the routes and travelled the coastal region with him, fearing that, if he entered the territory of Aleppo or of Ḥamā, the Muslims would rise against him on all sides and our true Faith would oppose him from every quarter.

Nevertheless, the Germans did not escape raids upon them, as al-Muẓaffar moved against them with his troops and assembled forces to oppose them. He made a big attack from which the emperor's outlying detachments suffered. He and his vanguard had caught up with the enemy. Had he been joined by al-Ẓāhir with his troops, he would have destroyed them, 'but the final moment for everything is written.'[1] People differed in their estimation of the enemy's numbers. I read some writings of specialists in warfare, who estimated their horse and foot at 5,000, after they had set out, as was reported, 200,000 strong. See how God deals with his enemies! I also read a book which stated that, when they left Lattakia making for Jabala, sixty-odd horses were found in their tracks that had perished and been stripped of their flesh. Nothing remained but their bones, such was the hunger of the enemy and the weakness of the horses. They continued their march, while the Muslims skirmished around them, plundering, killing and taking prisoners, until they came to Tripoli (may God facilitate its conquest). The news of their arrival came early on Tuesday 8 Sha'bān {11 September}.[2] All the while, the sultan remained firmly courageous and steadfast, not allowing himself to be distracted from the guarding and defending of Acre or from keeping watch on the besieging enemy. He continually raided them and carried out attacks, trusting his cause to God and relying on Him, cheerfully fulfilling the requests of people and rewarding with his bounty all the sufis, lawyers, shaykhs and literary men who paid him a visit. When the news reached me, I was much affected until, having gone in to see him, I was conscious of such strength of mind and courage as gladdened my heart and made me convinced that Islam and the Muslims would be victorious.

[138] The arrival of the busses from Egypt

During the middle period of Sha'bān [approx. middle of September] Bahā' al-Dīn Qarāqūsh, the governor of the city, and the commander of the fleet, who was the Chamberlain Lu'lu', wrote to tell the sultan, 'Only enough provisions remain in the city to last until half-way through Sha'bān, no more.' However, 'Yūsuf kept this to himself and did not reveal it to them',[3] neither to elite nor commoner, for fear it would spread and reach the enemy and weaken Muslim morale. He had previously written to Egypt for the dispatch of three busses

1 Koran xiii, 33.

2 *Nawādir* lacks the figure for the day of the month, but B provides '8'. *Fatḥ*, p. 287 has 6 Sha'bān, which is 8 September, but that was a Saturday.

3 Koran xii, 77. 'Yūsuf' refers both to the Biblical Joseph and to the personal name of Saladin.

laden with foodstuffs and supplies and all that was needed for the besieged to last them through the winter.

The three busses set sail from Egypt and put to sea, where the sailors sought the wind that would carry them to Acre. The wind became fair for their passage and they arrived at Acre just before the middle of Sha'bān, when the provisions had run out and the inhabitants had nothing left to eat. The enemy's fleet came out to oppose them, as the Muslim troops watched from the shore and all cried 'There is no god but God' and 'God is great'. The Muslims uncovered their heads, supplicating God to decree that He bring them safe into harbour. The sultan was on the shore like a bereft mother, watching the battle and calling upon God for victory. He knew what others did not know about the crisis of the garrison and his heart was troubled but God kept him firm. The battle raged around the busses on all sides, while God defended them and the wind strengthened. Voices were raised high by both parties and prayers rent the veils, until eventually, with God's grace, the ships came safely into harbour, to be met as rains are met after drought by the population of Acre, who were reprovisioned by their cargoes. It was a night of nights. The ships entered harbour on the evening of Monday 14 Sha'bān {17 September}.

Account of the siege of the Tower of Flies

When it was 22 Sha'bān [25 September] the enemy sent numerous vessels to besiege the Tower of Flies, a tower standing in the sea, built on the rock at the entrance to Acre's harbour which is defended by it. Once past it, a ship is safe from any enemy attack. The enemy wished to take it to put the harbour under their control and to prevent the entry of any busses, thus cutting off [**139**] the city's supplies. They put a 'turret' on the masts of the busses and filled each with firewood and naphtha with the intention of sailing the busses in and, when they drew close to the Tower of Flies and were alongside, setting fire to the 'turret' on the mast and attaching it to the Tower of Flies to throw it on to the roof, kill the defenders and so capture it. They placed lots of combustible material in the buss to throw on to the Tower when it was set alight. They loaded a second buss with wood and kindling with the aim of sending it amongst the Muslim busses, setting it on fire so that it would burn the Muslim vessels and destroy all the supplies they contained. In a third buss they placed soldiers beneath an arched covering where no arrows or any other weapons of war could reach them, so that, when they had set alight what they wanted to, they could enter the covered space and be safe. They ignited what they planned to and moved the buss towards the Tower. Their hopes were greatly increased since the wind was favourable for them. When they had set fire to the buss with which they intended to burn the Muslims' vessels and also the 'turret' with which they wished to burn those on the Tower, they fed the flames and threw on naphtha. However, as God willed and planned, the wind direction changed and one buss with everything in it was consumed in flames. They tried hard to put it out but were unable. The soldiers on board perished, except for those whom God chose to save. Then the buss that was prepared to burn our ships caught fire. Our own men leapt on board and brought it into harbour. As for the buss with the arched covering, those on board became anxious and fearful and thought of retreating. There was a dispute and a great commotion, and the vessel capsized, killing all on board, because they were in the covered space and unable to get out. This was a major sign of God's power and a wonderful miracle of support for God's religion. Praise be to God, it was a memorable day.

Account of the German's arrival to join their God-forsaken army

To return to our account of the German emperor, he had halted at Tripoli to allow his army to recuperate. He sent to those besieging Acre to inform them that he was coming. They were apprehensive at that, because the marquis, the lord of Tyre, was his chief councillor and right-hand man. King Guy,[1] the ruler of the Coastal Lands, was in the camp and he was the person to whom all referred in their affairs. He realised that with the arrival of the German emperor he would have no authority left. When the last ten days of Sha'bān [21-30 September] came, the emperor made up his mind to travel by sea, as he knew that, if he did not go by sea, he would fail and find the difficult routes blocked. So they prepared ships, which were sent to him from every direction. He and his army, their horses and equipment, were embarked and they set sail to join the besiegers. Hardly an hour had passed **[140]** before a strong wind arose. The waves swelled all around and they were likely to perish. Three busses were lost and the rest returned to await a fair wind. For several days they waited until the wind turned favourable. They sailed again and so came to Tyre (may God facilitate its conquest). While the marquis and the emperor remained there, they sent the rest of the forces to the siege camp before Acre. The two of them remained in Tyre until the eve of 6 Ramaḍān [7 October]. The emperor went on by sea on his own and arrived at the camp at sunset on that day with a small retinue. This was the information given by spies and deserters. His coming made a great impression on both sides.

After waiting several days, he wished that his arrival might have some visible effect. He reproved his fellow Christians for the length of the siege and he thought it a good plan to bring the Muslims to a general battle. They warned

[1] The original names Godfrey.

him about venturing on this course and of its possible outcome. He replied, 'It's essential that we make a sortie against their advance guard to taste their manner of fighting, to learn their strength and gain an insight into their methods. For gaining knowledge there is nothing like seeing for oneself.' So he moved out against the Muslim outposts, followed by most of the Franks, horse and foot. They proceeded until they crossed the depression which is between their hill and Tell al-'Ayyāḍiyya, on the latter of which were our advance units' tents. The duty troops that day were the Royal Guard of the sultan, who held their ground against them, fought hard and made them sample the taste of death. The sultan heard of this and rode out from his tents with his troops. He came to Tell Kaysān and when the enemy saw the Muslim forces winging their way arrow-like towards them and overwhelming them like swathes of black night, they turned on their heels in retreat. A large number of them were killed or wounded, as the sword was at work on the napes of their necks while they fled. The emperor reached his encampment at sunset that day, hardly crediting his own escape so full of fear was he. Night separated the two sides, after many of the enemy had been killed or wounded and the Muslims had lost two, although a sizeable number had been wounded. The battle went against the enemies of God (to God be the praise).

When the emperor became aware of what the advance guard, a detachment of our army and a mere part of the whole, had done to him and his men, he decided that he should return to assaulting the city and busying himself with the siege. He fashioned amazing engines and strange contrivances that, by causing a great fear for the city, terrified the onlooker and made him worried, fearful indeed, that these engines of war would lead to its fall. One of his new ideas was a huge engine called a 'crawler',[1] beneath which a large number of fighting men could position themselves. It was covered with sheets of iron with wheels beneath on which it could be moved **[141]** from inside, with soldiers within, to butt against the city wall. It had a large head with a strong iron neck, called a 'ram', with which the wall was butted with great force, because lots of people were pulling on it. By repetition of the blows it would demolish the wall. There was another engine, which was a testudo with men inside, dragged along in a similar way, except that its head was pointed like a ploughshare, while the head of the ram was rounded. The latter destroys by its impetus, while the former destroys through its sharp point and its impetus and is called a 'cat'. There were also screens and large formidable ladders. At sea they prepared a formidable buss, on which they built a turret with a prow. When they wished to lower it on the wall, it could be lowered mechanically and remain as a bridge to the place on to which it had been lowered and one across which the soldiers

[1] The Arabic *dabbāba* derives from the verb *dabba*, 'to crawl, creep'. In modern usage it means 'a tank'.

could pass. Their plan was to bring it close to the Tower of Flies to allow them to capture it.

Account of the burning of the ram and other engines

When the enemy saw that their engines were all finished and ready, they began an assault on the city from all directions, while the inhabitants of the city, seeing this, doubled their determination to aid God's religion and strengthened their hearts to hold fast. On Monday 3 Ramaḍān,[1] the day on which the troops of Syria arrived,[2] the sultan's son, al-Ẓāhir, the lord of Aleppo, came with his levies and his troop. He was one of his grown-up senior sons, experienced and one on whom the sultan relied in many of his affairs. He came alone the evening of the day mentioned, punctilious in waiting on his father and eager to show filial respect. In the morning he returned and joined his troops, then marched in with them, organised in divisions and in good order, on the Tuesday morning. His father was delighted at his arrival and rejoiced greatly, pleased with him for the troops and levies that he had gathered and organised. On that day there came Sābiq al-Dīn, the lord of Shayzar, 'Izz al-Dīn ibn al-Muqaddam and Majd al-Dīn, the lord of Baalbek, as well as a host of Muslim soldiers, who arrived excellently turned out, handsomely organised and fully equipped.

The sultan [**142**] was upset with a slight bilious fever, but he rode out on that day, which was a festive day from numerous points of view. On that day the enemy made an assault on the city in numbers that none but God could reckon. The inhabitants, the brave warriors within and the wise and experienced Muslim commanders there ignored them until the claws of their ambition were firmly fastened on the city, and they had dragged their engines we have mentioned close enough to be up against the walls and a large group of them had gathered[3] in the moat. Then our men shot crossbow bolts at them, stones from the trebuchets and also arrows and fiery missiles. With one great shout, they opened the gates and sold their bodies to their Creator Lord, content with his promised bargain. From all sides they dashed on the enemy and surprised those in the moat. God put terror into the hearts of the enemy, who, turning their backs in defeat, began a precipitate flight, retreating towards their tents and the safety of their ramparts, because of all the wounding and slaughtering they had witnessed and experienced. A large number remained in the moat and fell to the sword, God hastening their souls to Hell-fire. Seeing the enemy in

---

1 This date would be 4 October 1190, but that was a Thursday. Probably one should correct to 13 Ramaḍān {15 October} as *Fatḥ*, p. 294, gives this as the date of the destruction of the 'crawler' and the arrival of al-Ẓāhir.

2 At this point there is an intrusive rubric, 'The arrival of al-Ẓāhir'.

3 Reading as in B: *taḥaṣṣala*.

defeat and rout, the Muslims dashed towards their ram and set fire to it with naphtha, able to do so because its defenders had abandoned it and fled. It burnt with a horrible blaze and its flames rose up visibly into the sky. Shouts of 'Allah is great' and 'There is no god but God' and grateful thanks to glorious and mighty God were raised on high. The fire on the ram was so fierce that it spread to the 'cat', which was also burnt. The Muslims fixed chains with iron hooks to the ram and dragged it away, while it was still blazing, and brought it into the city. It was fashioned with great and impressive mechanisms. Water was thrown over it and eventually, after several days, the iron was cooled. We heard from within the city that the iron in it was weighed and came to 100 Ṣyrian *qinṭār*s, one *qinṭār* being 100 rotls and a Syrian rotl equalling four and a quarter Baghdad rotls. The 'head' was sent to the sultan and presented to him. I saw and examined it. It was similar to the rod which is attached to a mill-stone. It was claimed that whatever was rammed with it would be demolished.

This was one of Islam's best days. An indication of the happy fortune of the sultan's son, al-Ẓāhir, is that his coming coincided with Islam's victory and the burning of that frightening and terrible engine. Another example of that occurred with the burning of the turrets, as we have already explained. May God bring good fortune to Islam through this son and continue its victories in his reign with excellent regularity. The enemy were afflicted with intense disappointment and they carried away such of their machines as survived. The initiatives on which they had wasted their money came to a halt and their cunning plans were baffled. The sultan rejoiced in the auspicious prominence of his son and found a blessing in the fact that victory was linked time after time and again and again with his coming.

[143] The burning of the buss prepared to take the Tower of Flies

When it was Wednesday 15 Ramaḍān {17 October} our men went out of the city in galleys taking the enemy by surprise and they hurled phials of naphtha at the buss which caught fire. The flames climbed mightily high out at sea and our voices blended with shouts of 'There is no god but God' and 'God is great'. Thus God dealt with its threat. The Germans[1] were greatly saddened at that. They were overwhelmed with grievous disappointment and a general dejection fell upon them.

[1] B has: 'The German emperor and his troops ...'.

The prince's expedition to raid the Syrian lands adjacent to him

On Thursday 16 Ramaḍān of this year, that is 586 {18 October 1190} a pigeon-post letter, which a bird had brought from Aleppo, arrived enclosed in a letter that came from Ḥamā, telling that the prince, the lord of Antioch, had marched out with his army to raid the Muslim villages. The troops and lieutenants of al-Ẓāhir, the sultan's son, observed this and posted ambushes, which emerged to oppose him. Hardly was he aware of them before his men were falling to the sword. Seventy-five of their army were slain and a large number taken prisoner. He himself took refuge in a place called Shīḥā[1] until they hurried back to his lands (may God facilitate their conquest).

The capture of two of the enemy's busses

During the middle ten days [of Ramaḍān] [12-21 October] the wind forced ashore two busses that were making for the enemy containing men, women and children, a large amount of supplies and numerous flocks. The Muslims took all as booty. The enemy had recently seized a bark of ours, carrying money and men, which tried to enter **[144]** the harbour but was taken. The seizure of these two busses served to cancel and set right that loss. Later on reports were constantly coming from the mouths of spies and deserters that the enemy planned to come against the Muslim forces in a pitched hand-to-hand battle. The sultan's constitution was upset with a bout of bilious fever. In the circumstances he was obliged to withdraw the troops to a hill close to the hill of Shafar'am.

The army moves to Shafar'am

When the sultan had made up his mind to move back because of that indisposition, he did so and the move took place on Monday evening 19 Ramaḍān {21 October}. He made his camp on the top of the hill and the men camped on the high ground around to prepare for the winter and to have relief from the mud.[2] At this time Zayn al-Dīn Yūsuf ibn Zayn al-Dīn, the lord of Irbil, fell seriously ill with two intermittent fevers. He asked permission to depart, but this was not granted. He asked permission to move to Nazareth and this was allowed.

---

1 Probably identical with the village and district called Shīḥ in the 'Amq, 'formerly counted in the province of Antioch' (see Ibn Shaddād, *Description d'Alep*, p. 126).

2 Reading *al-waḥl*, as in B and in *Fatḥ*, p. 296.

Account of his death (may God have mercy on him)

Zayn al-Dīn remained in Nazareth for some days having his illness cared for. Towards the eve of Tuesday 28 Ramaḍān {30 October} his condition worsened and he died, while his brother Muẓaffar al-Dīn was present at his bed-side. People grieved for him because he was young and far from home. The sultan granted the town of Irbil to his brother, Muẓaffar al-Dīn, and asked him to give up the cities that he was holding, namely Ḥarrān [**145**] and Edessa, together with the lands and districts that were associated with them. The sultan also assigned him the town of Shahrazūr. He swore an oath to the sultan and agreed that if he received those places, he would hand over the lands he had, that is to say, Edessa, Ḥarrān, Ṣumayṣāt, al-Muwazzar[1] and all their territories. The sultan summoned al-Muẓaffar Taqī al-Dīn 'Umar, the son of his brother Shāhinshāh, to take his place and to fill the gap caused by the absence of Muẓaffar al-Dīn. While awaiting the arrival of Taqī al-Dīn, Muẓaffar al-Dīn Kūkbūrī ibn Zayn al-Dīn 'Alī remained in the royal camp. On midday 3 Shawwāl {4 November[2]} Taqī al-Dīn arrived, bringing back with him Mu'izz al-Dīn Sanjar Shāh, lord of Jazīrat [Ibn 'Umar], who was the son of Sayf al-Dīn.

Account of the Mu'izz al-Dīn affair

Mu'izz al-Dīn, that is, Sanjar Shāh ibn Sayf al-Dīn Ghāzī ibn Mawdūd ibn Zankī, was the lord of Jazīrat [Ibn 'Umar] at this time. The facts concerning him are that he came to wage Jihad - and we have mentioned the date when he arrived - but was overcome by tiredness, weariness and impatience, so much so that his messengers and letters came time and time again to the sultan seeking leave to depart, while the sultan was making his excuses, namely, that there was a to-and-froing of the enemy's envoys concerning the question of peace and it was not possible to break up the army until it became clear how the situation would end, either in peace or war. Mu'izz al-Dīn spared no effort in asking for leave until the feast day at the end of Ramaḍān came. At dawn of that day he presented himself at the door of the royal tent and asked permission to enter. The excuse was made that an indisposition had upset the sultan's constitution. However, he did not accept the excuse and repeated the request. He was then allowed to enter. Having presented himself before the sultan he made a direct petition for leave to depart. The sultan told him why this was inadmissable, saying, 'This is a time for the troops to come and muster, not a time to disperse them.' Mu'izz al-Dīn bent over his hand and kissed it like one

---

1 According to Yāqūt, iv, p. 679, a district in the Jazīra, which contained Nisibis.
2 The date is adjusted, as *Fatḥ*, p. 299, adds that it was a Sunday.

taking his leave. Then, straightaway, he rose up and departed, ordering his men to upset their cooking pots, with the food still in them, strike their tents and follow him.

When the sultan heard what he had done, he ordered a letter to be written to him in which he said, 'You initially sought to become my dependant and you approached me about that several times. You declared that you feared for your self and your city from your relatives. I accepted you and gave you succour and support. You acted high-handedly with the property, blood and honour of your people. I sent to you and forbade you to act so on several occasions but you did not refrain. This present crisis for Islam then ensued and we summoned you. You came with troops that I and other people know well, but you have stayed for this little while. You became restless and have taken this step, leaving without goodwill and without a conclusion of matters with the enemy. Look to yourself, see to whom you may attach yourself other than me and guard yourself against whoever may attack you. I have no longer [**146**] any concern for your welfare.' He handed the letter to a courier, who caught up with Mu'izz al-Dīn near Tiberias. He read the letter, but did not turn about, and carried on the way he was going.

As we have already explained, al-Muẓaffar Taqī al-Dīn had been summoned to the field of war because of the departure of Muẓaffar al-Dīn. He met Mu'izz al-Dīn on the way at a place called the defile of Fīq. Seeing that he was in a hurry and observing signs that everything was not well with him, he asked him what was the matter. Mu'izz al-Dīn told him of his situation and blamed the sultan for not having bestowed on him a robe of honour and not having allowed him to depart. Al-Malik al-Muẓaffar understood that he had left without leave from the sultan and against his wishes. He said to him, 'The best course for you is to return to his service and to stay close until he gives you permission. You are a child and you do not know the disaster that can come from this.' He replied, 'It is impossible for me to return.' 'You should return without question,' he said, 'there is no peace at all for you in leaving in this manner.' He still insisted on going away, but Taqī al-Dīn spoke roughly to him, 'You will return whether you want to or not.' Taqī al-Dīn was very bold and decisive and no respecter of persons. Realising that Taqī al-Dīn would arrest him if he did not himself choose to return, Mu'izz al-Dīn turned back in company with him. As he came to the camp, al-'Ādil, with us in attendance, went out to meet al-Muẓaffar and we found Mu'izz al-Dīn with him. They both took him into the sultan and asked for pardon for him, which was granted. Mu'izz al-Dīn, fearing for himself, requested that he should remain close to Taqī al-Dīn and permission for this was given. He stayed close to him until the time he departed.

'Imād al-Dīn's request for leave to depart

'Imād al-Dīn Zankī, the uncle of Mu'izz al-Dīn, whom we have mentioned, pestered the sultan for leave to depart. He complained of the onset of winter for which he had made no preparation. The sultan argued that messengers were going to and fro between us and the enemy concerning peace. Perhaps it might be arranged and it ought to be arranged with him present, as it was a shared decision. The sultan asked to be allowed to bring him winter tents but he refused, and also to supply him with money for expences but he refused again. His messengers came frequently to the sultan on this matter, while the sultan repeated his arguments. For some of this matter I acted as go-between. 'Imād al-Dīn had a determination to leave that beggared all description, while the sultan had an unbounded desire to cling on to him until matters between us and the enemy should be decided. In the end 'Imād al-Dīn wrote a petition in his own hand requesting permission to depart, in which he was both mild and hard. The sultan took it and wrote on the reverse in his own noble hand:

> Whoever loses such as me,
> Would that I knew what gain has he!

'Imād al-Dīn read this and his petitioning ceased completely.

A series of reports came in of the weakness of the God-forsaken enemy and of the incidence of shortages in their territory and army. A *ghirāra* of wheat in Antioch reached ninety-six Tyrian dinars, but that only added to their endurance, doggedness and stubbornness.

[147] Account of the enemy's move to Ra's al-Mā'

When their situation became difficult and shortages made them suffer, a large number of them came to give themselves into our hands because of their intense hunger. The rest made up their minds to move against us, their hopes fed by the illness that had befallen the sultan. They thought that he would not be able to take an active role. They came forth, both horse and foot, on Monday 11 Shawwāl 586 {12 November 1190}, carrying stores and tents. They came to the wells that the Muslims had dug beneath the Tell al-'Ajūl[1] when they were camped there. According to reports, they brought with them supplies for four days. The sultan was informed of the nature of their move, and he ordered the advanced detachment, which was at Tell al-'Ayyāḍiyya, to give way before them, back as far as Tell Kaysān. The enemy camped at the

---

1 *Nawādir*, by error, has Tell al-'Ijl. Correct from B.

wells after late afternoon prayer on the day mentioned. They spent the whole of that night surrounded by our advanced units. At daybreak one of those troops came to report that the enemy had started to move. Early in the night the sultan had given orders for the removal of the baggage to Nazareth and al-Qaymūn. The baggage left, but the troops remained. I was one of those who stayed in attendance on him.

The sultan ordered the army to form up as right wing, left wing and centre, in battle formation, and he himself mounted up, while the herald gave the cry for all to do so. They moved off and the sultan took up a position on one of the hills of al-Kharrūba. The right wing ended with its flank at the hill and the left wing's flank reached to the river,[1] near the sea.[2] On the right wing were his sons, al-Afḍal, lord of Damascus, al-Ẓāhir, lord of Aleppo, and al-Ẓāfir, lord of Buṣrā, and also the son of 'Izz al-Dīn, lord of Mosul, 'Alā' al-Dīn Khurramshāh. On the extreme right was his brother, al-'Ādil, with the following positioned close to him, Ḥusām al-Dīn [ibn] Lājīn, the *Ṭawāshī* Qaymāz al-Najmī, 'Izz al-Dīn Jurdīk al-Nūrī, Ḥusām al-Dīn Bishāra, lord of Bānyās, Badr al-Dīn Dildirim al-Yārūqī, lord of Tell Bāshir, and a large number of emirs. On the left wing were 'Imād al-Dīn Zankī, lord of Sinjār, his nephew Mu'izz al-Dīn, lord of Jazīrat [Ibn 'Umar], and on the extreme right al-Muẓaffar Taqī al-Dīn, the sultan's nephew. 'Imād al-Dīn Zankī himself was absent with the baggage-train because of an illness, but his troops remained. Also on the left wing were Sayf al-Dīn al-Mashṭūb and all the Mihrānīs and Hakkārīs, and Khushtarīn and other Kurdish emirs. In the centre was the Royal Guard.

The sultan commanded that from each troop a number of skirmishers should advance and surround the enemy, accompanied by the advanced guard. [**148**] He concealed some divisions behind the hills, in the hope that they might find an opportunity to surprise the enemy. God's enemies continued to advance while our men engaged them from all sides. They were following the river bank on the east side until they came to the head of the river. They circled around it and eventually crossed to the west side, where they camped. The fighting had deprived them of some of their champions and laid other men low. They camped on a rise there and pitched their tents that reached from there to the river. Many of them were wounded that day and several of them killed. When one of their number was wounded, they would carry him, and when someone was killed, they would bury him while still moving on, so that the number of their dead and wounded would not be ascertained. They took up this position on the Tuesday we have mentioned,[3] after midday.

---

1 The River Na'mān (the classical Belus) that flows into the sea a little south of Acre.

2 This sentence represents the text in B and in *Nawādir*'s footnote. A reversal of the position of the Muslim wings (as in *Nawādir*'s main text) is impossible.

3 Not, in fact, mentioned, but it would be 13 November.

Our troops retired to positions where they could wait and watch patiently. The sultan ordered the left wing to encompass the enemy with their extreme flank reaching the sea and the right wing to cover the river on the east side, while the skirmishers engaged them with constant flights of arrows that gave them no respite. The night was passed in this manner. The sultan with us in attendance went to the top of the Hill of al-Kharrūba, where he had camped during the previous year. He took his quarters in a small tent and around him the troops did likewise in view of the enemy. Hour by hour, until morning, intelligence of the enemy came to him. With daybreak on Wednesday 13 Sha'bān {14 November} someone brought news that they had begun to move at dawn, so he mounted up - this was the morning of Wednesday 13 Sha'bān - drew up his divisions and advanced to the al-Kharrūba hills nearest to the enemy, where he could observe all their dispositions. He was out of sorts and weak in body, but strong in heart. Then he sent to the troops with orders to engage, to press hard and charge from every direction. He ordered the main divisions to surround them, in such a way as to be neither close nor distant, to be a support for those actively engaged until the day was well advanced. The enemy proceeded along the west bank of the river, making for their tents while being heavily engaged from all sides, in fact, hard pressed from every direction but the river. The battle became hot and many of them were laid low. Their dead they buried and their wounded they carried away. They had formed their infantry into a wall, loosing a hail of bolts and arrows. No-one could reach them except with arrows, which [**149**] were flying over them like locusts. Their cavalry made their way in the centre, with the result that on that day not one of them was seen. Our drums were beating and our trumpets braying as voices were raised with shouts of 'There is no god but God' and 'God is great'. All the while, the sultan was reinforcing the skirmishers with bodies of troops that he had with him, so that in the end only a small band remained with him, as we observed the course of events. The enemy standard was raised high firmly planted on a cart pulled by mules. They defended this banner, which was very high like a minaret, a white cloth brightly marked with red in the shape of the Cross. They continued on their way in this manner until, at midday, they came opposite the bridge of Da'ūq, constrained by thirst, worn out by fatigue and weakened by wounds. Their situation was serious and the severe heat left them suffering from thirst.

That day the Muslims fought a fierce fight and gave Jihad its due. They assailed them mightily and surrounded them like a ring of hunters, but the enemy did not leave their infantry and charge. Most of the action that day was by the Royal Guard, who gave them a taste of death, although many of their own were wounded, such as Ayāz the Tall. In that battle he rivalled the greatest deeds that are told of earlier generations. He was wounded repeatedly, but continued to fight. Sayf al-Dīn Yāzkūj, one of the valiant warriors of

Islam, was wounded many times and has many exploits to his name. That day very many were wounded.

Our men continued to beset them until at noon of that day they camped at the bridge of Da'ūq, which they cut and demolished fearing that our men might cross over towards them. The sultan withdrew to Kharrūba Hill, leaving an advanced guard to watch them. All night until dawn reports kept on coming in. During that night he resolved to make a surprise attack on those left in their camp. He wrote to the city to tell them, so that they would attack from that direction as we did from this. No reply came back from the city, so he gave up that plan because of the communication delay.

On Thursday morning 14 Sha'bān [15 November] someone brought news that the enemy were showing signs of breaking camp. The sultan mounted up and disposed the divisions, but did not allow our men to engage for fear that they might be taken by surprise because the enemy had drawn close to their tents. He stationed the divisions on the east bank of the river to proceed opposite the enemy until they arrived at their tents.

Of their nobles the following were wounded during this foray, Count Henry and the marquis. The son of the German emperor remained behind **[150]** in their camp with a large force. After the enemy had returned to their tents, the reserve battalions they had there made a sortie against the Muslim advance units. They charged them and a fierce battle developed in which, after severe fighting, many of the enemy were killed or wounded, while on the Muslim side three persons were killed. Losses for the enemy included an important person, a commander amongst them, who was mounted on a large horse, clothed in mail down to its hooves. He himself wore armour the like of which had never been seen. After the termination of the battle they asked the sultan for his body, which was handed over to them. His head was sought for, but could not be found.

The sultan returned to his tent and brought the baggage-train back to its place. All the men returned to their positions, as did 'Imād al-Dīn, whose fever had now left him. The sultan's health remained upset. This was the reason why this force that ventured out had survived, as he was unable to direct the action himself. I saw him weeping when the battle was in progress since he was unable to engage the enemy and I saw him ordering his sons, one after the other, to take matters in hand and to join in the battle. When someone said to him, 'Disease has become rife on the plain of Acre, so mortality is great on both sides', I heard him quote the following, 'Kill me and Mālik, kill Mālik with me.'[1] By that he meant, 'I am content to perish if God's enemies perish.' Great strength was renewed thereby in the hearts of the soldiers of Islam.

1 At the battle of the Camel (36/656), Ibn al-Zubayr (see *EI*^{2}, i, pp. 54-55), struggling with Mālik al-Ashtar, a partisan of 'Alī, called out thus to his men (*Kāmil*, iii, p. 251).

Account of the battle at the ambush

On Friday 22 Shawwāl {23 November} the sultan decided to set an ambush for the enemy. His determination to do this was strong. He selected a body of brave warriors and valiant horsemen and ordered them to move by night and lie in ambush at the foot of the rise which is to the north of Acre, at some distance from the enemy forces. Nearby was al-'Ādil's position, where the battle that is named after him took place. He ordered a small group of them to make themselves visible to the enemy, move towards their tents and tempt them out. If the enemy came out against them, they should retire in the direction of the ambush. They carried this out, went at night to the hill mentioned above and set the ambush below it. At daybreak on Saturday 23 Shawwāl {24 November} a small band of them rode forward on picked horses as far as the enemy's encampment. They shot at them and with the incessant hail of arrows they stung them into action. [**151**] About 200 knights came after them, armed to the teeth and mounted on good horses, all fully equipped and armed. They rode at them with no infantry in support. They were full of eagerness to attack our men because they were so few. The latter gave way before them, fighting as they withdrew, until they reached the ambush. Our warriors there came out with a rush as they reached them and with a shout as of one man charged against the enemy like lions on their prey. The enemy held firm stolidly and fought fiercely, but then turned in flight. God's elect overwhelmed them and dealt sword blows upon them, overthrowing a large number of them. The rest survived to become prisoners, as indeed they did, and their horses and equipment were taken.

The good news came to the Muslim camp and cries of 'There is no god but God' and 'God is great' rang out. The sultan rode to meet the Jihad warriors. I was in his retinue when he went to Tell Kaysān where we met the first troops to arrive. He halted there to greet the returning troops, while people called down blessings on them and thanked them for their excellent exploit. The sultan reviewed the prisoners and looked into their circumstances. One of those captured that day was the commander of the king of France's troops, sent by him as reinforcements before his own arrival. The treasurer of the king was also taken.

The sultan, after all had been accounted for, returned to his tent full of joy and delight. He summoned the captives and ordered the herald to announce that anyone who had taken a prisoner should bring him. Our men brought in their prisoners. I was present at that gathering. The sultan honoured the nobles amongst them. He bestowed a fur robe especially[1] on the commander of the French king's troops and ordered for each of the rest a fur top-coat, for the cold

1 B reads *farwa malīḥa* (a beautiful fur). *Fatḥ*, p. 308, has *farwata-hu al-khāṣṣa*, 'his own personal fur'.

was intense and they had suffered from it. He also had food brought for them which they ate and he ordered a tent to be pitched for them close to his own. At all times he treated them generously. Sometimes he invited the commander to his table. He then ordered that they should be bound and conveyed to Damascus. They were taken there in honoured state. He allowed them to write to their comrades and to have the clothes and other things they needed brought to them from their camp. When that was done, they travelled to Damascus.

The troops rest from the Jihad

When winter descended and the sea became rough and there was no danger of the enemy seeking a pitched battle, or of making great efforts to attack the city, or to further the siege operations on account of the heavy and incessant rains, the sultan gave leave to the Muslim armies to return to their countries to enjoy a portion of rest and to restore their horses until the time for action. The first to depart was 'Imād al-Dīn, the lord of Sinjār, because he had been so anxious [**152**] to request leave. He left on Monday 25 Shawwāl[1] 586 [26 November 1190]. After him on the same day his nephew, Sanjar Shāh, lord of Jazīrat [Ibn 'Umar] left. This was after both of them had been showered with marks of honour, gifts and presents, more than were bestowed on others. On 1 Dhū'l-Qa'da {30 December} 'Alā' al-Dīn, the son of the lord of Mosul, took his esteemed and honoured departure, taking with him choice gifts. Al-Malik al-Muẓaffar Taqī al-Dīn and his troops delayed until after the start of the year 587 [late January 1191], as did the sultan's son al-Ẓāhir. The latter left for Aleppo on the morning of Wednesday 9 Muḥarram [6 February 1191] and al-Muẓaffar left on 3 Ṣafar {2 March}. Only a small group of emirs and the Royal Guard remained with the sultan.

Account of the visit of Zulfandār

Zulfandār[2] made his visit during the month of Dhū'l-Qa'da 586 [December 1190]. The sultan received him and gave him a generous welcome, providing a banquet for him the day of his arrival and behaving towards him with great affability. Zulfandār's purpose was to obtain an order for the restoration of

---

1 The printed text has 15 Shawwāl, which would be 15 November, but that was a Thursday. The correction is made on the authority of *Fatḥ*, p. 311, line 3.

2 'Izz al-Dīn Maḥmūd, known as Zulfandār, was a senior emir from Mosul who had fought for the Zengids against Saladin at the Horns of Ḥamā and Tell al-Sulṭān in 570-1/1175-6. In Ibn al-Athīr, *al-Bāhir*, pp. 175, 183, he is called Zulfdār, in Persian 'Curly'. Should he be thought of as Zulfnadār, 'Baldy'!!

properties which he had possessed in the districts of Nisibis and al-Khābūr and which had been taken away. The sultan signed an order for their restoration and ensured that subsequent action concerning them should follow the Holy Law. He bestowed a robe of honour on him and other marks of distinction and Zulfandār departed happy and delighted, expressing his gratitude for his favours.

How the sultan was busy getting the relief force into the city

When the sea was rough, the threat from enemy ships was removed and the galleys that they had at sea were pulled up on to dry land. The sultan then occupied himself with getting relief forces into Acre, transporting provisions, supplies, money and equipment, and getting out the emirs who had been there because of their many complaints about their long spell of duty, their endurance of fatigue and broken nights, and their constant fighting night and day. The commander of the relief going in was one of the emirs, the Emir Sayf al-Dīn al-Mashṭūb. He went in on Wednesday 16 Muḥarram 587 [13 February 1191], the same day that the previous commander, the Emir Ḥusām al-Dīn Abū'l-Hayjā', came out, **[153]** along with his men and the emirs who had been there. With al-Mashṭūb went a large number of emirs and leading members of the army[1] Each person who went in was instructed to take with him a whole year's supplies.

Al-'Ādil moved with his troop to Haifa on the coast[2], which was the place from where the ships were loaded that came to Acre and where they went when they left. The sultan stayed there, urging men to enter Acre and protect the provisions and stores, so that none of the enemy might interfere with them by a sudden attack. Seven busses full of provisions, stores and money, which had arrived from Egypt fully laden, managed to get into Acre. The sultan had ordered them to be prepared some time earlier. They arrived on Monday 2 Dhū'l-Ḥijja in the previous year (586) [31 December 1190]. One ship was wrecked on rocks that were near the harbour. All the fighting men within the city moved to the seaward part of the city to meet the busses and unload their cargo. Learning that all the garrison soldiers had shifted seawards, the enemy took advantage of this, assembled in great numbers and made a mighty assault against the city from the land side. They approached the wall and climbed a single ladder but, as God willed it, the ladder broke under them. The garrison then confronted them and killed many of them. They withdrew disheartened and disappointed. As for the busses, the sea became very rough and forced the ships against one another on to the rocks, where they foundered. Everything on

1 This translates *al-khalq*. Should one read *al-ḥalqa*, i.e., the Royal Guard?
2 Reading *al-baḥr*, not *al-nahr* (river), although B has the latter reading too.

board was lost and a great many people perished. It was said that they numbered sixty souls. They carried vast supplies which, had they been saved, would have sufficed the inhabitants of the city[1] for a whole year, but that was by the decree of the Mighty One, the All-Knowing. However, it brought a major setback upon the Muslims, which caused the sultan extreme anguish. He asked for it to be made good through his Jihad efforts. 'But what is with God is better and more lasting.'[2] This was the first sign that the city was going to be taken and overcome.

The collapse of a section of the wall, which was the second sign

On the eve of Saturday 7 Dhū'l-Ḥijja 586 [5 January 1191] God decreed and ordained that a large section of the city wall collapsed. It fell with its full weight on the barbican and demolished a large part of that too. This encouraged the enemy, who became eager and enthusiastic to make an assault. They came from everywhere towards the city like the advancing darkness of night. The defenders, aroused[3] and with zeal kindled, fought fiercely and killed and wounded many of the enemy, who eventually gnashed their teeth and despaired of gaining any advantage. Our men stood like a dam where the section had fallen. They gathered all the masons and craftsmen that were in the city and put them to work at that spot, protecting them with bows, crossbows and trebuchets. It took only a few days to put right and the construction became better, stronger and more solid than it had been before (praise be to God).

[154] The capture of the enemy's ships

Already huge numbers of the Franks had deserted, forced out by hunger to join us. They said to the sultan, 'We will put to sea in barks and plunder the enemy. What we win will be shared between us and the Muslims.' He granted them permission for this and gave them a bark, which is a small vessel. They embarked and fell in with some enemy merchant ships, which were making for their camp and whose goods were mostly worked silver or silver bullion. They attacked and fought until they finally captured them and took a vast amount of plunder. The prisoners they took they brought before the sultan. This was on

1 Reading *ahl al-balad*, as in B.

2 Koran xxviii, 60.

3 *Nawādir* has *fa-taḥāyā*, and B *fa-ntakhaw* (correct to *fa-ntakhā*).

13 Dhū'l-Ḥijja 586 [11 January 1191].[1] I was there on this occasion and one of the things they presented to him was a silver table with a perforated silver cover. The sultan gave them everything and did not take a thing. The Muslims rejoiced at God's victory over the enemy through their own hands.

Account of the death of the son of the German emperor

After winter had come with its incessant rainfall and change of airs, the plain became very unhealthy and, as a result, there was great mortality amongst the enemy. In addition to that there were the severe shortages and the fact that the sea was closed to them, from which supplies had been reaching them from every quarter. Daily, from 100 to 200 were dying, according to reports, and some said more than that. The German emperor's son became very ill. He was stricken by a sickness in the stomach, from which he perished on 22 Dhū'l-Ḥijja [20 January 1191].[2]

The Franks grieved greatly for him and lit impressive lamps, so that not a single tent of theirs was left without two or three lights burning within it. Their whole camp was like one blazing fire. The Muslims rejoiced at his death as much as the infidels grieved for his loss. One of their nobles, called Count Tibault,[3] perished and Count Henry fell ill and his life was despaired of.

On the 24th of the month [22 January] two barks with a total of fifty and more persons were seized from the enemy and on the 25th of the same [23 January] a large bark of theirs was taken with all its cargo. That included a robe encrusted with pearls, a garment for the king. It is said that his nephew was on board, who was also seized (to God be the praise).

[155] Account of Asad al-Dīn's raid

This Asad al-Dīn is the lord of Ḥimṣ, Shīrkūh ibn Nāṣir al-Dīn Muḥammad ibn Asad al-Dīn Shīrkūh the Great. What is to be told is that the sultan had instructed him to keep a watch on the Franks in Tripoli and to undertake the protection of the Muslims and the peasants in those regions. It was reported to him that the Franks of Tripoli had sent out their herds and horses to the plain there, along with their cattle and pack-animals. He decided to attack them with his troops. He marched out, taking them by surprise, and attacked the herds, taking from them 400 head of horses and 100 head of cattle. Forty of the

---

1 *Fatḥ*, p. 316, gives the date as Monday 22 Dhū'l-Ḥijja and the equivalent Monday would be 21 January.

2 *Fatḥ*, p. 316, gives 12 Dhū'l-Ḥijja [10 January 1191].

3 *Nawādir* reads Yanbāṭ, but the correct form is found in *Fatḥ*, p. 316, i.e., Tībāṭ.

horses died, but the rest survived. He returned to his base without losing a single man (to God be the praise). His letter with news of this arrived on 4 Ṣafar 587 { 2 March 1191}.[1]

On the eve of that day the wind cast an enemy ship ashore at al-Zīb[2] and wrecked it. On board were a large number whom, when our men caught sight of them, they pounced on and captured down to the last man. I was present when fifteen of these persons were paraded before the sultan.

The night of the new moon of Rabīʻ I [29 March] our men emerged from Acre and attacked the enemy, doing much slaughter amongst them. They seized a large number from their tents, of whom twelve were women, as was reported.

Account of several events in the year 587 [1191]

On 3 Rabīʻ I [31 March] it was the turn of the Royal Guard to act as advanced guard. A large crowd of the enemy came out against them and a hideous battle took place between them, in which several of the enemy were killed, including, by report, one of their great men. On the Muslim side the only loss was a serving man of the sultan, called Qarāqūsh, a large, brave man of many great exploits. He met a martyr's death that day.

On Saturday 9 Rabīʻ I [6 April] the sultan heard that sometimes a group of the enemy would venture out and take their ease because we were at a distance from them. He decided to send his brother, al-ʻĀdil, with a large body of Muslim troops under his command, ordering him to set an ambush for the enemy behind the hill where the battle known after him took place. The sultan himself and several of the great men of his family and followers went and prepared an ambush behind Tell al-ʻAyyāḍiyya. Among his family members with him were al-Muẓaffar Taqī al-Dīn with the latter's son, Nāṣir al-Dīn Muḥammad, and his own son, al-Afḍal, and of his younger sons, al-Malik al-Ashraf Muḥammad, al-Muʻaẓẓam Tūrānshāh and al-Malik al-Ṣāliḥ Ismāʻīl. The civilians present included Qāḍī al-Fāḍil and the secretariat. I was one of the company on that **[156]** day.

Some of our brave warriors rode forward on good mounts, skirmishing and plainly offering battle to the enemy, but none came out that day. It was as if they had been given intelligence of our planned ruse. However, that day did not end without a sort of victory.

During that day forty-five Frankish prisoners arrived who had been captured at Beirut and, having been sent to the sultan, reached him at this place that day. I witnessed at that time such soft-heartedness and clemency on his part as I

1 The day of the week is specified by *Fatḥ*, p. 323, i.e., Saturday {2 March}.

2 *Nawādir* has al-Dhīb, whereas *Fatḥ*, p. 324, has *ʻalā sāḥil al-Zīb*, 'on the shore of al-Zīb'.

have never seen surpassed. Amongst them there was a old man, very advanced in years, without a tooth left in his head and with only just enough strength to move. The sultan said to the interpreter, 'Ask him, "What brought you to come here when you are this old? How far it is from here to your[1] land?"' He replied, 'Between me and my land is a journey of ten months. As for why I came, it was just to go on pilgrimage to the Sepulchre.' The sultan had pity on him, gave him gifts, freed him and sent him back to the enemy camp on horseback. His young sons had asked him to allow them to kill a captive but he refused. I asked him the reason for his refusal, as I was the intermediary for their request. He said, 'So that they will not, as youngsters, grow accustomed to shed blood and make light of it, when they as yet do not distinguish between Muslim and infidel.' His merciful care for Muslims that is implied in this is quite clear.

When the sultan despaired of any move by the enemy, he returned to his encampment during the evening of that day, namely Sunday 10 Rabīʿ I [7 April].

The arrival of Muslim forces and of the king of France

Starting from this date the sea became navigable and the weather improved. The time for the return of troops to the conflict came for both sides. The first to arrive amongs the Muslim forces was ʿAlam al-Dīn Sulaymān ibn Jandar, one of the emirs of the sultan's son al-Ẓāhir, the lord of Aleppo. He was an old man of note and much military experience, a person of wise counsel, whom the sultan respected and honoured for he had long served with him. After him came Majd al-Dīn ibn ʿIzz al-Dīn Farrūkhshāh ibn Shāhinshāh, the lord of Baalbek. They both came in Rabīʿ I [April]. Afterwards a succession of Muslim troops arrived from every direction.

The enemy's troops, on the other hand, were threatening the advance guard and any Muslim troops that came near them with the imminent arrival of the king of France, who to them was a great man **[157]** and respected leader, one of their great kings to whom all present in the army would be obedient. When he arrived, he would have authority over everyone. They kept on threatening us with his coming until he eventually did arrive (God curse him) in six busses, bringing him, his supplies, the horses that he required and his personal retinue. He arrived on Saturday 23 Rabīʿ I [20 April].

---

[1] Reading *bilādika*, as in B.

A rare event and a good omen

A falcon the king valued had accompanied him from his own country. It was of impressive size, white in colour and of a rare type. He cherished and loved it greatly. The falcon escaped from his arm and flew off. He called it back, but it did not respond. In the end it alighted on the city wall of Acre. Our men caught it and sent it to the sultan. Its arrival caused much astonishment and was a happy omen of victory. To my eyes its colour was a dazzling white. I have never seen a more handsome falcon. The Muslims considered this an auspicious event. The Franks offered 1,000 dinars for it, but this was not accepted. After this the count of Flanders arrived. He was a great noble and a man of note amongst them, who had besieged Ḥamā and Ḥārim during the year of Ramla.[1]

A strange occurrence

On the 12 Rabīʿ II [9 May] a letter came from Lattakia which told that some of the Frankish deserters had been given barks to attack the enemy at sea. Having received them they landed on the island of Cyprus on one of their feast days. A large number of the island's inhabitants had gathered in a church near the sea. The deserters celebrated the feast-day service with them and then, when they had finished, they laid rough hands[2] on all in the church, men and women, seized every last one of them, even the priest, and carried them off to be thrown into the ships and taken to Lattakia. They took twenty-seven women and large sums of money, which they divided up, it being said that each one of them received 4,000 dirhams in silver bullion.

Later on, Badr al-Dīn, the prefect of Damascus, arrived on 17 Rabīʿ II [14 May]. Our men raided the enemy's flocks and seized them, in all 120 head. Their horse and foot came out in pursuit, but they did not win back any of them (praise be to God).

News of the king of England (God curse him)

This king of England was a mighty warrior of great courage and strong in purpose. He had much experience of fighting and was intrepid in battle, and yet he was in their eyes below the king of France in royal status, although being richer and more renowned for martial skill and courage. **[158]** The news

1 The latter phrase refers to Saladin's defeat at 'Mons Gisardi' in late 1177. The count of Flanders, Philip of Alsace, on an earlier crusade at that time raided widely in N. Syria.

2 Adding from B *yadahum* after *ḍarabū*.

concerning him was that, after he had arrived at the island of Cyprus, he decided not to go further without its being his and under his authority. He therefore invaded it. The ruler[1] marched out against him, having gathered a large force, and fought him fiercely. The king of England sent to the Frankish camp [at Acre] seeking some reinforcements to help him achieve his purpose. King Guy[2] sent him his brother with 160 mounted men. The Franks at Acre continued to wait and see what would be forthcoming from both parties.

On Sunday the last day of Rabīʿ II [26 May] letters came from Beirut with the news that five of the king of England's ships and a tarida[3] with a great host on board, men, women, supplies, timber and engines of war and so on, had been taken while making their way to the enemy army. This was a great victory, which the Muslims joyfully proclaimed.

On Thursday 4 Jumādā I [30 May] the enemy attacked the city and erected seven trebuchets. Letters coming from Acre reported serious alarms and requested diversionary operations against the enemy. The sultan informed the troops of his intention to move camp to engage the enemy more closely. The following morning he moved towards them until he halted at al-Kharrūba, where he arranged the army into right wing, left wing and centre. He sent people to reconnoitre the enemy and ascertain the state of their defensive ditches, whether there were any forces in ambush there. They returned with news that they were free of any such. He himself went forward with a small group of his mamlukes. Coming to their ditches, he climbed a hill known as Tell al-Fuḍūl, which was close to the enemy and overlooked their tents. He observed the trebuchets, which of them were functioning and which were out of action. He then returned to his encampment. I had been in attendance on him.

During the following morning some robbers brought him an infant child aged three months, whom they had stolen from its mother.

The story of the infant child

The Muslims had thieves who would enter the enemy's tents, steal from them, even taking individuals, and then make their way back. It came about that one night they took an unweaned infant three months old. They brought it to the sultan's tent and offered it to him. Everything they took they used to offer to him and he would reward and recompense them. When the mother missed the child she spent the whole duration of the night pleading for help with loud

---

1 Isaac Ducas Comnenus, who was in rebellion against Isaac Angelus and styled himself emperor.

2 The original has 'Godfrey' here. In fact, Guy not only sent his brother, Godfrey of Lusignan, but also went to Cyprus himself (Nicholson, *Chronicle*, p. 188 and note 123).

3 See above, p. 50, note 2.

lamentations. Her case came to the notice of their princes, who said to her, 'He has a merciful heart. We give you permission to go to him. Go and ask him for the child and he will restore it to you.' So she went out to ask [**159**] the Muslim advance guard for assistance, telling them of her troubles through a dragoman who translated for her. They did not detain her but sent her to the sultan. She came to him when he was riding on Tell al-Kharrūba with me and a great crowd attending upon him. She wept copious tears and besmirched her face with soil. After he had asked about her case and it had been explained, he had compassion for her and, with tears in his eyes, he ordered the infant to be brought to him. People went and found that it had been sold in the market. The sultan ordered the purchase price to be paid to the purchaser and the child taken from him. He himself stayed where he had halted until the infant was produced and then handed over to the woman who took it, wept mightily, and hugged it to her bosom, while people watched her and wept also. I was standing there amongst the gathering. She suckled the child for a while and then, on the orders of the sultan, she was taken on horseback and restored to their camp with the infant.

Consider this compassion which encompasses all humanity. O God, You created him merciful, show him Your ample mercy, O mighty and generous One! Consider, too, the testimony of the enemy to his gentleness, generosity, mercy and compassion.

> Many a fair one received testimony from her rivals.
> There is none that denies beauty its due.

On that day Ẓahīr al-Dīn ibn al-Balankarī, who was one of the foremost great emirs of Mosul, came to join us. He came, having abandoned Mosul and seeking to serve the sultan.

After the sultan had returned to his encampment, hardly an hour passed before news arrived that the assault on Acre had been renewed. He rode back immediately towards the city, but arrived only after the battle had ceased as nightfall separated the two sides.

Account of the sultan's move to Tell al-'Ayyāḍiyya

On the morning of Tuesday 9 Jumādā I [4 June] the sultan heard that the Franks had pressed hard on the city and set up trebuchets. He commanded the herald to call the troops to arms and all responded as the sultan mounted up, both foot and horse. He moved to al-Kharrūba and strengthened the advance guard by sending forward a detachment of the Royal Guard. However, the enemy did not emerge, but intensified their assault on the city. The sultan pressed hard with fierce fighting and attacked them in their defensive ditches. He kept that up until they gave up their assault at midday on the Tuesday mentioned. The enemy returned to their tents, despairing of taking the city. The sultan retired to a small tent which was set up for him there, to shelter from the sun. He stopped for the midday prayer and to rest awhile. He strengthened the advanced units and ordered the troops to return to the camp to take a little rest. I was attending upon him and while he was engaged as described, someone from the advance guard came and reported that the Franks had recommenced their assault, when they became aware that he had retired, more fiercely [**160**] than previously. He ordered people to go after the troops and order them back. The troops returned towards the enemy in division after division. He ordered them to spend the night in armour and he himself remained with the intention of passing the night there. I took my leave of him at the end of that Tuesday and returned to my tent. He and all the army remained in battle order throughout the night. A detachment of them were ordered by him to close with the enemy.

Just before daybreak on Wednesday 10 Jumādā I [5 June] the army moved to Tell al-'Ayyāḍiyya, facing the enemy, and a small tent was pitched for him there. The men were ordered to take up their positions around him on the hill as had been the case in the previous year, but lightly equipped as the baggage-train remained at al-Kharrūba. All that day he engaged the enemy with fierce attacks and repeated violent blows, which were not slackened, to prevent them from assaulting the city. He personally went around the divisions, urging and encouraging them to wage the Jihad, all that to keep the enemy too busy to press their attack on the city. When the enemy saw their serious engagement and impressive tenacity, they feared an attack on their tents, slackened their assault and busied themselves with guarding their defensive ditches and protecting their camp. Seeing that their assault had abated, the sultan withdrew to his tents on Tell al-'Ayyāḍiyya and posted men at the ditches to keep him informed of the enemy's movements hour by hour, if they returned to the assault. Throughout all this the enemy were still determined to persist in their close siege and their attacks.

Their efforts to press hard on the city

The enemy's pressure on the city and their extreme efforts to fill in the moat went so far that they were throwing in all their dead horses and, finally, they were even throwing in their own dead. People said that whenever one of their number was wounded mortally and beyond hope, they would throw him in. Reports of all this came in constant letters from our men in the city. The garrison itself was divided into different parties, one going down into the moat and cutting up the corpses and horses that were thrown in to make them easy to carry, one carrying away what the former had cut up and throwing it into the sea, another giving protection and defending them so that they could manage their task, and yet another at the trebuchets and guarding the walls. They were worn out with tiredness and exhaustion. Their complaints at all this were unbroken. This was a trial such as no-one had ever borne and no stout-hearted man could endure. Yet they were enduring it, 'and God is with those that endure'.[1] Meanwhile, the sultan did not interrupt his attacks nor the pressure on their trenches,[2] through his own efforts and those of his officers and his sons night and day, to hinder their assault. The enemy directed their trebuchets at the Ox Spring Tower.[3] Stones from the trebuchets rained on it night and day, until they had produced a visible effect. The more they increased their attacks on the city, the more the sultan increased **[161]** his on them and made surprise raids on their defences. Eventually, a man came out from their positions to ask for someone to parley with. When the sultan was informed of this, he replied, 'If you have anything to propose, let one of you come and speak with us. We have nothing to discuss with you.' The state of affairs continued without a break both night and day until the king of England arrived.

Account of the arrival of the king of England

On Saturday 13 Jumādā I 587 [8 June 1191] the accursed king of England came after having come to terms with the ruler of the island of Cyprus and taken control of it. His coming had great pomp. He arrived in twenty-five galleys, full of men, weapons and stores. The Franks manifested great joy and delight at his coming. Indeed, that night in their joy they lit huge fires in their camp. Those fires were impressively large, indicating sizeable reinforcements. Their princes had been threatening us with his arrival and deserters had been telling us that they were putting off the great push against the city that they wanted to make until his arrival. He was wise and experienced in warfare and his coming had a dread and frightening effect on the hearts of the Muslims. The sultan, meanwhile, was facing all this with steadfastness, confidence in future reward and trust in God Almighty. 'Whoever trusts in God, He will be his sufficiency.'[4]

---

1 Koran ii, 249.

2 Correct edition to *khanādiqihim*, as in B.

3 Perhaps over the eastern gate that was named after the spring ('Ayn al-Baqar) just outside the walls (see Le Strange, *Palestine*, pp. 330-334).

4 Koran lxv, 3.

The sinking of a Muslim buss

This was the third sign that the city would be taken. On 16 Jumādā I [11 June] a large and imposing buss arrived from Beirut, loaded with seige engines, weapons, provisions and stout fighting men. The sultan had ordered it to be fitted out in Beirut and dispatched, and a great company of fighting men had been embarked to force an entry into Acre despite the enemy blockade. Its fighting complement was 650 men. The accursed king of England confronted the buss with a number of galleys. It is said that he had forty sail. They surrounded our vessel on all sides and attacked it fiercely. As fate had it the wind dropped. The contest continued fiercely and a great many of the enemy were killed. Our men set fire to a large enemy galley with many on board, who perished every one. The crew of the buss were quite outnumbered and when their captain, an excellent, brave man, well skilled in warfare, saw signs of their imminent defeat and that they would inevitably be killed, he said, 'By God, we will not die without glory. We will surrender nothing to them on board this buss.' They fell upon the ship with pickaxes to scuttle her. They kept on until they had opened gaps on all sides. The ship filled with water and all the crew and all the equipment, provisions and other cargo sank. The enemy gained possession of nothing at all. The captain's name was Ya'qūb, a man from Aleppo. The enemy picked up one of the crew, [**162**] took him on board their galleys and saved him from drowning, but they mutilated him and sent him to the city to report the disaster. Our people were greatly saddened by this, but the sultan faced it with confidence in his future reward for his efforts in the path of God and with steadfast endurance of his trials. 'God will not neglect the reward of those who do right.'[1]

Account of the burning of a siege tower

The enemy had constructed a large frightening siege tower of four stories. The first story was of wood, the second of lead, the third of iron and the fourth of copper. It overtopped the city wall and could accommodate fighting men. The city garrison were greatly fearful of it and were tempted to ask for terms from the enemy, who, as far as we could judge by eye, had brought it to within only five cubits of the wall. The defenders began to rain down incendiary missiles on it night and day until God decreed that it caught fire and burned up. A tongue of flame rose high into the sky and voices proclaimed aloud their thanks to God. This was considered some reparation for the previous setback and a cancellation of its effect, a blessing after a disaster and an encouragement after

---

1 Koran ix, 120.

despair. This took place the day the buss sank and had a great effect on the Muslims, assuaging their grief and disappointment.

Account of several incidents

When it was Friday 19 Jumādā I [14 June], the enemy made a great assault on the city and put it under dreadful pressure. We had agreed with the defenders that, whenever there was an enemy attack, they would beat their drum. This they now did and the sultan's drum replied. Our troops mounted and the sultan pressed hard on the enemy from without. The Muslim troops attacked them in their tents, crossing over their defensive ditches and seizing their cooking pots from their trivets. A good amount of booty taken from their tents came before the sultan, when I was present.

The engagement continued until the enemy ascertained that there had been an attack and that they had suffered a reverse. They then gave up their assault on the city and commenced to fight our forces. The battle was fierce and grew in violence until the time of midday. On both sides all were greatly afflicted by the heat. The two forces retired to their tents, exhausted by fatigue and the heat. That was the end of fighting for that day.

Another incident

On Monday 23 Jumādā I {17 June} the city drum sounded and was answered by the sultan's drum. Fighting flared up between the two sides and the enemy determinedly pressed hard on the city, confident that our men would not attack their tents **[163]** and that they feared to do so. The troops gave the lie to their expectations by attacking and plundering them. The enemy withdrew [from the city] to give battle. Great shouts came from them and they caught a large body of Muslims within their trenches and ramparts. A considerable engagement followed in which two Muslims were killed and many wounded. The enemy had several losses.

The strangest thing that occurred in this battle was that an important and well-known man from Māzandarān arrived that day wishing to fight for the faith. He came when the battle was at its height. He met the sultan and asked permission to join the Jihad. He charged vigorously and met a martyr's death that same hour.

When the enemy saw that the Muslims had entered their trenches and penetrated within their ramparts, their religious zeal and sense of honour roused them to action. They moved out, mounted men accompanied by infantry, beyond the defences and charged the Muslims as one man. The Muslims stood solidly firm and did not move from their positions. The fighting raged fiercely and violent blows were exchanged, but the Muslims remained steadfast like noble heroes and joined the battle with élan.

Seeing this unconquerable steadfastness and defiant bravery, the enemy at this juncture sent an envoy. The request being made, he was allowed to approach. He came first to al-ʿĀdil, who accompanied him into the presence of the sultan, taking with him al-Afḍal too. The envoy delivered his message, the gist of which was that the king of England sought a meeting with the sultan. After he had heard this message, the sultan answered immediately without thought or hesitation, 'Kings do not meet unless an agreement has been reached. It is not good for them to fight after meeting and eating together. If he wants this, an agreement must be settled before it can happen. We must have an interpreter we can trust to act between us, who can make each of us understand what the other says. Let the envoy be our mutual interpreter. If we come to an agreement, the meeting can happen later, God willing.'

Another incident

On Saturday 28 Jumādā I {22 June} the enemy came out, horse and foot, on the seaward side north of the city. The sultan learnt of this and rode out with the army. Fighting broke out between the two sides and on the Muslim side a Bedouin and a Kurd were killed. Several of the enemy were killed. One was taken prisoner with his armour and horse and was brought before the sultan. The fighting continued until nightfall separated the two parties.

Another incident

On Sunday 29 Jumādā I {23 June} many enemy foot-soldiers came out on the bank of the freshwater stream. A detachment of our advance guard met them and a serious battle ensued. Some Muslim infantry arrived and a close quarters struggle followed. The enemy seized a Muslim and, having killed him, [**164**] burned his body. The Muslims then seized one of them, and killed and burned him. I saw the two fires blazing at the same time.

From our men in the city there was a constant stream of reports that the enemy was waxing ever stronger. They also complained that they were fighting uninterruptedly night and day. They reported the great fatigue they endured on account of all the various tasks they had constantly to put up with since the arrival of the accursed king of England. Then the latter fell seriously ill and was on the verge of death. Furthermore, the king of France was wounded, but this only made them more determined and stubborn.

Account of the flight of two servants of the king's sister[1]

The story is as follows. The servants belonged to the sister of the king of England and were secretly Muslims because they had lived in Sicily in the service of the ruler there. She had been the wife of the ruler of Sicily. When the latter died and her brother passed through the island, he took her with him to the army besieging Acre.[2] Once the two servants had arrived and were in the vicinity of Muslims, they ran away to the Muslim camp. The sultan welcomed them and bestowed great gifts upon them.

Account of the flight of the marquis to Tyre

When it was Monday the last day of Jumādā I {24 June} the marquis became very apprehensive that, if he remained, he would be arrested and they would give Tyre to the former king, who had been the sultan's prisoner, because of the period of captivity he had endured for the final triumph of the religion of the Messiah. When the marquis learnt that this was true, he fled to Tyre. They sent priests after him to bring him back, but he refused and travelled by sea to Tyre. They were upset and very distressed by this for he was a man of sound counsel, courage and experience.

The arrival of the rest of the Muslim forces

On Monday[3] the last day of Jumādā I {24 June} the troops of Sinjār arrived, led by Mujāhid al-Dīn Yarunqush. The sultan gave him a respectful welcome. He was a pious and intelligent man who loved to fight for the faith. After he had been honoured and entertained in the sultan's tent, he was given a position on the left wing by the sultan, who was extremely delighted by his arrival at this time. After that a large contingent of the Egyptian forces arrived, such as 'Alam al-Dīn Kurjī, Sayf al-Dīn Sunqur al-Dawādār and many others. They were followed by 'Alā' al-Dīn, the son of the lord of Mosul, with his troops. The sultan met him at al-Kharrūba, where they camped until early morning of the following day, 2 Jumādā II {26 June}. That morning he brought his force opposite the enemy, where he reviewed them. The sultan entertained him in his

---

1 Reading *li-ukht al-malik*, as in B.

2 Joanna, Richard I's sister, had married William II of Sicily, who died in late 1189.

3 *Nawādir* has 'Tuesday' and the editor (in the list of corrections) wished to read that instead of 'Monday' in the previous paragraph. However, 'Imād al-Dīn has 'Monday' in both places (*Fatḥ*, pp. 342 and 343).

tent and sent him gifts. [**165**] Rare presents such as were suitable to his noble rank were sent to him and he was stationed on the right wing.

On Friday 4 Jumādā II {28 June}[1] another detachment of the Egyptian forces arrived. The illness of the king of England worsened to the extent that it preoccupied the Franks and discouraged them from making their attacks. This was a great blessing from God, for the defenders in the city had become very weak and the noose around them had become extremely tight. The trebuchets had demolished the equivalent of a man's height of the wall. Meanwhile, however, thieves were still entering their camp and snatching goods and individuals. They seized men with ease by coming to them as they were sleeping, putting a knive to their throat, then waking them and saying through gestures, 'If you speak, we shall cut your throat.' Then they would carry them away to the Muslim camp. That happened many times. Meanwhile, the Muslim forces were assembling and flocking in from all directions and eventually their gathering was complete.

Their envoys come to the sultan

I have mentioned already that an envoy came, on behalf of the king of England, asking for a meeting with the sultan. I have also said that the sultan made his excuses. After a break, the envoy returned taking up the same matter. He talked with al-'Ādil, who then passed on what he had to say to the sultan. In the end it was agreed that the sultan would allow him to come and that the meeting should take place on the plain with their troops surrounding the two of them and in the presence of an interpreter. After this permission had been given, the envoy delayed for several days, blaming his delay on the king's illness. It became widely known that the Frankish princes had met with him and expressed their disapproval of his actions. They said, 'This is endangering the Christian religion.' Later his envoy returned to say [speaking for the king], 'Do not imagine that my delay is owing to what has been reported. The reins of power are entrusted to me. I rule and nobody rules me. However, in recent days some disorder has afflicted my constitution and has prevented me from moving. This was the reason for my delay, nothing else. It is the custom of princes when they camp close to one another to exchange gifts. I have something suitable for the sultan and beg permission to convey it to him.' Al-'Ādil replied, 'You may do that on condition that you accept a comparable present.' The envoy was content with that and went on, 'The gift is some birds of prey that have been imported from beyond the sea. They are sick and it would be kind if you would bring us some birds and fowls to feed them and

1 *Nawādir* and B have Friday 3 Jumādā II, but *Fatḥ*, p. 345, has Friday 4 Jumādā II.

restore their strength before we deliver them.' Al-'Ādil joked with him, for he understood perfectly what they were talking about, and said, 'So the king needs chickens and fowls and wishes to get them from us on this pretext.' The conversation ended with the envoy saying, 'What is it you want from us? If you have anything to say, then declare it **[166]** and let us hear it.' In reply to this he was told, 'We did not make any request from you. It was you who asked us. If you have anything to say, then speak out so that we may hear it.'

The negotiations were broken off until Monday 6 Jumādā II [1 July] and then the envoy of the king of England came to the sultan, accompanied by a North African, whom they had captured a long time ago, a Muslim. He was given to the sultan, who, accepting the gift, showed him kindness and set him free. The envoy returned with honours to his master. Their purpose in these repeated embassies was to learn how strong or weak our morale was and our purpose in receiving the embassies was to learn how they stood in respect of the same.

Account of their powerful assault on the city and its close investment

They continued to maintain a constant battering of the city walls by their trebuchets and to increase the weight[1] of the missiles. They limited their military activity to that alone and, eventually, they made the city wall shake and weakened its structure. Fatigue and wakeful nights had worn down the defenders because they were so few and the tasks that fell to them so many. Very many of them spent several nights without sleeping at all, neither at night nor during the day, while the host that beseiged them were numerous enough to take turns to fight. The small body of defenders was divided between the walls, the moats, the trebuchets and the ships. The enemy trebuchets maintained their battering until the walls were tottering, and their tottering and weakness and the precariousness of the structure were evident to the enemy. Once aware of this they began an attack from all sides, dividing themselves into detachments and taking turns by groups. Whenever one group tired, it took a rest and another relieved it. They embarked on this with great seriousness of purpose, both foot and horse. This was on Tuesday 7 Jumādā II [2 July] and meanwhile their infantry and fighting men, both night and day, were building up the walls that ran around their trenches.

When the sultan learnt of this through the reports of those that observed it and through the signal communication we had with the city, namely the beating of the drum, he and all his forces rode out and that day a great battle took place between the two sides. He, like a bereft mother, moved on horseback from

---

1 The sense is borne out by the *tathqīl al-ḥijārāt* in the same context in *Fatḥ*, p. 349.

division to division, urging people to perform their Jihad duty. We have heard that al-'Ādil charged twice in person on that day, while the sultan went the rounds amongst the divisions, himself proclaiming 'On, on for Islam!' while tears flowed from his eyes. The more he looked towards Acre and saw the torment she was in and the great calamity overcoming her inhabitants, the more he redoubled his attacks and his encouragements to wage the Jihad. That day he consumed no food at all. He merely drank some cups of a drink that his doctor advised him to take.

[167] I failed to be present at this attack because I was afflicted with an illness that upset my constitution. I was in my tent at Tell al-'Ayyāḍiyya, though I could watch everything. When night fell, the sultan returned to his tent after the late evening prayer, overcome by tiredness, dejection and grief. He fell into a deep sleep.

When dawn came, he ordered the drum to be beaten and the troops took the stations they had the day before. During this day a message came from the town, in which they reported, 'We have been so utterly reduced to incapacity that there is nothing left but surrender. Tomorrow (that meant Wednesday 8 Jumādā II [3 July]), if you do not do something for us, we will seek terms and surrender the city and purchase our necks at least.' This was the worst possible news the Muslims received and the most grievous to our hearts. Acre held all the armaments of the Coast Lands, Jerusalem, Damascus, Aleppo and Egypt, indeed of all the Muslim lands and it contained the great military commanders and heroes of Islam, such as Sayf al-Dīn al-Mashṭūb and Bahā' al-Dīn Qarāqūsh and others. Bahā' al-Dīn Qarāqūsh had been constantly defending the city since the enemy descended upon it. The sultan was devastated by this more than anything else and it was feared that his health would be adversely affected. During all this he did not interrupt his calling upon God and his recourse to Him, patiently, trustingly, determinedly and zealously. 'God will not neglect the reward of those who do right.'[1]

He decided to attack the enemy in their camp. The herald called the Muslim forces to arms, the divisions were prepared and the horse and the foot gathered. That day our assault was fierce, but our troops were unable to help him to fall upon the enemy because the Frankish infantry stood behind their defences like a solid wall with their weapons, their crossbows, bolts and arrows. Some of our men attacked them on their flanks, but they held firm and resisted mightily. One of the men who broke into their defences related that there was a single Frank, a foot-soldier, who climbed on to the rampart of their trench and turned his back to the Muslims. Several alongside him were handing him stones, which he threw at the Muslims who were pressing against the rampart. The source said, 'About fifty arrows and stones hit him, which he shrugged off, and

---

1 Koran ix, 120.

nothing put a stop to the spirited resistance he was engaged in. In the end a Muslim Greek-fire specialist hit him with a naphtha missile and burned him alive.' A wise old soldier told me that he was one of a group that got in. He said, 'Within their rampart was a woman dressed in a green cloak, who kept shooting at us with a wooden bow until she had wounded several of us. Having overpowered and killed her, we took her bow and carried it to the sultan, who was greatly surprised.' The battle raged between the two sides, creating dead and wounded, until nightfall intervened.

[168] The parlous state to which the defenders were reduced and the start of talks between them and the Franks

The enemy assaults on the city intensified and their great numbers pressed hard upon it. They could take turns to fight but the defenders were few, both foot and horse, because many had been killed and few replacements were able to get in. The defenders' spirits sank when they looked death in the face and they were apprehensive that they were too weak to put up a defence. The enemy took control of the moats and began to fill them. They also gained the barbican. They had mined the wall and set fire to it after filling it [with combustibles]. The curtain-wall of the barbican collapsed and the enemy entered, although about 150 or more of them were killed there. Six of them were nobles and one of them said, 'Do not kill me and I shall make all the Franks go away.' One of the Kurds rushed forward and killed him and the remaining five. The next day the Franks hailed them, 'Spare the six and we will let you all go free in return for them.' 'We have killed them already,' was the reply. At that the Franks were greatly grieved and put a stop to their attacks for three days.

We heard that Sayf al-Dīn al-Mashṭūb had gone out in person to meet the king of France, who was in rank the leader of them all. He went out under truce and said, 'We have taken several cities from you. We used to break into a city but, nevertheless, if men asked us for terms, we would grant them and convey the defenders to a place of refuge with honourable treatment. We may surrender this city. Will you grant us guarantees for our lives?' The king replied, 'These princes of ours whom you captured and you too are my servants and my slaves. I shall consider what to do with you.' We heard later that al-Mashṭūb then answered him roughly and delivered a tirade, saying, among other things, 'We shall not surrender the city until we are all killed. Not one of us will be killed without first killing fifty of your great men.' He then left.

When al-Mashṭūb returned with this news, several in the city were fearful. They took a bark, a small vessel, and put to sea at night to return to the main Muslim force. That was on the eve of Thursday 9 Jumādā II [4 July]. The men of note amongst them were Arsul, Ibn al-Jāwalī the Elder and Sunqur al-Wishāqī. After Arsul and Sunqur had arrived at the royal camp, they went into hiding, nobody knew where, fearing the sultan's wrath. Ibn al-Jāwalī, however, was seized and thrown into the Armoury. At dawn that day the sultan rode out, letting it be known that he planned to surprise the enemy, taking with him shovels and tools to fill in the ditches. The troops gave him no help, but acted like malingerers. They said, 'We shall put all Islam at risk. There is no advantage in that.'

During this day three envoys came from the king of England, who asked for fruit and ice and mentioned that the commander of the Hospitallers would come out the next day, meaning Friday [5 July], to have talks about peace. The sultan received them with honour **[169]** and they went to the army's market-place, looked around and returned that night to their camp. That same day the sultan ordered Ṣārim al-Dīn Qaymāz al-Najmī, him and his men, to attack their camp. Several of the Kurdish emirs dismounted, such as al-Janāḥ, who was the brother of al-Mashṭūb. He and his contingent charged and reached the Frankish defences. Qaymāz al-Najmī in person set up his banner on their rampart and fought around it for a portion of the day.

That day 'Izz al-Din Jurdīk al-Nūrī arrived while this attack was being prosecuted. He and his contingent dismounted and joined in the fierce fight. A huge effort was made by our men on that day.

On Friday 10 Jumādā II [5 July] the enemy had a rest from their assaults, while the Muslim forces still surrounded them, having spent the night under arms and on horseback, waiting to see whether they could perhaps help their brothers who remained in Acre by attacking some section of the Frankish lines and break them so that the defenders could come out and, with both groups offering mutual support, burst through the enemy army while our men balanced their efforts from their side. Some would undoubtedly escape and some would inevitably be taken. However, they were unable to break out although that had been the settled plan. That night they had no chance to slip out because one of the mamlukes had run away and informed the enemy, who took special precautions and mounted a numerous guard.

On the Friday three envoys made their way out and met with al-'Ādil, with whom they talked for an hour and then returned to their comrades, for nothing was settled that day. The day came to an end with the Muslims still on the plain opposite the God-forsaken enemy and they passed the night like that.

On Saturday 11 Jumādā II [6 July] the Franks donned their armour and made major preparatory manouevres such that one would believe that a pitched battle was likely. They formed their battle lines and then about forty men came out through the gate beneath the dome.[1] They called to a group of mamlukes and

[1] What this dome structure (Arabic *al-qubba*) was is not known. *RHC Or*, p. 235, translated 'la porte qui était surmontée d'un pavillon'.

asked them for al-'Adl al-Zabadānī, said to be governor of Sidon, a freedman of the sultan. He came and initial talks took place on the matter of releasing the army that was in Acre. In return for that they made excessive demands and the day came to an end with nothing decided.

An account of letters that came from Acre

When it was Sunday 12 Jumādā II [7 July], letters came from Acre in which they said, 'We have pledged ourselves to die. We shall continue to fight until we are killed. While we still live, we will not surrender the city. Consider how you might act [**170**] to keep the enemy busy and distract them from attacking us. These are our intentions. Take care not to submit to this foe and give in to him. As for us, our cause is lost.' The swimmer who brought these letters reported that, when a great noise occurred in the night, the Franks believed that a large body of troops had crossed to Acre and got safely in. He went on, 'A Frank came and stood below the wall and shouted up to one of those on the wall, "By the truth of your religion, will you not tell me how many troops made an entry yesterday?" (meaning the eve of Saturday, for a noise had occurred at night and both sides had been alarmed, and yet nothing had really happened). He said, "1,000 mounted men," to which the Frank replied, "No, rather less than that. I saw them and they were wearing green."'

The armies of Islam came flocking to us one after the other and during those days the enemy's wiles were thwarted, after the city had been on the verge of being taken. On Tuesday 14 Jumādā II [9 July] the lord of Shayzar, Ṣābiq al-Dīn, arrived and on Wednesday 15 of the month [10 July] Badr al-Dīn Dildirim, accompanied by many Turcomans. The sultan had sent him gold to spend on them. On Thursday 16 Jumādā II [11 July] Asad al-Dīn Shīrkūh came. The city, however, grew ever weaker and the gaps in the wall became numerous. The defenders strove valiantly and to compensate for each breach they built an inner wall, so that they could fight on it, when the breach had completely collapsed.

The Franks remained very firm that they would not make peace or grant terms to those in the city until all the prisoners in Muslim hands were released and the coastal cities restored to them. They were offered the surrender of Acre and all that it contained apart from the people there, but they did not accept. Then they were offered one of their men who were prisoners in return for each one in the city, but again they refused. In addition to that they were offered the Holy Cross, but once again they refused. Their arrogance increased and their position grew stronger. Our scope for finding ways of dealing with them became limited. 'They plotted but God plotted and amongst plotters God is the best.'[1]

The garrison's peace talks and negotiation for their lives

When it was Friday 17 Jumādā II [12 July], the swimmer came from the port and his letters declared that the garrison was at its last gasp, as the breaches in the wall had multiplied and they were unable to keep up the defence. They looked death in the face and were certain that, whenever the city was taken by storm, they would, every last man, lose their heads and all the equipment, weapons, ships and all else would be seized. They therefore made terms on condition that they would give up the city and all the engines, equipment and ships it contained and hand over 200,000 dinars, 1,500 prisoners of common, unremarkable background and 100 prisoners to be specified by the Franks, whom they would select, and additionally the Holy Cross, provided that they themselves could leave **[171]** in safety, taking with them their personal wealth and goods and their children and womenfolk. They guaranteed to the marquis (for he had been reconciled and had returned) 10,000 dinars because he was the intermediary, and 4,000 dinars to his men. On that basis an agreement was reached between them and the Franks.

Account of the enemy's taking control of Acre (may God facilitate its conquest)

When the sultan had perused their letters and understood the contents, he expressed his great disapproval and was upset by the whole business. He assembled the leaders and the great men of state who were his councillors, informed them of the situation and consulted them about what to do. Their views left him confused, divided in mind and disturbed. He decided to send a letter that night by the swimmer and to condemn their coming to terms in this manner, while he was in such a situation as this. Then, the next thing the Muslims knew the banners of Unbelief, its crosses, emblem and beacon were raised over the walls of the city. This was at midday on Friday 17 Jumādā II [12 July].

The Franks as one man gave a great shout, while the Muslims were overcome by the disaster. The grief of the true monotheists was intense and the wise amongst them limited their utterances to the recitation of 'To God do we belong and to Him do we return'.[2] Great perplexity and confusion

1 Koran iii, 54.
2 Koran ii, 156. This is the conventional Muslim response to bad news.

overwhelmed our people and the army resounded with cries, moans, weeping and wailing. Every man's heart shared in this according to his faith. Indeed every person had a share according to the strength of his religion and sense of pride. The upshot was that the agreement between the garrison and the Franks was confirmed as previously set out and the marquis entered the city with four banners belonging to the princes. A hostage for him had been given, Muḥammad ibn Bārīk, who was one of Islam's brave warriors. The marquis set up one banner on the citadel, another on the minaret of the main mosque (on Friday!), another on the Templars' Tower and the last on the Battle Tower in place of the banner of Islam. The Muslims were confined in one district of the city and the followers of Islam who witnessed this event experienced something that made them wonder greatly at life.

I was present in attendance on the sultan, who was more affected than a bereft mother or a distracted love-sick girl. I consoled him with such words of consolation as came to mind and reminded him to think on what he had already faced for the coastal lands and for Jerusalem the Noble and how all that had come about and to put his mind to securing the release of the Muslims [**172**] held in the city. That was on the eve of Saturday 18 Jumādā II [13 July].

What resulted was that the sultan decided that the best course of action was to withdraw from his present position, for there was no longer any purpose in maintaining close contact. He ordered the baggage-train to be transferred to the position he had first been in at Shafar'am. He remained where he was with an unencumbered force to see what the enemy would do and what the fate of the garrison might be. During that night and before daybreak our men moved, while he remained minus the baggage, imploring God that their overweening pride and foolishness might perhaps induce them to come out to attack him and he might then take some opportunity, dash himself against them and God would give the victory to whomsoever He wished. The enemy, however, did nothing of the sort. They were occupied with taking over the city and establishing control. He remained until the morning of 19 Jumādā II [14 July] and at dawn moved to where the baggage-train was. That day three of their men came out, accompanied by the Chamberlain Qūsh, one of Bahā' al-Dīn Qarāqūsh's men, for he was his spokesman and an intelligent person, to demand the money and prisoners that the surrender agreement had stipulated. They remained for a night, honourably received, and then set out for Damascus to view the prisoners. They departed on Tuesday 21 Jumādā II [16 July]. The sultan sent an envoy to the Franks to ask them how matters had gone and to enquire what period of time there might be to gather what the surrender terms and the truce had fixed.

Account of a battle that occurred in the meantime

When Thursday the last day of Jumādā II came {25 July}, the Franks marched out on the seaward side, north of the city, and from near the dome.[1] They spread out far and wide, both foot and horse, and formed divisions for battle. The advance guard informed the sultan of this and he had the drum beaten as a sign to mount up. He sent many men as reinforcements to the advance guard and waited until the Muslim forces had mounted and assembled. There was a fierce battle between the advance guard and the enemy before the main forces could join our men. The advance guard, strengthened by those he had sent, charged the enemy mightily and the latter broke before them. Their cavalry fled and abandoned the infantry, for they believed that there was an ambush beyond the advance guard. They hastened back to their camp and then the advance guard fell upon the infantry, killing about fifty of them and wounding a great number. The sword was kept busy amongst them until they entered their trenches.

During that day the Frankish envoys, who had been sent to Damascus to enquire into the state of the prisoners, arrived and they brought with them four of the distinguished captives. In addition, during the evening envoys came to the sultan to arrange the matter of the prisoners and the Muslims who were in Acre. A to-and-fro of envoys between the two parties was kept up until Friday 9 Rajab [2 August].

[173] Account of Ibn Bārīk's mission

That same day Ḥusām al-Dīn Ḥusayn ibn Bārīk al-Mihrānī came out along with two of the king of England's men. He reported that the king of France had gone to Tyre (may God facilitate its conquest), while they made some mention of settling the matter of the prisoners and asked to see the Holy Cross, enquiring whether it was in the camp or had been taken to Baghdad. The Holy Cross was brought to them and they looked upon it and reverenced it, throwing themselves to the ground and rubbing their faces in the dust. They humbled themselves in a manner the like of which had never been seen. It was also mentioned by them that the princes agreed with the sultan that what had been specified should be handed over in three 'terms' or instalments, each being a month. The sultan sent one of the envoys who had come to him to the king of France in Tyre with splendid gifts, much perfume and fine garments. Ibn Bārīk and his companion returned to the king of England.

---

1 See above, p. 159, note 1.

The morning of Saturday 10 Rajab [3 August] the sultan moved the Royal Guard and his special staff to a hill adjacent to Shafar'am, while the troops stayed in their positions as they were. The sultan's position was close to his initial position with only a river course between the two. There was a steady stream of envoys concerning the drawing up and implementation of the agreement until the enemy received what they sought, the prisoners and the money specified for that term. In all it was the Holy Cross, 100,000 dinars and 1,600 prisoners. They sent their trusted men who testified to everything, apart from the prisoners to be specified on their side, for they had not finished selecting and naming them so that they could be fetched. They kept procrastinating and wasting time until the first term elapsed, which it did on 18 Rajab [11 August]. At that time they sent demanding the prisoners. The sultan said to them, 'Either you send our men to us and you receive what has been specified for this term, while we give you hostages for the rest which you will get in the remaining terms or you give us hostages for what we hand over to you until you send our men out to us.' They replied, 'We shall do none of that, but do you deliver to us what this term demands and be satisfied with our word, until we hand over your men to you.' The sultan refused this, as he knew that, if they received the money, the Cross and the prisoners, while they still had our men, he could not be sure that they would not act treacherously and then the loss for Islam would be so great that it could hardly be repaired.

[174] The Franks move their tents out

When they saw that the sultan had refused their demand, they moved their tents out beyond their defensive ditches with all pomp and show. This was during Wednesday 21 Rajab [14 August]. The man who came so bravely forth was the king of England with a large host of cavalry, infantry and turcopoles.

Account of the killing of the Muslims who were in Acre

When the king of England saw that the sultan hesitated to hand over the money, the prisoners and the Cross, he dealt treacherously towards the Muslim prisoners. He had made terms with them and had received the surrender of the city on condition that they would be guaranteed their lives come what may and that, if the sultan delivered what was agreed, he would free them together with their possessions, children and womenfolk, but that, if the sultan refused to do so, he would reduce them to slavery and captivity. The accursed man deceived them and revealed what he had hidden in his heart. He carried out what, according to the subsequent reports of his co-religionists, he had intended to do after taking the money and the prisoners. He and all the Frankish forces, horse and foot, marched out at the time of the afternoon prayer on Tuesday 27 Rajab [20 August] and came to the wells beneath the Tell al-'Ayyāḍiyya. They brought their tents forward as far as that and then moved on into the middle of the plain between Tell Kaysān and al-'Ayyāḍiyya. Our advance guard had withdrawn to Tell Kaysān when the Franks moved their tents forward to Tell al-'Ayyāḍiyya. The enemy then brought out the Muslim prisoners for whom God had decreed martyrdom, about 3,000 bound in ropes. Then as one man they charged them and with stabbings and blows with the sword they slew them in cold blood, while the Muslim advance guard watched, not knowing what to do because they were at some distance from them. The Muslims had already sent to the sultan and informed him of the enemy's move and their new position and he had sent reinforcements. When the enemy had finished, the Muslims attacked them and a great battle ensued, in which men were killed and wounded on both sides. It continued until nightfall.

In the morning the Muslims investigated what had happened, found the martyrs where they had fallen and were able to recognise some of them. Great sorrow and distress overwhelmed them for the enemy had spared only men of standing and position or someone strong and able-bodied to labour on their building works. Various reasons were given for this massacre. **[175]** It was said they had killed them in revenge for their men who had been killed[1] or that the king of England had decided to march to Ascalon to take control of it and did not think it wise to leave that number in his rear. God knows best.

The enemy's move to the sea shore to the west

On Thursday 29 Rajab [22 August] all the Franks broke camp, struck their tents, loaded them on to their pack-animals and set off across the river to the western side. They pitched camp on the route to Ascalon and made plain their intention of proceeding along the coast. The king of England ordered the rest of the people to enter the city [of Acre] where they had blocked up the breaches in the wall and repaired the damaged parts. The commander of the army that marched away was the king of England (God curse him) with a large body of cavalry and infantry.

1 This probably refers to the six whom the Franks had wished to ransom (see p. 158).

Account of their march towards Ascalon

On Sunday 1 Sha'bān [25 August] at first dawn the enemy's campfires were lit. It was their custom to do so whenever they planned to move off and thus they told our forward screen of what they intended. The sultan ordered the baggage-train to be removed and the troops to remain on horseback. This was done but the troops lost many personal effects. Many items belonging to the camp followers were also lost as there were not beasts to carry all that they had. Every man had been acquiring what he needed over several months and each of the camp followers had stuff that would take numerous journeys to transport from one position to another, but it was not possible for anyone to stay behind in the present position because of its closeness to the Franks in Acre and the danger they presented.

When the day was well advanced, the enemy began their march along the coast. They divided into three bodies, each one independent. The sultan strengthened our forward screen and sent most of our forces to march along opposite them. They fought fiercely while on the move. His son, al-Afḍal, sent to the sultan to report: 'A group of them became separated from their comrades and we engaged them closely so that they withdrew seeking their tents. Had we been in force we could have taken them.' The sultan sent a large number of the troops and he himself came to where the sands begin. He ordered the baggage-train to take the main road to al-Qaymūn. Having come to the beginning of sands with myself in attendance, we met al-'Ādil who informed the sultan that that group had rejoined the first body and that most **[176]** of the enemy had crossed the Haifa River. They made camp when the remainder had caught up with them. There was nothing to be gained in marching after them apart from tiring the horses and wasting arrows. Having ascertained that, the sultan withdrew from them and ordered a detachment of the army to follow behind the baggage-train to bring the weaker ones up with the strong and to drive off any of the enemy's skirmishers who might catch up with them. He himself, with me still in attendance, went on towards al-Qaymūn, where he arrived during the afternoon of that day. He stopped where the vestibule of his tent had been erected with a cloth screen surrounding it, nothing more. He summoned several persons, had something to eat and consulted them about what to do.

The second stage

The general conclusion arrived at was that they would depart the morning of the following day and the sultan had posted pickets around the Franks to pass the night there, keeping a watch on what they might do. The morning of Monday 2 Sha'bān [26 August] the sultan sent off the heavy baggage, but he himself remained, looking out for news of the enemy. None reached him until the day was well advanced. He followed the tracks of the baggage-train until he came to a village called al-Ṣabbāghīn. For a while he sat there in expectation of news of the enemy,but no news came. 'Alam al-Dīn Sulaymān ibn Jandar had taken the sultan's position of yesterday and he had left Jūrdīk close to the enemy. He also despatched a large force that passed the night near to the enemy, but no news at all came to him.

He continued until he came up with the baggage-train, which was at a place called Serpents' Springs.[1] Having arrived there he caught sight of tents and asked what they were. He was told that they were the tents of al-'Ādil, so he turned aside to stop with him. We went on and stopped at our tents. The sultan stayed a while with him and then came to his own tent. During this stage information was totally lacking. Barley became expensive, reaching a dirham for a 'quarter'[2] and dry biscuits rose to two dirhams for a rotl.

The sultan waited until past midday and then he mounted and rode to a place called al-Mallāḥa, which would be a camping place for the enemy if they moved from Haifa. He had got there first to reconnoitre the site, to see whether it was suitable for a pitched battle or not. He reconnoitred the whole area of Caesarea as far as the wooded area and returned after the time for the evening prayer, worn out by fatigue. I was in attendance upon him and asked him what news he had heard of the enemy. He said, 'Some of our men have come to us with information that up to late afternoon today the enemy have not left Haifa.' He was referring to Monday 2 Sha'bān [26 August]. 'We are now waiting for news and shall take action accordingly.'

After a night's sleep the morning saw him at Tell al-Zalzala, waiting for the enemy. The herald summoned the army to a review and the troops mustered in battle order and battle gear. They left their tents and ranged themselves as right wing, left wing and centre. Thanks be to God, all was as the responsible officers[3] of Islam would prefer. He then returned to his encampment, as did the troops. The day was now far advanced and the sultan went to his tent. He took a short period of rest [177] after lunch and after several emirs had attended to discuss what was to be done. Later he prayed the midday prayer and held a session until the evening prayer time to dispense monies to replace wounded horses and the like, from 100 to 150 dinars, sometimes more, sometimes less. I have never seen anyone more heartily expansive or looking more cheerful when distributing cash. It was agreed during the evening of that day that the baggage-train should leave for Majdal Yābā.[4]

---

1 In Arabic: 'Uyūn al-Asāwida.

2 In Arabic: *rub'*, possibly a 'quarter' of a *wayba* (perhaps 12-15 litres).

3 This interpretation of *awliyā'* is based on the phrase in Saladin's document appointing al-Muẓaffar Taqī al-Dīn to govern Egypt, quoted by the latter's son, Muḥammad, in his *Miḍmār al-ḥaqā'iq*, p. 157: 'We have given him full administrative freedom over the salaries sanctioned by God for all the officers (*awliyā'*) and the men.'

4 About 21 km inland from Jaffa.

The third stage

The baggage-train stopped at Majdal Yābā the next morning, while he stayed all night where he was, unencumbered. The troops had set out towards the enemy and the baggage had left at the evening prayer. Only light belongings and equipment were left with the men that remained with the sultan. He passed the night in his position until the morning of Wednesday 4 Sha'bān [28 August] and then rode to the head of the river that flows to Caesarea, where he camped without heavy baggage. At this encampment dry biscuits reached four dirhams for a rotl and barley two and a half dirhams for a 'quarter'. Bread was nowhere to be bought at all.

Close to the time of the midday prayer he went to his tent, ate some bread and prayed. He then rode to the route the enemy would take to renew his scouting for a site to give battle and did not return until afternoon prayer. He sat for a while, took a little rest and then mounted again, having ordered the men to prepare to depart. He struck his tent and the troops did likewise late on Wednesday 4 Sha'bān [28 August].

The fourth stage

The move was made to a hillock back from the previous one but in the same general area. The baggage-train halted there and the sultan came back from his ride a little after sunset. At this camp he was brought two Franks who had been snatched by the advance guard. He commanded their execution and they were slain. Many of our men fell upon them with swords to vent their anger.

He spent the night there and next morning waited in this position because it was not confirmed that the enemy had made any move. He had sent to the baggage-train to get it to return the previous night on account of the shortage of foodstuffs and fodder that troubled our people. At his customary time he rode towards the enemy and viewed Caesarea before returning to the baggage-train near to midday. News arrived that the enemy had not yet left al-Mallāḥa. Another two men taken from the fringes of the enemy host were brought before him and they were most cruelly done to death, as he was still in an extreme rage at what had been done to the prisoners at Acre.

He then took a little rest and after the midday prayer received visitors. I presented myself before him, when an enemy knight of distinction had been brought into his presence. **[178]** He had been captured and his appearance announced that he was a leading man amongst them. An interpreter was summoned and he was questioned about their circumstances. The sultan asked him, 'How are food prices with you?' He replied, 'The first day we left Acre a man could eat his full for six *qīrāṭs*.[1] Then prices kept going up until it cost eight to satisfy oneself.' He was asked why they delayed so in their stages.

---

1 Used to weigh gold and silver, in the case of the latter 1 qīrāṭ was 0.186 g (Hinz, *Islamische Masse und Gewichte*, p. 2).

'Because we are waiting for ships to come with men and supplies,' he said. When questioned about losses in dead and wounded the day they departed, he replied, 'Many.' Asked about the horses that perished that day, he said, 'As many as 400 horses.' Then the sultan ordered his head to be cut off but forbade any mutilation. The Frank asked the interpreter what the sultan had said. When told, his face fell and he said, 'I will free a prisoner from Acre for you.' 'Alright,' the sultan said, 'but an emir.' 'I cannot free an emir,' he replied. Our admiration and his fair appearance interceded for him. Indeed, I have never seen such a perfect frame with such elegance of body and refinement of manners. The sultan ordered him to be left for now and his case deferred. After he had been fettered, the sultan upbraided him for the treachery they had shown in killing the prisoners. The Frank acknowledged that it was bad, but that it had been done merely by the will of the king alone.

After afternoon prayer the sultan rode out as was his custom. All this took place on Thursday 5 Shaʿbān [29 August]. After his return he ordered the knight's execution, which was carried out. Two others were brought in after him and they were executed on the sultan's orders. He passed the night in this camp and at dawn he was told that the enemy had moved off towards Caesarea and that their first detachments had drawn near to the city. He decided to retire a further stage on the route the enemy was taking.

The fifth stage

The sultan and the army moved to a hill near to the one where we had been. A halt was made and the tents pitched. The sultan proceeded to scout the areas lying on the enemy's route to see which were most suitable for a battle. He halted around midday and summoned his brother, al-ʿĀdil, and ʿAlam al-Dīn Sulaymān ibn Jandar, whose opinion about what to do he sought. After a little rest, when the muezzin called to prayer, the sultan prayed the midday prayer, then mounted up to reconnoitre the enemy and get wind of their latest moves. Two Franks who had been seized were brought to him and he ordered their execution. Then two others were brought in, whom he also had put to death. This was on Friday 6 Shaʿbān [30 August]. Towards the end of the day yet two more were produced and executed. When day ended, he returned from his ride at the time of sunset prayer. Having performed his devotions he held audience as usual. He summoned his brother, al-ʿĀdil, and then dismissed the others present and closeted himself with him until a late hour.

The night over, the herald announced a review of the Royal Guard alone. The sultan rode towards the enemy and halted on some hills looking towards Caesarea, where the enemy had arrived during Friday. He continued his review there until the day was well advanced, then dismounted and ate. He then joined his brother and after the hour of midday prayer he went back and took a little rest. He performed his ablutions and prayed, before being brought fourteen

Franks and a Frankish women taken captive with them, who was the daughter [**179**] of a distinguished knight. With her was a Muslim captive whom she had received. The sultan freed the Muslim woman and the rest were herded into the Armoury. They had been brought from Beirut, having been captured in a very numerous travelling party. They were put to death. All this was on Saturday 7 Sha'bān [31 August], while the sultan was at this position, waiting for the enemy to start their march, resolved to meet them whenever they did.

The sixth stage

On the morning of Sunday 8 Sha'bān [1 September] the sultan rode out as was his custom. After a halt someone came with news that the enemy was ready to move. Our divisions had spent the night in their positions around Caesarea. The sultan ordered food to be dispensed and entertained his staff. A second person arrived to report that the enemy had set out. Having ordered the drum to be beaten, he and the troops mounted. With me in attendance, he came to the enemy's army and ranged the divisions around him, then ordered battle to commence. He sent the skirmishers forward and the arrows on both sides were like rain. The enemy army was already in formation with the infantry surrounding it like a wall, wearing solid iron corslets and full-length well-made chain mail, so that arrows were falling on them with no effect. They were shooting with crossbows and wounding the Muslims' horses, their cavalry and infantry. I saw various individuals amongst the Franks with ten arrows fixed in their backs, pressing on in this fashion quite unconcerned. Another company of their infantry rested while marching beside the sea, not being engaged in the fight. When those engaged in the battle became tired or were debilitated by wounds, the company that had been resting would take their place and the previously active company would take a rest. Meanwhile the cavalry was in the middle of them, not leaving the infantry's protection except when making a charge, not otherwise. They were also divided into three main divisions, Guy[1], the former king, accompanied by a number of the resident Franks in the vanguard, the kings of England and France in the middle, and the sons of the Lady, the lords of Tiberias, and another detachment in the rear. In the midst of the army was a tower on wheels. Their banner, which was as I have described it previously, also proceeded in their midst on wheels like a huge beacon.[2]

This was the formation of the enemy as I saw it and according to the information of captives and deserters from their ranks. They marched on in this fashion, while the fighting raged between the two sides. The Muslims were shooting arrows on their flanks, trying to incite them to break ranks, while they controlled themselves severely and covered the route in this way, travelling very steadily as their ships moved along at sea opposite them, until they

[1] 'Godfrey' in the text.

[2] For a description of King Richard's standard, see Nicholson, *Chronicle*, p. 237.

completed each stage and camped. Their stages were short ones [**180**] for the sake of the foot-soldiers. Those resting [from the fighting] were carrying the baggage and tents because they were short of beasts of burden. Consider the endurance of these people, bearing exhausting tasks without any pay or material gain. They camped beyond the river of Caesarea (may God facilitate its conquest).

The seventh stage

On the morning of Monday 9 Sha'bān [2 September] there came men who reported that the enemy was on the march. The sultan rode out at first light and drew up the divisions. From each one he selected skirmishers and then set off to seek the enemy. We came upon them as they were proceeding in their normal fashion in three divisions. The skirmishers encompassed them and peppered them with arrows as they were marching along in the manner I have described. Whenever a division weakened, the one next to it came to its help, offering mutual protection. The Muslims beset them on three sides with fierce attacks and the sultan urged the divisions to close with them. I saw him actually riding among the skirmishers as the enemy's arrows flew past him. He was attended by two pages with two spare mounts and that was all, riding from division to division and urging them forward, and ordering them to press hard upon them and bring them to battle. The drums throbbed and the bugles brayed and shouts of 'There is no god but God' and 'God is great' were being raised. All the while the enemy kept steadfastly in perfect formation, undismayed and undisturbed. Many charges were made, but their infantry with bolts and arrows wounded our men and their horses. Our men continued to engage them from every direction, making charges, and the enemy would give way a little and then counter-attack. They came eventually to a river called the River of Reeds,[1] where they camped. The midday heat had come and they pitched their tents. Our troops withdrew, for whenever they camped we despaired of achieving any success and so broke off the fight.

This day one of the brave knights of Islam was killed, Ayāz the Tall, a mamluke of the sultan. He had done much slaughter amongst them and had killed a great number of their knights and champions. His bravery became widely known in both armies, since he had had many encounters which gave credence to the tales of the ancients. It reached the point that, when the Franks recognised him anywhere, they avoided him. His horse fell under him and he met a martyr's death. He was buried on a hill overlooking al-Birka and the Muslims grieved for him greatly. A mamluke of his was killed defending him.

The sultan camped with the baggage-train at al-Birka, which is a place where many streams meet. He remained there until after the evening prayer

[1] In Arabic: Nahr al-Qaṣab.

and fed the troops, who then rested a while. After the evening prayer he set out again and came to the River of Reeds, where he again camped. We were drinking from the higher reaches while the enemy were drinking from the lower, with only a short distance between us. Barley at this stage reached [**181**] four dirhams for a 'quarter'. Bread was plentifully to be had, priced half a dirham for a rotl. There the sultan remained, waiting for the enemy to move so that he could move in parallel. The enemy spent the night there as did we.

Account of a battle

A detachment of the Muslim army, which was keeping an eye on the enemy, ran into a detachment of theirs, which was also keeping a watch on the Muslim army but was not wearing armour.[1] Having caught them, our men attacked and a big battle followed, in which several of the enemy were killed. The enemy's main body became aware of what was happening and rushed to help them. The engagement continued and the Muslims lost two men, while three of the enemy were taken prisoner.

These were brought before the sultan who asked them their latest news and was told that the king of England had been visited by two Bedouin in Acre. They had informed him that the Muslim army was few in numbers and depleted and this was what had encouraged him to take the field. However, the day before - meaning Monday - he saw some stout fighting on the part of the Muslims and was impressed by the number of their divisions. Yesterday about 1,000 of his men had been wounded and several killed. This was what had necessitated his staying in camp today to rest the army. After having seen the stiff resistance met with yesterday and the great size of the Muslim force, he summoned the two Bedouin, confronted them with what they had done and had them decapitated.

This day, that is, Tuesday 10 Sha'bān [3 September], we remained [initially] at this present position as the enemy also stayed where they were.

The eighth stage

At midday on the Tuesday, however, the sultan decided to break camp and advance towards the enemy. The drum was beaten and all moved off. The sultan entered the wooded area around Arsūf, into the very middle of it, as far as a hill near which was a village called Dayr al-Rāhib,[2] where he camped. Nightfall came upon us and our men were left scattered amongst the woods. Until the morning of Wednesday 11 Sha'bān [4 September] the sultan was

---

1 This description in *Nawādir* (*ghayr musallaḥīn*) is absent from B. It certainly cannot mean 'unarmed'. In the parallel passage *Fatḥ*, p. 381, has 'without equipment, carelessly'.

2 Literally, 'Monk's Monastery'.

waiting for the rest of the army, and then the Muslim forces were again in touch with one another. He rode out to scout for a site suitable for a battle and an encounter with the enemy. He passed the whole day there.

One of the reports of the enemy during that day was that they spent it camped at the River of Reeds and that reinforcements from Acre in eight large busses had joined them. The Muslim pickets were all about them, keeping in contact with news of their latest moves. A fight took place between our pickets and the enemy's foragers, in which there were wounded on both sides.

[182] Account of negotiations that took place this day

The enemy made a request to our advanced squadron for someone to hold talks with. The commander of the squadron was 'Alam al-Dīn Sulaymān ibn Jandar, for it was his turn. When someone went to them to hear what they had to say, it was a request for al-'Ādil so that they could talk with him. Having asked permission, he went to them and spent the night - I mean the eve of Thursday [5 September] - with the advanced squadron, holding talks.

The gist of what they had to say was, 'Fighting between us has now gone on a long time and brave men have been killed on both sides. We have come here to aid the Frankish residents of the littoral. Make peace, you and they, and each of us can return to his own place.' The sultan wrote a note to his brother, al-'Ādil, the morning of Thursday 12 Sha'bān [5 September] in which he said, 'If you are able to spin out the talks with the Franks, then perhaps they will remain where they are today, so that the Turkomans can catch up with us, for they are now quite near.' During this day al-'Ādil met with the accursed king of England and the son of Humfrey[1] acted as their interpreter.

Account of the meeting of al-'Ādil and the king of England

When the enemy asked for al-'Ādil, he had been given permission to go to them. He came up to the advanced guard and when the king of England learnt that he had come there, he asked for a meeting, which was granted. They met *tête-à-tête* without their retinues, while the son of Humfrey acted as interpreter. He was one of the nobles of the Franks of the littoral. I saw him the day peace was made and he was a handsome youth, although he was clean-shaven as is their fashion.

In the conversation that took place between them the king of England started to talk of peace, but al-'Ādil said to him, 'You desire peace but you do not

[1] In the text: Ibn al-Hunfarī. The son of Humfrey III of Toron was also called Humfrey (Humfrey IV).

mention your demands that I might mediate your differences with the sultan.' The king of England replied, 'The basic condition is that you should restore all the lands to us and return to your own countries.' Al-'Ādil gave a harsh answer and a quarrel followed which led to the enemy's departure after the two of them had separated.

When the sultan realised that they were on the move, he ordered the baggage-train to move and put the Master of the Horse,[1] Aslam, in charge. He held his position and drew up the troops in battle order and waited to receive news of the enemy. The lesser baggage also left and drew near the heavy baggage, but then an order from the sultan arrived for them to return, which they did, arriving back when night had already fallen. During that night they became greatly disorganised.

The sultan summoned [**183**] his brother, al-'Ādil, to learn from him what had happened between him and the king. He was closeted with him privately for that purpose. This was on the eve of Friday 13 Sha'bān [6 September].

The enemy marched on and came to camp at a place also called al-Birka, in sight of the sea. On the Friday morning the sultan ordered the baggage-train to proceed to a village called Burayka.[2] The sultan stayed where he was and organised the divisions of the army, while seeking intelligence of the enemy. Two of the Franks were brought before him who had been seized by the advanced guard. He ordered them to be beheaded. A report arrived that this day the enemy had not moved from their latest position. The sultan also remained in his position and met with his brother, al-'Ādil, to discuss the present situation and what to do with the wretched enemy. He passed the night there.

Account of the battle of Arsūf, which wounded Muslim hearts

When it was Saturday 14 Sha'bān [7 September], the sultan was informed that the enemy had moved out towards Arsūf. He rode out and drew up his divisions for battle, with every intention of bringing the enemy to a pitched battle that day. He sent forward a picked body of skirmishers from each division. The enemy marched on until they were close to the woods and plantations of Arsūf. The skirmishers loosed their arrows against them and then the divisions pressed them close from every direction. The sultan made them engage closely, but held some back in reserve. The enemy were tightly beset and the fighting was fierce and blazed into flame on both sides. Amongst the enemy there were dead and wounded and they quickened their march in the hope of reaching the site where they could camp. Their situation became

---

1 Arabic: *amīr ākhur*.

2 The reading in B, although not with full diacritical points.

serious and the noose about them tightened, while the sultan was moving between the left wing and the right, urging the men on in the Jihad. Several times I encountered him, when he was attended by only two pages with two spare mounts and that was all. I met his brother in a similar state, while the arrows were flying past them both.

The enemy's situation worsened still more and the Muslims thought they had them in their power. Eventually, the first detachments of their infantry reached the plantations of Arsūf. Then their cavalry massed together and agreed on a charge, as they feared for their people and thought that only a charge would save them. I saw them grouped together in the middle of the foot-soldiers. They took their lances and gave a shout as one man. The infantry opened gaps for them and they charged in unison along their whole line. One group charged our right wing, another our left and the third our centre. Our men gave way before them. It happened that I was in the centre, which took to wholesale flight. My intention was to join the left wing, since it was nearer to me. I reached it after it had been broken utterly, so I thought to join the right wing, but then I saw that it had fled more calamitously [**184**] than all the rest. I determined to join the sultan's guard, which was in reserve to support all the others as was customary. I came to him but the sultan had kept no more than seventeen fighting men there and had taken the rest into battle, but the standards were still there and the drum was beating without interruption. When the sultan saw this reverse that had befallen the Muslims, he returned to his guard and found there this scanty number.

He stood amongst them while men were fleeing on all sides, but he was commanding the drummers to beat their drums without stopping. He ordered men to rally to him all those he saw fleeing. However, the Muslims were, in fact, in a complete rout. The enemy made a charge and they fled, but then the enemy halted for fear of an ambush, so our men halted and made some resistance. Then there was a second charge and our men fled but fought as they fled. The enemy halted again, as did our men. A third charge followed, which brought them to the tops of some hillocks there and a ridge of hills. Our troops fled again until the enemy halted and then they also halted. All who saw the sultan's troop holding its position with drums beating were ashamed to pass beyond it and feared the disaster that might follow, so they rallied to his troop and a large number assembled there.

The enemy stood facing them on the tops of the hills and hillocks, while the sultan was with his troop and men were gathering around him. Eventually, the whole army rallied and the enemy feared that there might be an ambush in the woods, so they withdrew, making for their camping place. The sultan went back to a hill where the woods began and halted there, but not in any tent.

I was in attendance on him, offering consolation, which, however, he was unable to accept. He was protected from the sun by a kerchief and we asked him to take some food. Something light was brought to him, from which he took only a little. The troops sent their horses to be watered, for the source of water was far away. He sat waiting for people to return from watering their mounts, while the wounded were brought before him and he was giving orders for them to be treated and carried away. That day many foot-soldiers were killed and a lot on both sides were wounded. Among those that stood firm were al-'Ādil, the *Ṭawāshī* Qaymāz al-Najmī and al-Afḍal, the sultan's son, who was shaken by this day. A boil that was on his face burst and much blood flowed over his face, but he was steadfast and confident of his future reward through all of this. The troops of Mosul with their commander, 'Alā' al-Dīn, stood firm this day and the sultan thanked him for that. Our men enquired after one another and many of the army were found to have met a martyr's death, notable among whom were the Emir of the Hunt[1] Mūsak, who was a brave and well-known man, Qaymāz al-'Ādilī and Buzghush,[2] brave men of note. The sultan grieved for the latter. Many men and horses were wounded and the enemy had many killed. One was captured and brought before the sultan, who ordered his head to be cut off. Four horses were taken from them.

The sultan had ordered the baggage-train to go to al-'Awjā[3] [**185**] and had said that our camp would be there. I asked for leave to go on before him to our camp. He sat waiting for the troops to be assembled and for any news of the enemy that might come in. The enemy had, in fact, already camped at Arsūf, to the south of it.

The ninth stage

After the midday prayer I came to the baggage-train, which had stopped across the river known as al-'Awjā in a pleasant green and fertile place along its banks. The sultan arrived towards the end of the day. The men crowded together at the bridge, while the sultan stopped on a hill overlooking the river and did not cross to his tent. He ordered the herald to proclaim throughout the army that they should cross back to him. On account of the battle his heart was full of feelings that God alone could know. The troops, too, were either wounded in body or wounded in the heart. Until first dawn on Sunday 15 Sha'bān [8 September] the sultan waited and then the drum was beaten, the men mounted up and he returned towards the enemy, eventually drawing near to Arsūf.

He arranged his divisions for battle in the hope that the enemy would come out and he could march to confront them. However, that day the enemy made no move because of fatigue and the wounds that they had suffered. The sultan

1 In Arabic: *amīr shikār*.

2 Following B and ignoring other readings. *Bozğuş* (or *Bozkuş*), 'gray falcon' is expressly mentioned as a mamluke name (Clauson, *An Etymological Dictionary*, p. 388).

3 Al-'Awjā flows into the sea between Arsūf and Jaffa. See Le Strange, *Palestine*, pp. 55-56.

remained facing them until the end of the day. He then returned to his position of the night before and passed the eve of Monday 16 Sha'bān [9 September] there.

On the Monday morning, with the beating of the drum, he and the troops rode out and went towards the enemy. Reports came that the enemy had already set out in the direction of Jaffa. The sultan manoeuvred into very close contact with them, drew up his divisions in battle order and sent the skirmishers forward, encompassing the enemy with the Muslim forces. They released a cloud of arrows that wellnigh blotted out the sky. The battle raged furiously. His aim was to provoke them into a charge, so that, when they did charge, he would hurl his troops against them and God would give the victory to whomsoever He willed. They did not charge, however, but controlled themselves and marched on in their battle lines according to their custom, until they came to the River al-'Awjā, the river whose upper reaches had been our camp. They camped lower downstream and some of them crossed over, while the rest remained on the east bank.

Learning that they had made camp, our army disengaged and the sultan returned to the baggage-train. He stopped in his tent and took some food. He was brought four Franks who had been taken by the Bedouin, and with whom there was a woman. They were taken to the Armoury. The sultan spent the rest of the day in that camp writing letters to his far-flung territories to mobilise the rest of his forces. Someone arrived with a report that during the battle of Arsūf, the enemy had had many horses killed and that the Bedouin had followed this up and counted them. They came to more than one hundred. The Muslims, too, had lost many horses. The sultan ordered the camel train to leave, proceed to Ramla and spend the night there. He himself passed the night in this present position.

[**186**] *The tenth stage*

On Tuesday 17 Sha'bān [10 September] after the morning prayer he set out accompanied by the lesser baggage-train, making for Ramla. He was brought two Franks whose decapitation he ordered. From the Muslim advanced guard there arrived men who reported that the enemy had moved off in the direction of Jaffa. The sultan travelled on to Ramla where he stopped among the main baggage-train. Two other Franks were brought to him and he questioned them about the state of the Franks. They replied that they would probably stay in Jaffa for some days, as they had it in mind to repair the place and fill it with men and supplies.

The sultan summoned his councillors and consulted them about what to do with Ascalon, whether to demolish or preserve it. It was agreed that al-'Ādil, with a detachment of the army, should stay behind close to the enemy to gather intelligence about them and to pass it on, and that the sultan himself should go to Ascalon to demolish it for fear that the Franks might gain control of it intact, destroy the garrison and use it to take Jerusalem (may God grant us its reconquest) and cut our communications with Egypt. The sultan feared this and realised that the Muslims would be incapable of holding it because of their recent experience with Acre and what had happened to the garrison there. Our troops were loathe to enter Ascalon, but the strength of the Muslim forces was conserved for the protection of Jerusalem. Because of all of this it was settled that Ascalon should be demolished. The camel train moved off in the first part of the evening and he ordered his son, al-Afḍal, to follow after the baggage half-way through the night. He himself, with me in attendance, set out just before dawn on Wednesday [11 September].

The eleventh stage, when he was at Ascalon
When it was Wednesday 18 Sha'bān [11 September], the sultan arrived at Yubnā and camped there at midday, where the troops rested. He then travelled on and came into the territory of Ascalon after the afternoon prayer. His tent was pitched far from the town to the north of it in pleasant, handsome country. He passed the night anxious about demolishing Ascalon and slept only a little. At dawn he called me to attend him. I had left his presence half-way through the previous night. I arrived and he began a discussion about the town's demolition. He summoned his son, al-Afḍal, whom he consulted on this matter while I was in attendance. The discussion lasted a long time. The sultan said, 'By God, I would prefer to lose all my sons rather than demolish a single stone of it. Yet, if God decrees it and prescribes it as a way of preserving the best interests of the Muslims, what else can I do?'

[187] Account of the demolition of Ascalon

He sought the guidance of God, Who led him to understand that the best course was to demolish the town because the Muslims were incapable of holding it against the Franks. He summoned the governor, Qayṣar, one of his senior mamlukes and one of the wisest, and ordered him to put pickaxes to work. This was at dawn on Thursday 19 Sha'bān [12 September]. I saw him after he had passed through the market and the encampment personally urging the men to start the work of destruction. He assigned sections of the wall to the men. To each emir and detachment of troops he appointed a particular stretch of curtain wall and a particular tower to destroy. Our men entered the town and great cries and weepings arose. It was a verdant, pleasant town with strongly built, well-constructed walls and much sought after for residence there. The inhabitants were sorely grieved for the town and great were their wailings and weepings on leaving their homes. They started to sell what they were unable to transport. Things that were worth ten dirhams were sold for one. People got rid of their property for trifling sums, so that, for example, twelve chickens were sold for one dirham. There was chaos in the town and the inhabitants with their children and womenfolk went out to the army, for fear that the Franks would descend on the town. They offered many times the proper rate for the hire of mounts, some to go to Egypt and some to Syria, while some walked[1] since they could hire no beasts. Dreadful things happened and frightful strife, which perhaps did not fall only on the wicked.[2]

The sultan in person and his son al-Afḍal urged our men on in the work of demolition and the need to press on with it, fearing that, if word got to the enemy, they would come and demolition would be impossible. The men passed the night in a complete state of fatigue and exhaustion.

That night news came from al-'Ādil that the Franks had spoken with him about peace and that the son of Humfrey had come to him to discuss the matter, making a demand for all the coastal lands. The sultan thought that talks were in our interest because he saw in the hearts of men that they were tired and disillusioned with the fighting, the hardship and the burden of debts that was on their backs. In his reply to al-'Ādil he gave him permission to hold talks and the power to negotiate on his own initiative.

The morning of Friday 20 Sha'bān [13 September] found the sultan determined to carry on the demolition and to keep the men hard at work on it. He gave them a free hand with the granaries that were the stores of the town because of his inability to move them, because time was short and he feared a Frankish attack. He ordered the town to be torched, so the houses and residences were set on fire and burnt down. The inhabitants threw away the remnants of their goods and chattels because they could not transport them.

From the direction of the enemy there came constant reports that they were restoring Jaffa. Al-'Ādil wrote saying that the Franks were unaware of the demolition of Ascalon, to which the sultan replied, saying, 'String them along and spin out **[188]** your talks with them, so that we can perhaps manage to destroy the town.' He gave orders for the towers to be crammed full with combustibles and set on fire. On Saturday 21 Sha'bān [14 September] he rode out to urge on the men in their task of destruction and burning. He continued to keep the men at their work, going the rounds in person with his encouragement until his health was slightly affected and so he was unable to ride or to take nourishment for two days.

Information about the enemy was flowing in all the time and clashes and skirmishes were occurring between them and our advance guard or nearest units. These reports were coming in while he assiduously encouraged the demolition work. He transferred the baggage-train to a position near Ascalon,

---

1 Following the reading in B: *yamshūna*.

2 This last phrase echoes Koran viii, 25.

so that the grooms and the porters and others could help. Eventually, most of the wall was torn down. It was very strongly built, so much so that in places it was nine cubits thick, even ten in some. One of the masons mentioned to the sultan, when I was present, that the thickness of the tower they were undermining was a spear's length. The demolition and the burning of the town and its walls were kept going until the end of Sha'bān [22 September].

At that juncture a letter came from Jurdīk in which he reported that the enemy had widened their activities and had begun to leave Jaffa and raid the neighbouring lands. If the sultan moved, he could perhaps catch them unawares and gain some advantage. The sultan therefore decided to make a move and to leave some stonemasons at Ascalon to finish the demolition with some cavalry to protect them. He thought he should wait until the tower named after the Hospitallers had been burnt. It was a vast tower, overlooking the sea, like an impregnable fortress. I went in to inspect it and saw that its construction was the most solid that one could imagine, on which pickaxes would have no effect. He wished to burn it merely to leave it thereby in a demolishable state on which the work of destruction could be effective.

On Monday 1 Ramaḍān 587 [23 September 1191] he ordered his son, al-Afḍal, to take a direct part himself in this work along with his close staff. I saw him and his staff carrying timbers to burn the tower. Our men continued to bring timbers and cram them into the tower until it was full. The timbers were then lit and blazed into flame. The fire remained burning for two days and nights. This day, to settle his state of health, the sultan did not ride at all. I, too, was afflicted by some disorder of body which meant that I was absent from him that day. Three times people came to me to ask after my health on his behalf, notwithstanding the fact that he was preoccupied by this weighty matter. God Almighty have mercy on him, for with his death there died the best of moral qualities.

[189] His stop at Yubnā

That night, that is the eve of Tuesday 2 Ramaḍān [24 September], the sultan left camp half-way through the night because he feared the effect of the heat on his state of health. We prayed the dawn prayer and then set out, coming to Yubnā towards late morning on the Tuesday. He began by stopping in his brother al-'Ādil's tent and learning from him the latest news of the enemy. He then rode on and stopped in his own tent, where he spent the night at this locality.

Account of his march to Ramla

Wednesday 3 Ramaḍān [25 September] found Saladin on the move towards Ramla, where he arrived around noon. With the main baggage-train he made a long-term camp there. He organised the army into right wing, left wing and centre and fed the troops before taking a little rest. Between midday and afternoon prayer times he rode as far as Lydda. He viewed the town and viewed its church and the great size of its construction, then ordered its demolition and also the demolition of the castle at Ramla. Work started on both places that day and he divided the troops into two groups to raze both places. He allowed people to take what they wanted of the straw and barley in the royal granaries in both, and ordered their residents to move to other populous centres. Only a very few persons remained in either place. Our men kept up the destructive work until the evening. He then returned to his tent.

Thursday 4 Ramaḍān [26 September] dawned and the sultan organised stonemasons in both places and appointed people to oversee their work, while he came frequently in the late afternoon. Once the time of sunset prayer came, he spread food and all broke their fast, then retired to their tents.

It occurred to him to go secretly with a small band to observe affairs in Jerusalem (may God facilitate its deliverance). He set out early in the night and came to Bayt Nūbā, where he slept. In the morning he prayed and then travelled on to Jerusalem, arriving on Friday 5 Ramaḍān [27 September]. He passed the day investigating conditions in Jerusalem, its state of repair, its provisions, its military stores, its garrison and such like. During that day the servants of the *Ṭawāshī* Qaymāz seized a few local Christians, who had on them letters of recent date that the governor had written to the sultan, reporting the city's lack of grain, equipment and men. They planned to carry them to the enemy. After he had read the letters, those on whom they were found were executed. He continued to investigate the local situation and to order shortcomings to be met until Monday 8 Ramaḍān [30 September]. When Monday had come, all the troops left after the noon prayer and he spent the night at Bayt Nūbā.

This day there arrived Mu'izz al-Dīn Qaysar Shāh [**190**], the lord of Malaṭiyya and son of Qilij Arslān, as a suppliant, requesting help from the sultan against his brothers and his father, for they were purposing to take his city from him. Al-'Ādil met him north of Lydda and received him with honour and respect. Later the sultan's son al-Afḍal met him, after his tent had been pitched near Lydda.

On this day enemy foragers ventured out and were attacked by our advanced guard. Word came to their main force and some cavalry came out to help them. A battle between them and our advanced guard ensued. One of the prisoners said that the king of England was with them, that a Muslim went to lance him, but a Frank interposed his own body and was killed. The king himself was wounded. Thus it was reported, but God knows best.

The sultan's return to the army

When it was Tuesday 9 Ramaḍān [1 November], the sultan came to the army and was met by the troops, delighted at his return. The son of Qilij Arslān also came to meet him. The sultan dismounted out of politeness and received him with honour and respect. After taking up his quarters again, the sultan continued to encourage the demolition work, while reports about the enemy were constantly coming to him. There were clashes between them and our advanced guard, and the Bedouin were snatching some of their horses, mules and men.

Account of the arrival of the envoy of the marquis

During this time an envoy came from the marquis saying that he would make peace with Islam on condition that he be given Sidon and Beirut in return for showing open hostility to the Franks, marching on Acre, besieging it and taking it from them. He also stipulated that the sultan should begin by swearing to hold to that. The sultan sent back to him the courier al-'Adl bearing a reply to his request, with the aim of detaching him from the Franks. He was a wicked, accursed man, who had been apprehensive that the Franks might take his town, that is Tyre, from him. He therefore withdrew from them and retired behind the defences of Tyre, an impregnable town. This was why his suggestion was accepted.

The courier al-'Adl set out with the envoy on Friday 12 Ramaḍān [4 October]. The sultan made it a condition that the marquis should first besiege the enemy in Acre, capture the place and set free the prisoners there and in Tyre. Only then would he hand over the two towns to him. In the evening of that day the envoy of the king of England came out to al-'Ādil to put a series of peace talks in motion.

[191] Account of the sultan's departure from Ramla

When Saturday 13 Ramaḍān arrived [5 October], the sultan decided to withdraw the army to the hills to enable the troops to send their mounts out to pasture, for at Ramla we were close to the enemy and it was not possible to leave the mounts unattended because of the fear of attack. He therefore left and camped on a hill adjacent to the hill of Latrun with the heavy baggage and all the army apart from the advanced units, as is normal. This was after razing Ramla and Lydda.

After camping there that day he made a tour around Latrun and ordered its demolition. It was a strong and well-fortified castle of great renown. A start was made on the demolition.

Envoys went back and forwards between al-'Ādil and the king of England and they reported of the latter that he had entrusted the business of peace talks to al-'Ādil and that he relied on him utterly. Ten men came from the king to the advanced guard to see al-'Ādil and told him some good news, which he passed on to the sultan the evening of Wednesday 17 Ramaḍān [9 October].

Account of the death of the king of France

One of the things reported by al-'Ādil was that the king of France had died. He died in Antioch from a sickness he contracted. Another was that the king of England had returned to Acre. The reason for this was that he learnt beyond doubt that the marquis had made contact with the sultan, and he heard that an agreement had been arranged between the marquis and us and that the basis of the agreement was Acre. He therefore returned to Acre to frustrate this alliance and to win the marquis back to his side.

Al-'Ādil remained with the advanced guard and on Thursday the 18th of the month [10 October] the sultan rode out to their position and had a meeting with his brother al-'Ādil at Lydda. He questioned him about the latest news and then, at the time for the evening prayer, returned to his encampment. Two Franks, who had been seized by the advanced guard, were brought to him and they confirmed the truth of the death of the king of France[1] and of the king of England's return to Acre.

[192] Account of al-'Ādil's journey to Jerusalem and the arrival of news of the death of Qizil ibn Ildekiz

On Friday 19 Ramaḍān [11 October] circumstances demanded an investigation into the state of affairs at Jerusalem and an inspection of its state of repair. Al-'Ādil had returned from the advanced guard and knew that the forward units of the Franks were far away from us. He therefore decided that he should be the one to travel to Jerusalem and investigate affairs there. He set out that day for that purpose.

1 In fact, Philip Augustus had fallen ill and returned home at the beginning of August. He did not die until 1223 A.D.

On this day's date a letter arrived from al-Muẓaffar Taqī al-Dīn in which he told that Qizil, the lord of the Persian lands and son of Ildekiz, had been attacked by his own men and killed. It is said that this was done on the orders of his wife in support of the Sultan Ṭughril. Because of his murder much disturbance occurred in the Persian lands. According to reports we heard, he was killed early in Sha'bān of the year 587 [c. 24 August 1191], but God Almighty knows best.

The return of al-'Ādil from Jerusalem

When it was Sunday 21 Ramaḍān [13 October], al-'Ādil arrived from Jerusalem a little before the afternoon prayer. At the same date a letter arrived from the August Prophetic Divan[1] disapproving of al-Muẓaffar Taqī al-Dīn's hostile move against Khilāṭ, manifesting the utmost concern for Baktimur, and interceding for Ḥasan ibn Qifjāq and ordering his release. Muẓaffar al-Dīn had arrested him in Irbil. The letter also commanded that Qāḍī al-Fāḍil should proceed to the Divan to settle matters. The letter was sent on to Qāḍī al-Fāḍil to be read by him and the contents were communicated to al-Muẓaffar.

Information from the advanced guard at Acre and the case of the robbers who entered the enemy's tents

On Monday 22 Ramaḍān [14 October] robbers brought a horse and a mule after they had entered the enemy's camp and stolen them. The sultan had enrolled 300 robbers from amongst the thieving Bedouin [**193**] to infiltrate the enemy and steal their property and their horses, and also to carry off men alive. That is to say, as one of them was sleeping, a dagger would be held to his throat. Awakened, he would see the thief, armed with a dagger which was held at his throat, so he would keep silent and not dare to say a word. Carried off in that state away from his tent, he would be made a prisoner. Several of them did speak and had their throats cut, so those who subsequently found themselves in this predicament kept silent and chose to be taken rather than killed. This continued for a long time until the signing of the peace.

On the same date there came from our advanced force, stationed to keep watch on Acre at a place called al-Zīb, information from prisoners, brought by a courier. He told that the enemy had left Acre and scattered far and wide. Our troops keeping watch had charged and taken twenty-one of them prisoner. These prisoners told that it was true that the king of England had returned to

---

[1] This means the Abbasid caliphal court and administration at Baghdad.

Acre and that he was ill. They also gave information about the weak state of the people in Acre, their lack of money and provisions. This same date several enemy ships arrived, which were said to have come from Acre, bringing the king of England who had returned with a large force with the intention of marching to Ascalon and refortifying it. That he intended to march on Jerusalem was also rumoured, but God knows best.

The arrival of the prisoners mentioned above

When it was Wednesday 24 Ramaḍān [16 October], the prisoners came from al-Zīb. Their arrival was a source of delight to the Muslims and a harbinger of better things. At the same time an envoy from Qizil arrived, whom he had despatched before his death, and also an envoy from his cousin, Īnānj. In the evening of that day an envoy came from the king of England, bringing a horse for al-'Ādil in return for a gift that the latter had sent the king.

Account of the death of Ḥusām al-Dīn ibn Lājīn

On the same date news came of Ḥusām al-Dīn's death[1] in Damascus from an illness that struck him down. The sultan took his death very hard and grieved for him. There also came a letter from Sāma in which it was reported that the Prince [of Antioch] had raided Jabala and Lattakia, and that he suffered a great setback, having many of his men killed. He returned to Antioch chastened.

Al-'Ādil's envoy visits the king of England

On Friday 26 Ramaḍān [18 October] it fell to al-'Ādil to command the outlying pickets. The king of England asked for his envoy, so al-Ṣanī'a, al-'Ādil's secretary and a handsome young man, was sent to him. He came to the king at Yāzūr,[2] after the emergence of a large force **[194]** of their foot-soldiers who spread over that area. Having met with him, the king kept him for a long time and discussed the matter of peace with him, saying, 'I will not go back on what I said to my brother and my friend,' meaning al-'Ādil. He mentioned a proposition which the envoy repeated to al-'Ādil after he returned to him. Al-'Ādil wrote it on a piece of paper and sent it to the sultan. It arrived a little before afternoon prayer on the day mentioned and contained:

---

1 Ḥusām al-Dīn Muḥammad ibn 'Umar ibn Lājīn, a nephew of the sultan, had died on the eve of Friday 19 Ramaḍān / 11 October (*Fatḥ*, pp. 406-407).

2 A settlement about 5 km south-east of Jaffa.

> You will greet him and say, 'The Muslims and the Franks are done for. The land is ruined, ruined utterly at the hands of both sides. Property and lives on both sides are destroyed. This matter has received its due. All we have to talk about is Jerusalem, the Holy Cross and these lands. Now Jerusalem is the centre of our worship which we shall never renounce, even if there were only one of us left. As for these lands, let there be restored to us what is this side of the Jordan. The Holy Cross, that is a piece of wood that has no value for you, but is important for us. Let the sultan bestow it upon us. Then we can make peace and have rest from this constant hardship.'

After the sultan had read this message he summoned the leading men of his council and consulted them about what to reply. What the sultan decided to say in reply was:

> Jerusalem is ours just as much as it is yours. Indeed, for us it is greater than it is for you, for it is where our Prophet came on his Night Journey and the gathering place of the angels. Let not the king imagine that we shall give it up, for we are unable to breathe a word of that amongst the Muslims. As for the land, it is also ours originally. Your conquest of it was an unexpected accident due to the weakness of the Muslims there at that time. While the war continues God has not enabled you to build up one stone there. From the lands in our hands we, thanks be to God, feed on the produce and draw our benefit. The destruction of the Holy Cross would in our eyes be a great offering to God, but the only reason we are not permitted to go that far is that some more useful benefit might accrue to Islam.

This reply went back to the king by the hand of his own envoy.

Account of the flight of Shīrkūh ibn Bākhil al-Kurdī from Acre, where he was a captive

Towards the end of the day on Friday 26 Ramaḍān [18 October] Shīrkūh ibn Bākhil al-Zarzārī, one of the emirs imprisoned in Acre, arrived. This was his story. He fled on the eve of Sunday 21 Ramaḍān [13 October], for he had kept a rope hidden in his pillow and the Emir Ḥusayn ibn Bārīk had also concealed a rope in the privy. They agreed to escape and climbed down through a window that was in the privy. They descended the first wall and Shīrkūh also managed to cross the outer wall, but Ibn Bārīk had his rope break as he was coming down. Shīrkūh, who had got down safely, saw him injured by the fall. He spoke to him, but there was no answer. He urged him to move, but he did not stir, then he shook him in the hope that he might revive and come with him, but to no avail. He knew that, if he stayed with him, both would be taken, so he left him and went on. He fled with difficulty because of his chains and eventually came to Tell al-'Ayyāḍiyya when dawn had arrived. He hid on the slopes [**195**] until the day was well advanced, broke his chains and, under the protection of God Almighty, carried on until he came to where the army was camped at that time. He presented himself before the sultan and amongst what he had to report was that Sayf al-Dīn al-Mashtūb was being closely confined, that he had agreed a great ransom for himself of horses, mules and sundry other property, that the king of England had come to Acre and seized all the servants and mamlukes that al-Mashṭūb had there and his other chattels, leaving him nothing there, that the peasants of the Mountain were supplying the king copiously with provisions and that Ṭughril the Sword-bearer, one of the elite mamlukes of the sultan, had managed to escape before Shīrkūh himself.

A message which al-'Ādil sent me to take to the sultan in company with several emirs

On Monday 29 Ramaḍān [21 October] al-'Ādil summoned me during the morning and asked a number of emirs to be present, 'Alam al-Dīn Sulaymān, Sābiq al-Dīn, 'Izz al-Dīn ibn al-Muqaddam and Ḥusām al-Dīn Bishāra, and expounded to us the written and oral messages that his envoy had brought back from the king of England. That is to say, he told us that the essential basis of agreement depended on al-'Ādil's marrying the king of England's sister, whom he had brought with him from Sicily, for she had been the wife of its ruler, who died. Her brother brought her with him when he travelled here via Sicily. It was proposed that he would marry her to al-'Ādil, that the seat of their realm should be in Jerusalem, and that the sultan should give to al-'Ādil all the coastal lands that he held and make him king of the Littoral. This should be in addition to the lands and fiefs that were in his hands. The Holy Cross should be handed over to him. The villages would belong to the Templars and the Hospitallers while the castles would be held by the married pair and our prisoners would be released as would theirs. It was proposed that this should be the basis for a peace settlement and that the king of England should depart, making his way home over the sea, and the matter be concluded. This is what the king had said as al-'Ādil's envoy reported it.

Having learnt of this, al-'Ādil took the matter forward, summoned us to his presence and entrusted us with this message to the sultan. He appointed me the spokesman, while the others were just to listen. When this proposition was presented to him, if he approved of it and saw it to be to the benefit of himself and the Muslims, we were to be witnesses that he gave permission for it and approved it. If he rejected it, we were to bear witness that the peace talks had reached this final point and that he was the one who thought they should be stopped.

When we presented ourselves before the sultan, I set forth [**196**] the proposal and read the missive to him in the presence of the company mentioned above. He hastened to express approval of these terms, believing that the king of England would not agree to them at all and that it was intended to mock and deceive him. Three times I repeated my statement that he gave his approval, while he was quite plain about it and gave his testimony that he accepted it. Having verified this we returned to al-'Ādil and informed him of what the sultan had said. The company told him that I had repeated the proposal to the sultan when confirming his testimony and that he was adamant that he gave permission for it. Thus these terms were settled.

The envoy's return to the king of England with the reply to this missive

When it was Wednesday 2 Shawwāl [23 October], [al-Ṣanī'a] Ibn al-Naḥḥāl went as an envoy on behalf of the sultan and of al-'Ādil. When he had reached the enemy's camp and sent to inform the king of his arrival, he was sent news that the royal lady had been presented with the marriage plan by her brother and it made her very displeased and angry. Indeed, she rejected it utterly and swore by her religion with the most binding of oaths that she would not consent. How could she possibly allow a Muslim to have carnal knowledge of her! Her brother then proposed, 'If al-'Ādil becomes a Christian, I will finish the business. If she is willing, I will do it.' He left the door for negotiations open. Al-'Ādil wrote again to the sultan with the latest information.

Account of the seizure of a famous ship of the Franks, called 'the Armoured', which they greatly prized

On Saturday 5 Shawwāl [26 October] news came that the Muslim fleet had captured some Frankish ships, amongst which was the ship known as 'the Armoured'.[1] It is said that it held 500 men or even more than that, of whom a great number were killed. Our men spared four great persons of note. This greatly cheered the Muslims and victory drums were beaten and trumpets brayed. To God belong all praise and blessing.

1 In Arabic: *al-musaṭṭaḥ*. This could mean 'qui a un pont, un tillac' (see Dozy, *Supplément*, i, p. 652), but other references there quoted suggest that it could mean '(barca) armata.' Cf. *RHC Or*, p. 279, 'le blindé'.

The emirs' unanimity of opinion in the presence of the sultan

The sultan assembled the great emirs and his councillors of state on Sunday 6 Shawwāl [27 October] and consulted them about what to do if the enemy marched forth. Various reports had been coming in that they had agreed to take the field to engage the Muslim army. [**197**] The decision was made among the wise heads of the Muslims that they should remain in their position after reducing the size of the baggage-train. Then, if the Franks marched out, they would be ready to meet them.

During the evening that day two Franks on horseback deserted to us and told that the enemy were intending to move out on Tuesday and that they numbered about 10,000 mounted men. It was said that the Franks did not know their destination. A Muslim prisoner escaped from them and reported that they had announced a march to Ramla and they would decide there which place to make for. Having learnt this, the sultan ordered the herald to proclaim that the army should prepare to move with light baggage only. Our banners were raised and it was clear that he intended to stand and face the enemy if they marched out. On the Monday [28 October] he set out (strengthened by God and victorious with God's help) and came by night just south of the church at Ramla, where he camped and spent the night.

The Franks march out from Jaffa

On the morning of Tuesday 8 Shawwāl [29 October] he drew up the divisions for battle and entrusted the advanced guard to al-'Ādil. Those who were eager to fight for the Faith followed him. A number of people from Anatolia had arrived with that purpose and went forward as a body. When they reached the Franks' tents, the royal mamlukes charged for they had great courage, familiarity with the enemy's manner of fighting and confidence in their mounts and their equipment, and they loosed flights of arrows at them. The volunteer warriors and the arrivals from Anatolia watched them and were led astray by their bold attack. They tried to match what they did. They drew close to the enemy force and when the Franks saw how they pressed closely on them, their spirits bridled and their pride roused them to action. They rode out from amongst their tents, gave a great shout as one man and charged in a large body. The Muslims that survived were those whose mounts carried them away from their pursuers or whose survival had been decreed in pre-existence. Several were seized, of whom three persons, as it was said, were killed. The enemy transported their tents to Yāzūr and the sultan remained through that night until the morning in what had been their position.

Account of the death of al-Muẓaffar

The sultan rode out towards the enemy on Friday 11 Shawwāl [1 November], viewed them and then returned. He commanded me to request his brother al-'Ādil to wait upon him along with 'Alam al-Dīn Sulaymān ibn Jandar, Sābiq al-Dīn ibn al-Dāya and 'Izz al-Dīn ibn al-Muqaddam. When this group appeared before him, he ordered a servant to clear from his presence all but those he had summoned. I was one of the latter. He ordered everyone to be removed far from the tent. Then he drew a letter from his gown, broke the seal and read it. Tears started to his eyes and he was overcome by his weeping [**198**] and his wailing, so that we joined in without knowing what the reason was. During all this he told us that the letter was about the death of al-Muẓaffar and then the assembled company took to weeping all the tears that were due to him. Later, I urged the sultan to think of God and that His decree and will must be fulfilled. He said, 'God forgive me. "To God do we belong and to Him do we return."' Then he went on, 'The best course is to conceal this and keep it secret, lest it is communicated to the enemy, while we are in close contact with them.' He then summoned food and the company ate and dispersed.

The letter that came containing news of his death was not the letter reporting his demise that came to Ḥamā and was forwarded enclosed in a letter from the viceroy there. Al-Muẓaffar died on the Khilāṭ road when returning to Mayyāfāriqīn. His corpse was carried to Mayyāfāriqīn, but later a tomb was built for him in a famous madrasa in the territory of Ḥamā. He was taken there to be buried and I have visited his grave (God's mercy be upon him). He died on Friday 19 Ramaḍān 587 [11 October 1191].

Account of a letter that arrived from Baghdad

On Saturday 12 Shawwāl [2 November] a letter came from Damascus from the deputies there, enclosing a letter sent by the August Prophetic Divan in Baghdad (may God extol it), which contained three sections. The first expressed disapproval of al-Muẓaffar for his campaign against Baktimur and made much of this, so much so that it was said that the August Divan offered him no greeting. The second section contained disapproval of Muẓaffar al-Dīn for his seizure of Ḥasan ibn Qifjāq and a command to restore him to al-Karkhānī.[1] Again this was greatly stressed, to the extent that it was said, 'The August Divan has not given permission for anyone else to dwell there.'

Ḥasan ibn Qifjāq's story is as follows. He set out for Urmiyya with[2] Sultan Ṭughril, for the latter stayed with him in his tents after he fled from Persian

1 Probably the same as Karkhīnī, east of the Tigris near Daqūqa.
2 Reading *bi'l-sulṭān*, as in B.

lands, sought his help and married his sister. It occurred to Ḥasan that he might become his regent-guardian and use him to conquer territory. They therefore attacked Urmiyya, where, as is reported, Ḥasan killed the inhabitants, enslaved the women and children and waylaid caravans. His fortress was al-Karkhānī. When the Sultan Ṭughril found how powerful he was, he left him and went away, while Ḥasan returned to his lands, openly pursued his wicked career and preyed on caravans, according to reports. Muẓaffar al-Dīn, the lord of Irbil, courted him and in the end Ḥasan returned to him and joined the ranks of his followers, but Muẓaffar al-Dīn arrested him. The August Divan sent this message concerning Ḥasan because of Muẓaffar al-Dīn's seizure of his lands and the possibility that Ḥasan might seek the intercession of the Divan. Partiality for him demanded that this be done on his behalf.

As for the third section, it contained a command to dispatch Qāḍī al-Fāḍil to the August Divan as an envoy to settle certain fundamental matters and set out certain explanations. These were the contents of the letter and in answer to it the sultan replied, with reference to the first section, 'We did not give orders for any of this. Al-Muẓaffar crossed [the Euphrates] only in order to gather [**199**] troops and to return to the Jihad. Certain factors occurred which necessitated all of this, but we had ordered him to withdraw.' As for the second section, his answer was that he had alerted them to what Ibn Qifjāq was doing and the iniquities that he perpetrated throughout the land and he had ordered Muẓaffar al-Dīn to bring him with him to Syria, where he would be given a fief and could devote himself to the Jihad. His reply to the third section was that he apologised on behalf of Qāḍī al-Fāḍil, that he had many illnesses and he was too weak in body to journey to Iraq. Such was the gist of his reply.

The arrival of the lord of Sidon as an envoy from the marquis

On Tuesday 15 Shawwāl [5 November] a messenger came to report the arrival of the lord of Sidon on behalf of the marquis, lord of Tyre. A whole series of talks had taken place between us and his men, the upshot of which was that they cut off their support for the Franks and joined us against them, all based on a discord that arose between the marquis and the other princes because of a woman he married who had been the wife of the brother of King Guy, and whose marriage was dissolved through something that their religion necessitated.[1] Concerning this there was a great confusion of opinions. The marquis feared for his life, took his wife and fled under cover of night to Tyre. He relied on the sultan and his support for him. In all this there was much

---

1 In November 1190 Conrad of Montferrat married Isabella, daughter of Amalric I, whose marriage with Humfrey IV of Toron (in fact, the brother-in-law of King Guy) had been annulled as she had married when under the age of consent.

advantage for the Muslims, because of the marquis's break with the Franks, for he was one of their doughtiest, their most experienced in warfare and their most soundly based in counsel.

When news of the arrival of this envoy reached the sultan, he ordered that he be treated with honour and respect. A tent was pitched, around which a screen was set up, and in it were placed such cushions and furnishings as were fit for their nobles and princes. The sultan ordered that he be lodged at the baggage-train to rest and then brought to meet him.

Account of the ambush in which Ayāz al-Mihrānī met a martyr's death

On the 16 Shawwāl [6 November] the sultan ordered the Royal Guard to set an ambush for the enemy in the bottoms of some valleys there. They took with them a group of Bedouin. When the ambush was in place, the Bedouin **[200]** showed themselves in their customary way when they engage the enemy. Several of the enemy had been venturing out to gather fodder and fire-wood near to their camp. The Bedouin caught sight of them and shot at them. A battle ensued and a great clamour arose, which the Franks heard and so a group of their cavalry rode out, making for where the noise came from. The Bedouin withdrew in the direction of the ambush, while the enemy followed them, eager to catch them, until they drew near the ambush. The hidden troops emerged and gave them one great shout. The enemy fled back towards their tents. News of this spread amongst the enemy force and a huge number of them rode out and made towards the battle, which raged and became very intense. On both sides several were killed or wounded, and several of the enemy were taken prisoner and many horses taken from them.

The reason why the battle was broken off was that the sultan took into account such a turn of events. He sent the Master of the Horse, Aslam, Sayf al-Dīn Yāzkuj and their like as reserve support for the ambushing force. He said, 'If you see that the ambushers are being overwhelmed, take the field.' When they saw the great number on the enemy's side, they moved to engage them with cavalry and infantry. Seeing that the Muslim divisions had turned the reins of their horses towards them, the enemy retreated in the direction of their tents, with the sword in action on their backs. Once they had reached their tents, the battle concluded a little before the noon prayer on Wednesday 16 Shawwāl [6 November].

The sultan had ridden out to seek news of the ambush. I was attending him. The first to return from the battle were a group of Bedouin, who had with them five horses they had taken in the battle but who had left the field before the conclusion. Subsequently scouts and messengers kept on coming one after the other. In the battle, according to report, about sixty of the enemy were killed.

Several Muslims were wounded and several men of note on the Muslim side were killed, among them, Ayāz al-Mihrānī, who was a man of known bravery, and Jāwulī, the mamluke of al-Ghaydī. Ayāz al-Mu'aẓẓamī was also laid low. He was wounded a number of times and carried back to our ranks. Two of the enemy's knights, men of standing, were captured and two deserted to our side with their horses and equipment.

The sultan returned to his tent in a happy and delighted state, giving replacement horses to those who had lost theirs, showing great consideration for the wounded and compassion for the dead. During what was left of the day the envoy of the king of England came to al-'Ādil, finding fault with him for the ambush and seeking a meeting. Permission to visit was sought and given, and in due course he came.

[201] Account of what occurred between al-'Ādil and the king of England at their meeting

On Friday 18 Shawwāl [8 November] al-'Ādil went to the advanced guard, where a large reception tent was pitched for him. He took with him such foods, luxuries and presents as are customarily brought by one prince to another. When he acted with magnificence in such a manner, he was not the man to be outshone. The king of England came to see him in his tent and was treated with great respect. With the king came some of the food that is peculiarly theirs. By way of being pleasant the king offered some to al-'Ādil, who took some of it, while the king and the men who accompanied him partook of al-'Ādil's food. The latter presented what he had brought and the two of them conversed for the greater part of the day. They parted in amity and good spirits as firm friends.

Concerning the letter that the king of England sent to the sultan about a meeting and the reply it received

That same day the king asked al-'Ādil to request a direct meeting with the sultan for him. When this communication arrived, the sultan consulted several people about a reply. Not one of them had the same reaction as the sultan, who made this reply, 'When princes meet, their subsequent enmity is disgraceful. When something is arranged, then it is good to meet. Any meeting would only be to discuss important business, but I do not understand your language and you do not understand mine. Someone to interpret for us both, one whom you trust and I trust, is essential, so let that interpreter be an envoy until something is settled and a firm basis established. At that point there can be a meeting which will be followed by friendship and love.' The envoy said, 'When the king of England heard that, he fully appreciated its significance and realised that he could only achieve any aim by adapting to what would satisfy the sultan.

[202] The lord of Sidon comes before the sultan, delivers a message and discusses his mission

When it was Saturday 19 Shawwāl [9 November], the sultan held a session to receive the lord of Sidon to hear his message and what he had to say. He presented himself with several others who came with him. I was present at the reception when the sultan showed him great honour. He conversed with them and offered what was customary. When the food had been taken away, he went into private session with them. What they had to say was that the sultan should make peace with the marquis, the lord of Tyre. Several Frankish nobles had joined his ranks, such as the lord of Sidon and other men of note. His situation has already been mentioned. Our condition for making peace with him was that he should show open hostility to the Franks from overseas. The reason behind all this was his serious fear of them and the dispute he had fallen into with them because of his wife. The sultan offered agreement on certain conditions by which he aimed to cause dissension amongst them and that some of them should suffer a reverse.

When the sultan had heard his mission, he promised him to give him a reply at a later time. This same day the lord of Sidon departed.

Account of the arrival of the king of England's envoy

The evening of this same day the king of England's envoy arrived, namely, the son of Humfrey, one of their nobles, a lord and son of a lord. He came on a mission, with one of their important elders in his retinue, who was said to be 120 years old. The sultan summoned Humfrey's son into his presence and heard his message, which was that the king says, 'I wish for your friendship and love. You have said that you have granted these coastal lands to your brother. I want you to be an arbitrator between him and me and to divide the lands between him and me. It is essential that we have some hold on Jerusalem. My aim is that you divide the land in such a way that there should be no blame on him from the Muslims and none on me from the Franks.' The sultan immediately replied with fair promises and gave them leave to depart directly. They were greatly impressed by this.[1]

The sultan sent after them people who enquired into the question of prisoners, for it was separate from the peace talks. They said, 'If there is peace, it will cover all. If there is no peace, then there will be no talk at all about prisoners.' The sultan's aim was to undermine the peace talks, [**203**] for he turned to me at the end of the session after they had departed and said to me, 'If and when we make peace with them, we cannot be sure they will not be a danger to us. If death should happen to strike me down, these forces are hardly likely to assemble again and the Franks will grow strong. Our best course is to keep on with the Jihad until we expel them from the coast or die ourselves.' This was his own view and it was only against his will that he was persuaded to make peace.

The council he held to choose between the peace alternatives, peace with the king or peace with the marquis, lord of Tyre

On Monday 21 Shawwāl [11 November] the sultan gathered the emirs, magnates and councillors and told them of the treaty that the marquis sought and the terms fixed on by him, namely, that he take over Sidon and cooperate with us against the Franks, fighting them and being overtly hostile. He also told them what the king demanded to conclude a treaty of peace, that is, that he should have specified places amongst the settlements on the coastal plain and that we should have the uplands in their entirety or that all settlements should be held in condominium. Under either division they should have priests in the shrines and churches of Jerusalem. The king had given us the choice between the two divisions.

The sultan now explained to the emirs the position concerning the two proposals of peace and solicited their opinions about which side they inclined to, the king of England or the marquis, and which of the two divisions put forward by the king they preferred. The council thought that, if there was to be a peace, it should be with the king, for a sincere friendship of the [local] Franks towards the Muslims, such that they could mix together, was a remote possibility and an association[2] not safe from treachery.

The people dispersed, but discussion of peace continued backwards and forwards with envoys coming one after the other to arrive at the terms of a treaty. The basic proposal was that the king offered his sister to al-'Ādil as a bride and put forward that the two of them should have all the coastal plain,

[1] B and *RHC Or*, p. 288, read the singular verb *ta'aththara*, which would mean that the sultan was the one 'deeply impressed' or 'affected.'

[2] This is reading *wa-ṣuḥba(t)* from B, rather than *ṣiḥḥatu-hu* as in *Nawādir*.

both Muslim and Frankish parts, the former being hers through her brother and the latter being al-'Ādil's through the sultan. The final communication from the king on the topic was as follows: 'The assembled Christian folk have criticised me for subjecting my sister to a Muslim without consulting the Pope, who is the leader and head of the Christian religion. So I am now sending him an envoy who will return within three months. If he gives permission and she is happy about it, well and good, otherwise I shall marry you [**204**] to my niece, for which I do not need his permission.'

All this was happening while the war still raged and the fighting was doing them severe damage. On occasions the lord of Sidon went riding with al-'Ādil, observing the Franks as the Muslims engaged them in battle. Whenever the Franks saw him they redoubled their efforts in search of peace, fearing that the marquis would ally himself with the Muslims for then their military might would be broken. So matters continued until Friday 25 Shawwāl[1] [15 November].

The sultan's move to Tell al-Jazar

The sultan awoke on that Friday determined to make a move. He summoned his councillors and consulted them over how to answer the communication of the Franks. He reviewed for them what they had said and recalled their various opinions. Then he called in the envoys, and Humfrey's son acted as interpreter between him and the Franks from overseas. It was agreed that two envoys should be sent with them, one from him and one from al-'Ādil, since the discussions concerned him.

The gist of their communication was that, if the Pope allowed this union, it would be concluded and, if he did not allow it, they would marry al-'Ādil to the niece of the king, a virgin.[2] They remarked that in their religion it was only necessary to ask for the Pope's permission to give a royal princess in marriage who had been previously married, but virgins could be married off by their families. The reply to this was, 'If there is to be a marriage, let it be to the former, because we have already talked of her and we do not go back on our word. If it cannot be managed, we are not concerned with any alternative.' With this the meeting terminated and the envoys went to the tents of al-'Ādil so that the sultan's emissary might prepare himself and join them.

Later, from the advanced guard, there came a report that many Frankish foot-soldiers had spread out, having left the defences they had, but that this

---

1 Correcting the '15 Shawwāl' of the original.

2 This was Eleanor, the daughter of Geoffrey, Duke of Brittany, a son of King Henry II.

move appeared not to be hostile. The sultan proceeded to Tell al-Jazar[1] to scout out this position and was followed by the forces in general. It was only just noon when they came up with the sultan and we all camped at Tell al-Jazar. When the Franks had learnt that the sultan had withdrawn, they too retired. The sultan remained at Tell al-Jazar, but later set out towards Jerusalem. The Franks moved back into their own territory and the winter weather worsened with heavy rains.

The sultan went [**205**] to Jerusalem and gave his army leave. We stayed in Jerusalem the whole of that winter, while the enemy returned to their lands. The king of England placed a garrison in Jaffa before returning to Acre to look into its affairs. After he had been there a while, a messenger came from him, saying, 'The king says, "I desire above all a meeting with al-'Ādil, my brother, for it will be to the advantage of both sides. I have heard that the sultan has entrusted peace negotiations to my brother al-'Ādil."' The sultan convened a council to discuss whether al-'Ādil should go and it was agreed that he should, provided that he rendezvoused with our troops that were in the Jordan Valley, at Kawkab and in those regions, and that in his talks he should say, 'On many occasions there have been talks between us, which have yielded no useful result. If this time is to be like those others, there is no need for more talk, but if the aim is to settle some arrangement, then buckle down to the business.[2] I will only meet with you if I see something that is close to settling the situation.' It was arranged with al-'Ādil that, if he thought there was a basis for making peace, he should act accordingly. Otherwise, he should temporise and procrastinate until our armies assembled from the provinces. Al-'Ādil requested a written memorandum stating[3] on what terms peace may be made. A memorandum for him was drawn up, in which condominiums were mentioned and, as far as Beirut was concerned, the sultan said that, if the king persists in asking for it, it should be made a condition that the fortifications be destroyed and not rebuilt, and the same for al-Qaymūn.[4] If they sought to build on waste land,[5] that should be granted. The Holy Cross should be handed over, the Holy Sepulchre should have a priest and they should be given an opportunity to visit it as pilgrims on condition that they bear no arms. What brought us to this was the exhaustion of our troops through the continuous campaigning, their heavy debts and absence far from their homes, for there were some who stayed with the sultan and were unable to ask him for leave.

1 Between Ramla and Latrun, sometimes identified as the site of Saladin's 1177 defeat at Mons Gisardi (but see Lyons and Jackson, *Saladin*, pp.123-124).

2 This renders B: *fa-qārib*. In *Nawādir* correct *bathth ̀* to *batt*.

3 B's *inhā* is preferred to *Nawādir*'s *n.h.y*.

4 *Nawādir* and B: al-Qābūn.

5 Emending *waghar* in *Nawādir* to *wa'ar*. B has Zughar, but this is a place south of the Dead Sea and therefore inherently unlikely.

Account of al-'Ādil's journey

Al-'Ādil set out from Jerusalem on the evening of Friday 4 Rabī' I 588 [20 March 1192]. A letter came in due course from Baysān, reporting that Humfrey, along with the Chamberlain Abū Bakr, had met him as an envoy from the king of England, saying, 'We have agreed to divide the land and that everyone should keep what he holds. If, however, what we have is greater you can take from the extra that we hold something to make up for that and, if what you have in your hands is more, then we can do likewise. Jerusalem will be ours and you can have the Dome of the Rock.'

This was the content of the letter of which the sultan informed the emirs. The Emir Abū'l-Hayjā' approved of this and all thought that whoever had drafted this communication was in agreement with the understanding on the basis of which al-'Ādil had made his journey, it being the best course. A reply to this effect was sent to al-'Ādil. When **[206]** it was Tuesday 15 Rabī' I [31 March], the Chamberlain Abū Bakr, al-'Ādil's man, arrived with news that the king of England had gone from Acre to Jaffa and that al-'Ādil did not think that he should meet him except on the basis of a firmly concluded agreement. This chamberlain and the king had already had many negotiations, the result of which was that he conceded that we should have the Dome of the Rock and the citadel with the rest shared half-and-half, that from their side there should be no distinguished commander in the town, and that the villages around Jerusalem and what is within should be in shared possession.

Al-'Ādil's return from the Jordan Valley

Al-'Ādil came back on 16 Rabī' I [1 April] and, after he had been met by the sultan, they conversed together and al-'Ādil related the recent news.

Account of a Frankish raid

During the remainder of that day someone arrived with news that the Franks had raided a Bedouin encampment near to Dārūm and that they had seized many of them and taken from them about 1,000 head of sheep and cattle. The sultan was very upset by this and greatly grieved. He despatched a force, but they were unable to overtake them.

The departure of the envoy of the marquis

Yusūf, the servant of the lord of Sidon, had arrived previously as an envoy on behalf of the marquis, seeking peace with the Muslims. The sultan proposed certain conditions, such as that he should fight his own kind, breaking with them openly, that whatever Frankish territory he took on his own initiative after conclusion of the peace should be his and that whatever we might take on our own should be ours. Whatever we and he cooperated in taking, the territory itself should be his, while we should have any Muslim captives there and other goods and property. Other conditions were that he should release to us every captive within his possessions and that, if the king of England entrusted to him control of the lands through some arrangement made between them, the treaty between us and himself should conform to whatever is concluded between us and the king of England, apart from Ascalon and lands beyond it, for that does not come into the treaty. The coastal regions should be his and what we hold should be ours. Whatever is in the middle should be shared half-and-half. The marquis's envoy set out with these draft proposals.

[207] The return of the Muslim forces in 588 [1192]

The first to arrive was Asad al-Dīn Shīrkūh ibn Muḥammad ibn Shīrkūh, who returned on Monday 28 Rabī‘ I [13 April]. He came with a lightly equipped force in advance of the main body.

Account of Sayf al-Dīn ibn al-Mashtūb's release from captivity

Ibn al-Mashṭūb reached Jerusalem on Thursday 1 Rabī‘ II[1] [16 April] and went in, unexpected, to see the sultan, with whom was his brother al-‘Ādil. The sultan rose in welcome and embraced him, greatly delighted to see him. He cleared the room and they discussed some curious reports concerning the enemy. Sayf al-Dīn was questioned on what was said about the peace, but he said that the king of England had kept silent about that.

On this day the sultan wrote to his son al-Afḍal with instructions to proceed across the Euphrates to take over the lands of al-Malik al-Manṣūr, son of al-Muẓaffar. Al-Manṣūr had shown signs of rebellion because he feared the

[1] The original gives the month as Jumādā II. I have followed the date in *Fatḥ*, p. 420, which provides an exact match for the day of the week.

sultan was hostile to him. Al-'Ādil became involved and al-Manṣūr sent to al-'Ādil to get him to speak on his behalf, for he did look after his interests. This annoyed the sultan and made him very angry against al-Manṣūr for having caused this trouble in the family. No-one in the family had ever feared him before or demanded an oath from him. This was the reason for the king of England's dilatoriness in making peace, and why he thought that this was a rift that would muddy the waters of the Jihad for the sultan and constrain him to agree to what he was not happy with.

The sultan sent to al-Afḍal ordering him to travel to those regions and he wrote to al-Ẓāhir in Aleppo that, if his brother needed support, he should help him. He sent al-Afḍal off well provided for and in great style. Arrived at Aleppo, he was received with great honour by his brother al-Ẓāhir, who provided full hospitality for him and presented him with splendid gifts.

We return to the narrative concerning the enemy.

The return of the envoy from Tyre

On 6 Rabī' II [21 April] Yūsuf arrived from the marquis to renew peace talks. He said, 'Some sort of understanding has been reached between him and the [local] Franks.[1] If a settlement is achieved in the next few days, the French will depart [**208**] by sea. If it is delayed, peace negotiations with the marquis will be completely futile.' The sultan believed, because he was preoccupied with the east,[2] that the best plan was to make peace with the marquis. He feared that [al-Manṣūr] the son of Taqī al-Dīn might join with Baktimur and the result would be a distraction from the Holy War.

He therefore agreed to the requests of the marquis and drew up a detailed draft on the lines of what has already been mentioned. Al-'Adl set out with the reply to the mission of Yūsuf. That was after Friday congregational prayer on 9 Rabī' II [24 April].

Account of the assassination of the marquis

On the 16 Rabī' II 588 [1 May 1192] a letter came from al-'Adl, the emissary despatched to the marquis, with news that he had been killed and that God had hastened his soul to Hell-fire. The manner of his death was as follows. He lunched on Tuesday, the 13th of the month [28 April], with the bishop. As he

---

1 Conrad of Montferrat had now been accepted by all, including King Richard, as king of Jerusalem (as consort of Isabella, daughter of Amalric I). Guy of Lusignan was to be king of Cyprus.

2 That is, the family trouble with al-Manṣūr in Mesopotamia.

left, two of his men attacked him with daggers. He was slight of build. They kept striking him until God hastened his soul to Hell-fire. The two men were apprehended and questioned about the affair and who had put them up to it. They replied, 'The king of England put us up to it.' Two persons assumed authority and held the citadel until the news reached the princes, and they took over authority and the administration of the town.

The conclusion of al-Manṣūr's affair and what happened to him

When al-Manṣūr heard of the sultan's anger against him, he sent an emissary to al-ʻĀdil, asking him to intercede to reconcile the sultan with him and asking for one of two lots of territory, either Ḥarrān, Edessa and Ṣumayṣāt or Ḥamā, Manbij, Salamiyya and Maʻarrat [al-Nuʻmān], with guarantees from his brothers. Al-ʻĀdil approached the sultan several times, but he would not accept this and agreed to nothing suggested. All the emirs interceded vigorously with him, which stirred the well-spring[1] of his generous spirit and so he reverted to his Prophet-like[2] character, swearing on oath that al-Manṣūr could hold Ḥarrān, Edessa and Ṣumayṣāt on condition that, when he came across the Euphrates, he would be given the [other] places he asked for and would have his brothers' guarantees, and relinquish those places that he presently held. He entered into this promised arrangement and al-ʻĀdil stood guarantor for him.

Later, al-ʻĀdil asked for a signed document from the sultan, which he refused. After he had been importuned, he tore up the text of the oath on 29 Rabīʻ II [14 May]. The arrangement was over and discussion broken off. I had been acting as go-between for them both. The sultan was overcome with rage that he could be addressed in such a way on the part of one of his grandchildren.[3]

[209] Arrival of the Byzantine envoy

When it was 1 Jumādā I [15 May], an envoy arrived from Constantinople the Great and was received with honour and respect. He appeared in the sultan's presence on 3 Jumādā II [17 May]. The missive he brought included several requests, such as a request for the Holy Cross and that the Holy Sepulchre and all the churches of Jerusalem should be in the hands of priests sent by him, that there should be an understanding that his enemy should be our enemy and his friend our friend, and that the sultan should agree to attack Cyprus.

---

1 Literally, 'the tree'.
2 B has *al-ṭāhir*, 'pure'.
3 Al-Manṣūr Muḥammad was, in fact, Saladin's great-nephew.

The envoy stayed for two days and then an envoy called Ibn al-Bazzāz from Egypt was sent back with him. In the reply, all the requests were denied. It was pointed out that the king of the Georgians had offered 200,000 dinars for the Holy Cross and that had not been accepted.

Al-'Ādil's initiatives concerning the lands beyond the Euphrates

After al-Afḍal had set out, al-'Ādil softened the sultan's heart towards the son of Taqī al-Dīn, whose situation was much discussed. The sultan sent me to consult the emirs in the service of al-'Ādil about the case. I gathered them before him and explained the matter concerning which the sultan had sent me to them. The Emir Abū'l-Hayjā' was deputed to make a reply. 'We are his slaves and his mamlukes,' he said, 'while that person is a boy. Perhaps his fear has led him to ally himself with another party. We are unable to combine fighting Muslims with fighting infidels. If the sultan wants us to fight Muslims, he will make peace with the infidels, march to those parts and we will fight under his leadership. If, however, he wishes to persevere in the Holy War, he will make peace with the Muslims and be lenient.' This was the answer of them all.

The sultan relented and, when I had written a fresh copy of the oath for the son of Taqī al-Dīn, the sultan duly swore it and gave him his signed warrant for what had been agreed upon. Al-'Ādil then asked the sultan for the lands that were in the hands of Taqī al-Dīn's son, once he had moved from them. Many negotiations took place about what should be given in exchange, for which I was their go-between. What was finally agreed was that al-'Ādil should take over those lands and give up what [he already held] north of the Euphrates and what was this side of it, apart from Kerak, Shawbak, Ṣalt, Balqā' and his personal holding[1] in Egypt, after surrendering [the rest of] his fief. He was to provide annually 6,000 *ghirāra*s of corn, to be brought to the sultan from Ṣalt and Balqā' to Jerusalem. In the current year the produce of his lands would be his, while the produce from beyond the Euphrates went to the sultan in this year. He received a signed document to this effect from the sultan and then set out to pacify and reconcile the son of Taqī al-Dīn. He departed on 8 Jumādā I [22 May].

1 The *khāṣṣ* was that proportion of a fief reserved for personal expenses rather than the fulfilment of feudal obligations.

[210] The Franks' seizure of Dārūm

When the Franks saw that the sultan had given his troops leave to depart and that they had dispersed, they descended upon Dārūm with eager designs on it. It was a possession of 'Alam al-Dīn Qayṣar, who had his deputies there.

On Saturday 9 Jumādā I [23 May] the enemy made a fierce assault on the place with both horse and foot. The accursed king of England had suborned some Aleppan sappers from the Acre garrison. They were now able to mine this place and they set fire to the mine. The defenders of the castle asked for a truce to enable them to consult the sultan, but the Franks allowed them no truce. They attacked ever more strongly and took the place by force of arms. Those for whom God had decreed it met a martyr's death and others, for whom this was God's decree, were taken captive. This was a fate foreordained.[1]

Account of their attack on Majdal Yābā

Having taken possession of Dārūm, the Franks set out, after they had settled its affairs and stationed picked men there, and stopped at a place called al-Ḥasī,[2] which is near the hills rising to al-Khalīl. This was on 14 Jumādā I [28 May]. They camped there for a while and then made preparations to attack a castle called Majdal Yābā. They arrived there without their baggage, having left their tents where they had camped. A Muslim force was there, which resisted them and a big battle followed. On the enemy's side a count of some note amongst them was killed and on the Muslim side one knight met his death. The reason for this was that he dropped his lance and dismounted to pick it up. His horse prevented him from re-mounting and the enemy rushed him and killed him. They returned to their tents in what remained of the day disappointed of success. To God be the praise.

Account of an engagement at Tyre

On 16 Jumādā [I] [30 May] a letter came from Ḥusām al-Dīn Bishāra in which he reported that a hundred mounted men had remained behind in Tyre and about fifty had joined them from Acre. They became bold and came out to launch raids on Muslim territory. Our troops stationed to guard the territory on that front fell upon them and in a fierce fight that followed fifteen of the enemy

---

1 A close reference to Koran xxxiii, 38.

2 Tell al-Ḥasī is the site of Lachish, about 20 km south-east of Ascalon. The valley of al-Ḥasī runs from the Judaean Hills to the sea between Ascalon and Gaza.

were killed. There was not a single loss on the Muslim side. The enemy retired thwarted and foiled. To God be the praise.

[211] The Muslim armies return to the Jihad

When the sultan saw the more confident operations that the enemy had taken part in, he sent to his armies in all the provinces that they should hasten to join him. The first to arrive, with a large force of Turkomans, was Badr al-Dīn Dildirim, whom the sultan met with respect.

The arrival of Ibn al-Muqaddam

After Badr al-Dīn, on 17 Jumādā I [31 May] there came 'Izz al-Dīn ibn al-Muqaddam with a fine troop and excellent battalions. The sultan gave him, too, a respectful welcome.

Account of the enemy's departure from al-Ḥasī

The enemy broke camp at al-Ḥasī and moved to a junction of routes, where one led to Ascalon and another to Bayt Jibrīl and other Muslim fortresses. Hearing of this, the sultan ordered his forces to move in that direction. Abū'l-Hayjā', Badr al-Dīn Dildirim and Ibn al-Muqaddam set out and the other troops followed in succession. The sultan himself remained behind in Jerusalem because of some sort of indisposition that afflicted him. When the enemy became aware that the Muslim forces had taken the field, they withdrew, retracing their steps thwarted and foiled. Letters from the emirs arrived, telling of the enemy's departure for Ascalon in a similar state. To God be the praise.

The enemy make their dispositions for a march on Jerusalem

When it was Saturday 23 Jumādā I [6 June], a courier came from the army to report that the enemy had set out with horse and foot and a huge mass of camp followers. They camped at Tell al-Ṣāfiya. The sultan sent to the Muslim forces [212] with orders to keep watch and be on the alert and summoning the emirs post-haste to his presence to concert a plan for what corresponding action to take.

The enemy left Tell al-Ṣāfiya and moved towards Latrun, to the north of which they made camp. That was on 26 Jumādā I [9 June]. A group of the

Bedouin on the Muslim side had gone to raid Jaffa. They arrived on their way back without knowing of the enemy's movements and stopped along part of the road to divide their booty. The enemy's troops fell upon them and seized them. Six persons escaped and came to the sultan to tell him what had happened.

Our spies and intelligence gatherers came from the direction of the enemy with information that the enemy would stay in Latrun to bring up the provisions and equipment that were necessary for the military campaign. When they had acquired what they needed, they would march on Jerusalem.

On Wednesday [27 Jumādā I {10 June}] an envoy came from them, accompanying a mamluke of al-Mashṭūb, who had been with them and discussed the matter of Qarāqūsh, while they were talking about peace.

Account of their coming to Bayt Nūbā

Bayt Nūbā is a flat area amid hills, one day's march distant from Jerusalem. The enemy set out from Latrun on Wednesday 27 Jumādā I[1] [10 June] and camped at Bayt Nūbā. When he learnt of that, the sultan summoned the emirs and held a council to discuss what to do. The essence of what was decided was that sections of the city walls should be assigned to the emirs, while the sultan, with the rest of the army as a mobile force, should move out towards the enemy. When all the men knew their posts on the wall and had made all their preparations, then, if the need arose for them, they should take the field and, if it was necessary for them to maintain their position, they should do so. The orders were drawn up and dispatched to the emirs.

Account of an engagement that took place

The road from Jaffa was busy with people transporting provisions to the enemy. The sultan ordered the advance guard to do whatever it could with them. Badr al-Dīn Dildirim was with this unit and he laid an ambush around this road with a fair number of troops. A squadron of enemy cavalry, who were guarding the provisions caravan, passed by and he judged them weak in numbers. He therefore attacked them and a fierce battle ensued, in which fortune went against the enemy. Thirty of them were killed and several taken prisoner. The prisoners were brought to us in Jerusalem on Saturday 29 Jumādā I[2] {13 June}. [**213**] Their arrival had a great impact and the incident

1 *Nawādir* and B read Rabī' I.

2 The date given here cannot be reconciled with others in the narrative. If one accepts the 'Saturday', the date should be 30 Jumādā I. *Fatḥ*, p. 424, does indeed make 29 Jumādā I a Friday.

weakened the enemy's morale. Our advanced unit was much heartened in spirit and their zeal was aroused, so that they attacked the enemy force and stationed themselves on the fringes of the enemy encampment.

A further engagement

When the Muslims learnt that there were caravans uninterruptedly on the move, a detachment laid an ambush for them, taking along many Bedouin. A caravan with a large number of men came by and the Bedouin attacked. The cavalry escort chased them, as they gave way, retreating towards the Muslim troops. The Turks then appeared from the ambush, took some prisoners and killed others. Several of the Turks were wounded. This took place on Tuesday 3 Jumādā II [16 June].

Account of the taking of a caravan from Egypt

The sultan had ordered the Egyptian army to come, and had urged them to take care and be on the watch when they were in the vicinity of the enemy. They remained in Bilbays for some days until the caravans had assembled, but also until information about them had reached the enemy. They set out for Syria. Meanwhile, the enemy were keeping a close watch on their movements and hearing of them through the Bedouin whom they had corrupted.

When the enemy had gained reliable intelligence of the convoy,[1] the king ordered his army to stay close to the foot of the uplands and rode off with 1,000 knights and 1,000 infantry, each knight carrying a man mounted behind him.[2] Our troops, having been ordered by the sultan to be watchful and careful, proceeded to Tell al-Ṣāfiya where they passed the night, and took fodder for[3] their horses there. Then they continued to a spring called al-Ḥasī. The news that the enemy was on the move was communicated to the sultan, so he sent to warn the convoy. Those assigned this task were the Master of the Horse, Aslam, Alṭunbughā al-ʻĀdilī and several renowned warriors. He ordered them to take the convoy on a wide circuit in the desert and to keep them away from the enemy as much as possible.

It so happened that our troops had arrived at al-Ḥasī before the enemy did. They did not stay there, but went on and joined up with the convoy and the

1 The rest of this paragraph is somewhat freely and speculatively translated as the subjects of the various verbs are far from clear in the original.

2 This translation represents the reading of B, *murdifīn* (see also *Rawḍ*, ii, p. 198), which is preferable to *Nawādir*'s reading *murāfiqīn*, 'accompanying'.

3 Reading *'allaqa* as in B (see Dozy, Supplément, s.v.).

Egyptian army. They then brought the convoy back along that route, confident that they would find no frightening foe on the route nor be aware of any cause for alarm. They were eager to take the short way and so they took the people along that route. They came to a spring called al-Khuwaylifa, where they scattered to get [**214**] water. The Bedouin passed this news to the enemy who were camped at the source of al-Ḥasī. Immediately, they struck camp, made a night march and arrived just before dawn.

The commander of the Egyptian army was Falak al-Dīn, the half-brother on the mother's side of al-'Ādil. Aslam had advised him to make a night march to get through the route and to seek the security of ascent to the uplands. Falak al-Dīn feared that, if he moved by night, something might befall the convoy because it would become scattered. He therefore announced that there would be no departure until dawn.

Meanwhile, as we have heard, the king of England, when this news reached him, did not believe it. He rode with a small party and the Bedouin until he reached the caravan, and then circled around it, disguised as an Arab. He saw them quietly resting, deep in sleep. He went back and called his men to horse. The surprise attack was close to dawn. He caught them unawares and charged with both his horse and foot. It was a brave and stout man who was able to mount his horse and save his live. Our troops fled towards the caravan, followed by the enemy, who, when they saw the caravan, turned from fighting our troops to pursuing the caravan. It was divided into three: one part made for Kerak with a body of [loyal] Bedouin and the troops of al-'Ādil, another went deep into the desert with another group of Bedouin, and the third was overwhelmed by the enemy, who drove off their camels and loads, and all that they had. It was a disastrous incident, the like of which had not befallen Islam for a very long time.

With the Egyptian troops were several persons of note, such as Ḥusayn the Surgeon, Falak al-Dīn, the sons of al-Jāwulī and others. On the enemy side 100 knights were killed, according to one report, or ten according to another. On the Muslim side none but the following notables were killed, the Chamberlain Yūsuf and the young son of al-Jāwulī, who both passed as martyrs to the mercy of God. One camel load belonging to the sultan was with Aybak al-'Azīzī, who fought to protect it and got away safely. For that reason his standing rose in the estimation of the sultan. In general our people were dispersed about the desert and threw away their goods. Happy was the man who escaped with his life. The enemy gathered up all the horses, camels, textiles and other goods that they could, and they compelled the cameleers to look after the camels, the muleteers to handle the mules and the grooms to tend the horses. They set out to return to their army with a vast quantity of booty, stopped at al-Khuwaylifa where they drew water and then travelled on to al-Ḥasī.

Someone who was a prisoner of theirs related that during that night, a rumour passed amongst them that the sultan's army had moved against them, so they abandoned the booty and fled, remaining at a distance for some time. When it became plain to them that the army had not caught up with them, they returned to the baggage. During their absence a number of Muslim prisoners had run away. The source of this information was one of them. I asked him, 'How many camels and horses did you estimate there to be?' He said that the camels numbered about 3,000 and the prisoners were 500. The number of horses was comparable to this. Several people gave the same report. This disaster took place during the morning of Tuesday 11 Jumādā II {23 June}.

The sultan heard the news on the evening of that day after evening prayer. **[215]** I was sitting in attendance on him. A young man, one of the stable orderlies, brought the news. No news came into the sultan's ken more grievous to his heart than this or more upsetting to his spirit. I began to calm and console him, although he was hardly capable of accepting any consolation. Central to the whole affair was that the Master of the Horse Aslam had advised them to gain the uplands and then camp, but they had not done so. He and his men had gone up. When therefore the surprise attack happened, he was on the uplands and none of the enemy reached him, nor did they know he was there. When the Muslims fled, the Frankish cavalry followed them, while their infantry remained to seize the stuff that the Muslims left behind. Realising that the cavalry were far away from the infantry, the Master of the Horse came down on the latter with the cavalry that he had. They caught them totally by surprise, killing many of them, and gained back some mounts, including the mule on which our messenger was riding.

The enemy then made for their camp, where they arrived on 16 Jumādā II {29 June}. It was a great day for them[1] on which the joy and rejoicing shown were beyond description. They returned their tents to the plain at Bayt Nūbā and their determination to march to Jerusalem was confirmed. Their spirits were greatly raised by their acquisition of the money and the camels that had been carrying provisions and supplies, coming from Egypt with the Egyptian army. They posted a detachment at[2] Lydda to guard the road for those who were bringing up provisions and sent Count Henry to Tyre, Tripoli and Acre to summon all the fighting men there to come up to Jerusalem.

When the sultan learnt what they were doing, he turned to the city walls, assigned sections of them to the emirs and commanded them to prepare the means to withstand a siege. He then started poisoning the water sources outside Jerusalem, destroying the pits and the cisterns, so that around Jerusalem there remained no drinkable water at all. He was extremely thorough in this. In the

1 B reads *aẓīm* 'great' instead of *'indahum* 'for them'. One would like to keep both.
2 B has *'alā* rather than *min*, 'from'.

area around Jerusalem there is no hope of digging a well with plentiful water[1] because it is a large mountain of solid rock. The sultan sent to muster his troops from all quarters and lands.

The arrival of al-Afḍal

When the agreement had been reached with al-'Ādil concerning his crossing into the lands of the Euphrates, the sultan sent to al-Afḍal to order him to return from his expedition into those areas. He had got as far as Aleppo and, when the sultan's order to return came to him, he returned broken in heart and troubled in his mind. He came tardily to Damascus and did not present himself for service with the sultan.

When the reports about the Franks became serious, the sultan sent for him and demanded his presence. He could delay no longer, so he set out with those eastern troops who had come to Damascus. He arrived on Thursday 19 Jumādā II[2] [2 July]. When the sultan met him at al-'Āzariyya, the sultan dismounted to greet him to mend his feelings and enhance his authority. Al-Afḍal then left, with his brothers al-Ẓāfir and Quṭb al-Dīn under his command, to operate against the enemy around Jerusalem.

[216] The reason why the enemy withdrew to their own territory

On the eve of Thursday 19 Jumādā II [2 July] the sultan summoned the emirs to him. With great difficulty the Emir Abū'l-Hayjā' came and had a stool to sit on while in the presence of the sultan. Al-Mashṭūb with all the Asadiyya [emirs] and the whole complement of [other] emirs came before him. The sultan commanded me to address them to encourage them in the Jihad. I delivered whatever words God brought to my mind on that subject. For example I said, 'When the Prophet was in a critical situation, the Companions swore to be true even unto death when they faced the enemy. It is right for us more than for others to follow his pattern. The best thing we can do is to assemble at the Dome of the Rock and swear to support one another unto death. Perhaps through the blessedness of this purpose our enemy will be repelled.' All approved this and agreed to do it.

After being silent for a time, lost in thought, while those present held their peace and hardly dared to move[3] the sultan then began to speak. 'Praise be to

1 B has *mā' ma'īn*.
2 If the 11th was a Tuesday (see above), this Thursday should be the 20th. Several dates in the following pages are mutually irreconcilable.
3 Literally, 'as though there were birds on their heads'.

God and blessings on the Prophet of God,' he said, 'Know that today you are the army of Islam and its bulwark, as you are aware that the blood of the Muslims, their property and their offspring depend on your protection. There are no Muslims who can face the enemy but you.[1] If you turn your reins away, which God forbid, they will roll up these lands *as one rolls up a scroll*.[2] This is your responsibility, for you are the ones who took on this task and have been supported by public treasury monies. The Muslims in all lands depend on you. My blessings go with you.' Sayf al-Dīn al-Mashṭūb undertook to reply and said, 'We are your mamlukes and your slaves. You are the one who has shown us favour and raised us high, made us powerful and enriched us with your bounty. We have nothing but our lives and they are at your feet. By God, not one of us will give up fighting for you till he dies.' All responded in similar fashion and the sultan's heart was greatly cheered by this session and his spirits rose. He provided them with a meal and then they departed.

Thursday came to an end with the most intense preparation and activity. When it was time for the late evening prayer, they gathered to wait on the sultan as was normal practice and we stayed conversing until a good part of the night had past, but he was not at ease as he normally was. We prayed the prayer, which was the general signal to disperse. After prayer, we started to leave but he called me over. I took my seat before him and he said to me, 'Do you know what has happened?' I replied, 'What has happened?' He went on, 'Abū'l-Hayjā' sent to me today, saying, "The mamlukes and the emirs as a body have met with me today and criticised us for agreeing with you to make preparations for a siege. They said that this is not the best course and they fear that, when they are besieged, they will suffer what happened to those in Acre and then all the lands of Islam will be lost. The right plan is to meet in pitched battle. If God decrees **[217]** that we defeat them, we will gain all their remaining territory. In the other eventuality, our forces will survive although Jerusalem will go, but the lands of Islam have been sustained[3] by their armies for a while without Jerusalem."' Now, towards Jerusalem the sultan felt a great concern that would move mountains[4] and he was distressed by this communication. I remained in attendance upon him that night, a night wholly spent on the concerns of the Holy War. Part of their communication had been, 'If you want us, then you or one of your family should be with us, around whom we may unite, for otherwise the Kurds will not submit to the Turks nor the Turks to the Kurds.' In the end it was decided that one of his family, Majd

---

1 Reading with B: *laysa la-hu min al-muslimīn man yalqā-hu*.

2 Cf. Koran xxi, 104.

3 Reading *inḥafaẓat* as in the quoted passage in *Rawḍ*, ii, p. 199. Cf. *inḥafaẓa al-islām* in *RHC Or* iii, p. 313. *Nawādir* reads *inkhafaḍat* and B *inkhaṭafat*, with no clear meaning.

4 Literally 'which mountains cannot bear'. This is the reading of *Nawādir* and also of B. *RHC Or*, p. 313, read *al-khayāl* rather than *al-jibāl*, hence the translation in Wilson, *Saladin*, p. 349: 'that almost surpasses imagination'.

al-Dīn ibn Farrūkhshāh, the lord of Baalbek, should remain [in Jerusalem]. He had been tempted to remain himself, but then his better sense rejected that because of the risk to Islam it involved.

When dawn drew near, I expressed concern for him and told him to rest for a while in the hope that he would get a little sleep. I left and returned to my own residence. Hardly had I arrived before the muezzin gave the call to prayer. I applied myself to my ablutions and had only just finished when dawn broke. Normally I would perform the dawn prayer with the sultan, so I made my way to him, just as he was renewing his ablutions. We prayed together and then I said, 'I have had a thought which I would like to propose.' He gave his assent, so I went on, 'Your lordship is deeply worried and greatly exercised in the matter that he has taken upon himself. Earthly means have failed. Now it is proper to have recourse to God. This is Friday, the most blessed day of the week, during which prayers are answered, as the authentic Traditions of the Prophet have it. We are in the most blessed place that we could be in on this day. Let the sultan make his ablutions for the congregational Friday prayer and bestow some alms secretly, so that they are not known to be from you, and perform two ritual sequences[1] between the call to prayer and the commencement of the service, during which you commune privately with your Lord and entrust the management of your enterprise to Him, confessing your inability to fulfil what you have embarked upon. Perhaps God will take pity on you and answer your petition.' The sultan held to an admirable creed and was a total believer, who faced the obligations of the Holy Law with complete obedience and acceptance. We parted and then, when it was time for the Friday prayer, I prayed alongside him in the Aqsa Mosque. He performed two ritual sequences and I saw him prostrate himself and say some words, while his tears were falling on to his prayer rug. The Friday prayer was then completed with proper ceremony.

On the evening of that day, while we were in attendance as normal, a report arrived from Jūrdīk, who was with the advanced detachment, in which he said, 'The enemy all mounted up, stood in the field on horseback and then returned to their tents. We have sent spies to discover what they are up to.' Early morning on Saturday [4 July] another despatch came, reporting that our spies had returned and reported that the enemy had been in dispute about whether to march up to Jerusalem or depart for their own territory. The French were for going up to Jerusalem, saying, 'The only reason we have come from our countries is Jerusalem. We shall not return without it.' However, the king of England said, 'The water sources of this place have been poisoned. All around no water remains at all. Where will we drink from?' 'From the spring at

---

[1] That is, two *rak'as*, each of which consists of a bowing at the waist followed by two full prostrations.

Taqū'',[1] they replied. This place is about a league from Jerusalem. The king said, 'How [**218**] can we go to get water?' They said, 'We shall divide into two. One group will ride to the source of water with the animals and the other will remain in position before the city. There will be one watering a day.' 'In that case,' stated the king, 'the [Muslim] army in the field will overwhelm the group that goes with the animals, the troops in the city will make a sortie against those that stay behind and Christendom will be lost.' The discussion ended with a decision to nominate 300 arbitrators from amongst their notables. The 300 nominated twelve from their number and then the twelve selected three. They waited overnight for the decision of the three and whatever they ordered would be done. In the morning their decision was for departure and no disagreement was possible.

Early morning on 21 Jumādā II [4 July] they set out in the direction of Ramla, retreating the way they had come. Their troops, bristling with weapons, held their ground until there remained only the traces of where their camp had been and then they moved down to Ramla. Many reports of this came in and the sultan rode out with his troops. This was a day of delight and rejoicing, but the sultan feared an attack on Egypt because of the camels and other pack-animals they had acquired. The king of England had talked in such terms several times.

Count Henry's mission

When the sultan's mind was relieved by the departure of the enemy, he summoned Count Henry's envoy to hear what mission he came on. Having appeared before the sultan and been given permission to deliver his message, he said, 'Count Henry says the following, "The king of England has bestowed on me the lands of the coastal plain, which are now mine. Restore to me my lands so that I may make peace with you and be one of your sons."' The sultan became furiously angry, almost struck him and had him removed. He then asked to be allowed to appear to say a few more words. This was granted and he said, speaking for Count Henry, 'My lands are in your hands. Which of them will you give me?' The sultan dismissed him with an angry rebuke.

When it was Monday[2] 23 Jumādā II [6 July], he called the envoy again and gave this answer: 'Let our discussion be about Tyre and Acre, as was agreed with the marquis.' Later on the Ḥajjī Yūsuf, al-Mashṭūb's man, came from the Franks and reported that the king of England had summoned him and Count Henry, cleared the chamber and said to him, 'Tell your master that we, you and we together, are ruined. Our best course is to stop the bloodshed. You ought

1 *Nawādir* has Naqū'. It is Biblical Tekoah, a village about 12 km south of Jerusalem.
2 B supplies the day of the week.

not to believe that this is from any weakness of mine. No, it is for the good of all. Let al-Mashṭūb be the mediator between us and the sultan and not be deceived by our withdrawal. The ram backs away to charge.' The king called two men to go with the Ḥajjī to hear what al-Mashṭūb had to say. The ostensible aim was to discuss the freeing of Bahā' al-Dīn Qarāqūsh, but in reality it was to have peace talks. The Ḥajjī told us that the enemy had marched from Ramla and were making for Jaffa and that they were extremely weak and incapable of attacking any place. **[219]** Al-Mashṭūb was asked to come from Nablus to hear the communication, which he did. The answer was, 'Count Henry has been given Acre. We will make peace with him recognising what he has. Let him leave us to negotiate with the king of England over the remaining territories.'

A battle that took place before Acre

The sultan had stationed a force facing Acre because he feared that the enemy might make forays into the adjacent regions. When it was Sunday 22 Jumādā II [5 July], the enemy did march out of Acre to raid the towns and the countryside that were nearby. Our ambushes surprised them in several places, for our troops were aware of their foray. They ambushed them and captured or killed several. To God be the praise.

The return of their envoy to discuss peace

On Thursday 26 Jumādā II[1] [9 July] their envoy returned with the Ḥajjī Yūsuf, who had been given a message to deliver in the presence of their man, which was, 'The king, that is the king of England, says that he desires your love and friendship. He does not wish to be a pharoah ruling the earth and he does not think that of you. "It is not right," he says, "for you to ruin all the Muslims, nor for me to ruin all the Franks. Consider my nephew, Count Henry, whom I have made ruler of these lands. I hand him and his troops over to your authority. If you were to summon them [for a campaign] to the east, they would hear and obey. Many monks and men of religion have asked you for churches and you have not grudged them what they asked. Now I ask you for a church. Those matters which annoyed you in the negotiations with al-'Ādil I have declared

1 At this point *Nawādir* reads Friday 26 Jumādā II, as does B. This date would correspond to 9 July, a Thursday. Note too that *Nawādir*, p. 220, gives a date Friday 27 Jumādā II.

that I give them up. I have renounced them. Were you to give me a whip or a water-skin,[1] I would accept it and kiss it.'"

When the sultan had heard this message, he gathered his advisers and councillors and asked them what the reply to this message should be. There was not one who did not advise conciliation and a conclusion of peace because of the fatigue, exhaustion and burden of debts from which the Muslims suffered. It was agreed to make this response: 'If you make this sort of overture to us, goodwill cannot be met with other than goodwill. Your nephew will be to me like one of my sons. You shall hear how well I shall treat him. I will bestow on him the greatest of churches, the Holy Sepulchre, and the rest of the lands we shall divide. The coastal plain that is in your hands shall remain so and the upland castles that are in our hands shall remain ours. What is between the two regions shall be in condominium. **[220]** Ascalon and what is beyond shall be left in ruins, neither ours nor yours. If you want its villages, let them be yours. What I have disliked is discussion about Ascalon.' The envoy departed well satisfied. That was on the day after his arrival, on 27[2] Jumādā II [10 July]. The news came that they, after the return of their envoy, were setting out for Ascalon, with the intention of marching to Egypt.

On Friday 27 Jumādā II [10 July] an envoy came from Quṭb al-Dīn[3] ibn Qilij Arslān, whose message was, 'The Pope has come to Constantinople with a great multitude the number of which God alone knows.' The envoy added, 'I have killed twelve knights on the road,' and then, speaking [for his principal], 'Command someone to come to take over my lands, for I am incapable of defending them.' The sultan did not believe this news and paid no attention to it.

The return of the Frank's envoy a third time

The evening of Sunday 29 Jumādā II [12 July] al-Mashṭūb's man, the Ḥajjī, came, accompanied by Geoffrey, the king's envoy. He said, 'The king is

1 There are problems here. This is the apparent meaning of the text in *Nawādir*, which reads m.q.r.'a and q.r.ba. This text is repeated when quoted in *Rawḍ*, ii, p. 199. B replaces the second word with *qarya*, 'village', which might suggest that the first word should be read as *maqra'a*, 'field of marrows'. How then would one understand 'and kiss them'? *RHC Or*, p. 318, read *mazra'a wa-qarya*, translating the passage as 'Si vous me donniez une ferme ou un village.' However, this text continues (with what authority I do not know) with *qabiltu-hā wa-qābaltu-hā*, translated as 'je l'accepterais avec plaisir et je vous en rendrais l'equivalent.' Wilson, *Saladin*, p. 355, has 'Will you not, then, give me a barren spot, and the ruin of its shrine [reading *khirba*?].' 'Barren spot' is perhaps derived from another sense of the root *q.r.'*, i.e., 'to be bald'.

2 *Nawādir* has 22 Jumādā II, as does B, which must be an error.

3 Qutb al-Dīn Malikshāh, the eldest son of the Seljukid sultan Qilij Arslān and son-in-law of Saladin. He died in 1195.

grateful for the sultan's favours and has said, "What I request from you is that we should have twenty persons in the citadel of Jerusalem and that the local Christians and the Franks who live in the city should not be harrassed. As for the rest of the land, we have the coastal plain and the lowlands and you have the hill country."' The envoy told us on his own initiative the following helpful information: 'They have given up all talk of Jerusalem apart from being allowed to make pilgrimage. What they are proposing is only a ploy. They are eager for peace and it is essential for the king of England to return to his own country.'

He stayed during Monday the last day of the month [13 July] and on this occasion he had with him two falcons as a gift for the sultan. The latter summoned every one of his emirs and consulted them about what answer to make to this communication. The answer that was arrived at finally was 'You have no say at all in Jerusalem apart from a pilgrimage visit,' to which the envoy replied, 'But the pilgrims are to have nothing to pay.' From these words it was understood that he agreed. Our answer continued, 'As far as territory is concerned, Ascalon and what is beyond must be demolished.' The envoy said, 'The king has spent vast sums on the walls there,' so al-Mashṭūb asked the sultan to make Ascalon's fields and villages a recompense for his losses. The sultan agreed to that, but stipulated that Dārūm and other places should be demolished and their lands shared half-and-half. As for the rest of the country, they should have from Jaffa to Tyre, the towns and their districts, and if there was ever any dispute about a village it was to be shared equally. Such was the response to his mission.

The envoy left on Tuesday 1 Rajab [14 July] in the company of the Ḥajjī Yūsuf, having asked for an emissary of high standing whose oath could be taken if all the terms were settled. However, the sultan put off sending such an emissary until the peace terms were fully agreed, but he dispatched a handsome gift in response to theirs. In the matter of gifts he was not to be outdone.

[221] The return of their envoy

When a good part of the night was already over, the envoy came back during the eve of 3 Rajab [16 July]. The Ḥajjī presented himself during the night and told the sultan this news. Early in the morning of Thursday 3 Rajab [16 July] their envoy was given an audience and delivered his message, which was, 'The king humbly requests you to leave him these three places intact. What importance do they have in the light of your power and greatness? The only reason for his repeated demands is that the Franks have not countenanced their demolition. The king himself has totally given up Jerusalem and only asks that there should be monks and priests in the Holy Sepulchre. Will you not leave him these lands and let there be a general peace? The Franks will keep what they now hold from Dārūm to Antioch and what you hold will be secure, the situation will be resolved and he can depart. If peace is not concluded, the Franks will not allow him to depart and he cannot gainsay them.' Just look at this guile in eliciting what one wants by soft words at one moment and by harsh ones at the next! He was obliged to leave and this is how he operates despite this obligation! We pray to God to keep the Muslims safe from his evil, for they had never been tried by anyone more devious or more bold.

Having heard this message, the sultan summoned his emirs and councillors of state and asked them what his reply should be. The net result of their advice was the following reply: 'With the people at Antioch we are in negotiation and our envoys are with them. If they come back with what we want, we shall include them in the peace, but if not, we will not. As for the lands which he asks us for, the Muslims will never consent to hand them over to him, but in any case they are not important. Let the king accept Lydda on the plain in return for what he has spent on Ascalon's walls.' He sent the envoy off on the morning of Friday 4 Rajab [17 July].

The arrival of his son, al-Ẓāhir, lord of Aleppo

When it was Saturday 5 Rajab [18 July], his son, al-Ẓāhir, arrived, for whom he had great love and special affection because of the signs of his being blest by good fortune and for the qualities of competence and the promising indications of kingship that he saw in him. The sultan went out to meet him, which he did beyond al-'Āzariyya, because he came by the Jordan valley. When they met the sultan dismounted and received him with honour and respect, embraced and kissed him between the eyes. He lodged in the [former] Hospitallers' residence.

Account of the envoys's fourth mission

When it was Sunday 6 Rajab[1] [19 July], the Ḥajjī Yūsuf arrived alone. He reported that the king had said to him, 'It is impossible for us to demolish one stone of Ascalon. Such a thing shall not be spoken of us in the land. The boundaries of these lands are well known and there is no dispute **[222]** about them.' At that point the sultan made preparations to march out towards the enemy, to show his strength and determination to meet in battle.

1 *Nawādir* and B have 7 Rajab, surely an error.

The sultan takes the field

On 10 Rajab [23 July] the sultan heard that the Franks had set out for Beirut. He therefore left Jerusalem and stopped at a place called al-Jīb. Al-'Ādil had arrived back from the lands around the Euphrates during the morning of Friday 11 Rajab [24 July]. He had entered the Dome of the Rock, prayed there and then set out to follow the sultan. The latter moved from al-Jīb to Bayt Nūbā. He sent to the troops in Jerusalem, urging them to march out to join him. I caught up with the sultan at Bayt Nūbā, for I had stayed behind the night he made his preparations to leave.

On Sunday 13 Rajab [26 July] he departed for Ramla and camped there around midday on some high ground between Ramla and Lydda, remaining there the rest of that day. When it was Monday 14 Rajab [27 July], he rode out with a light force till he came to Yāzūr and Bayt Dajan,[1] looked out towards Jaffa and then returned to his camp, where he remained for the rest of the day. He gathered his councillors and consulted them about laying siege to Jaffa. Their joint opinion was that that should be done.

Account of the siege of Jaffa

When it was the morning of Tuesday 15 Rajab [28 July], the sultan set out for Jaffa and came to camp there at midday. He drew up his army as right wing, left wing and centre. The extremes of the right and left wings rested on the shore, while the sultan was in the middle. The commander of the right wing was his son al-Ẓāhir and that of the left was his brother al-'Ādil and the main forces lay between them.

On 16 Rajab [29 July] our men began the assault, disdainfully belittling the task involved. The sultan arranged the troops in battle order and brought up the trebuchets and set them up before the weakest place in the walls near the East Gate. During the day he sat on the remnant of a wall opposite the trebuchets. He set the sappers to work on the wall, shouts were raised and great was the commotion. The assault was pressed hard and the sappers mined from north of the East Gate to the corner along the curtain wall. The Muslims had already demolished that part during the previous siege and the Franks had rebuilt it. The sappers made progress with the mine and were soon inside it, so our people had no doubt that the place would be taken that very day.

Meanwhile the enemy forces were growing. The king had previously gone to Beirut and that was what encouraged **[223]** the sultan to besiege Jaffa. The end of the day saw fierce fighting from which the enemy suffered much, but

---

1 At the half-way point between Jaffa and Ramla.

they showed such firm and determined resistance as undermined the morale of our men. The sappers had meanwhile succeeded with their mining but when it was near to completion, the enemy started to make it collapse on them. They caused it to cave in at several places. The miners were fearful and many came out. Our men lost enthusiasm for the fight and realised that to take the town was [after all] difficult and required more effort. The sultan showed suitable determination and ordered the sappers to begin mining along the rest of the curtain wall from the tower to the gate and he ordered the trebuchets to be sited opposite the wall that was already mined, which was done.

The sultan remained there that night until about a third of it had passed and then he returned to where the baggage-train was, some way from the town on a hill over against it. When morning came two trebuchets had been erected and a third was set up during the rest of that day. The sultan rose eager for the fight and the assault, but found nothing but slackness among the troops because of the setting up of the trebuchets and their belief that the trebuchets would only be effective after some days. When the sultan learnt that the men were slacking and shirking, he urged them to attack and the fighting became intense and fierce. They made the enemy taste its bitterness and the town was on the point of falling. In our hearts we were sure of it and eager to bring it about. The enemy grew weak, although many of the Muslims were wounded by arrows and bolts from the town. Among them was the Chamberlain Abū Bakr, Khutlukh, the governor of Baalbek, who was hit in the eye, Ṭughril al-Tājī, Sarāsunqur, wounded in the face (the latter two amongst the sultan's favoured mamlukes), Ayāz and[1] Jarkas, one of the senior mamlukes, who was wounded in the hand.

When the enemy saw what had befallen them, they sent two emissaries, a local Christian and a Frank, to ask for and discuss terms. The sultan demanded the arrangement made for Jerusalem and the same ransom tarif. They agreed to this, but stipulated that they should be given until Saturday, that is, 19 Rajab [1 August]. The terms agreed would then become effective, unless any help came to them. The sultan, however, refused any respite, so the envoys went back but later returned again to ask him for this respite. He again refused and meanwhile our men continued the fight half-heartedly because of the to-and-fro of the envoys, content to take things easy, as is normal. The sultan ordered the sappers to stuff the mines [with combustibles] after they had been completed.[2] This was done and then it was set on fire. Part of the curtain wall collapsed. The enemy had realised that the mine had been set on fire and knew that that part of the wall would fall, so they fetched huge timbers and got them ready behind that spot. When that section fell, they lit fires, which prevented any entry at the breach. On the orders of the sultan, our men attacked and pressed

1 B adds this expected 'and' between the two names.
2 Correcting the reading in *Nawādir* to *intihā'i-hā*.

the enemy closely. My God, what fighting men they are! How strong they are and how great their courage! Despite everything, they had not closed any gate of the town and they continued to fight outside the gates. The battle remained at its most fierce, until nightfall separated the two sides. Nothing was achieved against the town during that time after the mines had been set on fire along the rest of the curtain wall. The sultan was very worried by this and his thoughts were very troubled, while he regretted that he had not accepted their terms. He passed that night [**224**] in his encampment, having decided that he would set up a full five trebuchets to pound the curtain wall that was weak because of the mines, the fires and the counter-mining on the enemy's side.

The conquest of Jaffa, that is, the beginning of the second conquest, and the events that happened there

By the morning of Friday 18 Rajab [31 July] the trebuchets were set up and the rocks for them gathered from the river beds and distant places because of the lack of stones on the spot and they kept up a pounding of the weakened curtain wall. The sultan and his son al-Ẓāhir led a strong assault. The troops of al-'Ādil also made an assault on the left wing, although he himself was ill. Shouts were raised, drums were beaten and trumpets brayed, while the trebuchets hurled their missiles and the enemy were met by death and destruction from every direction. Our sappers intensified their efforts to set fire to the mines and hardly had two hours of daylight passed before the curtain wall collapsed. Its collapse was like the clap of doom and our men called out, 'Ah, the wall has fallen!' There was no-one, even of the least faith, who did not advance to the attack and there was not an enemy heart that did not tremble and shake. They, nevertheless, were more fierce and determined in the fight and more eager for and devoted to death. When the curtain wall fell, a cloud of dust and smoke went up and darkened the sky. The light of the day was blotted out. Nobody dared to enter the breach, fearing to confront the fire. When the darkness cleared, spear-points had replaced the walls and lances had blocked the breach. Even looks could not penetrate. The endurance and steadfastness of the enemy and the soundness of their operations seen by our men greatly impressed them. I witnessed two men on the wall's walk-way who were stopping those who would climb up from the breach. One of them was hit by a trebuchet missile which knocked him down inside. His companion took his place, ready to face the same sort of fate, faster than one could wink, so that only a sharp-eyed man could tell there was any difference.[1]

[1] B has a variation: ... *li-mithl dhālika fa-laḥiqa-hu bi-asra' min* ... etc. This supports the translation of Wilson, *Saladin*, p. 365, which points up the speed of the two fatalities rather than of the replacement itself. That does not fit the end of the sentence so well.

When the enemy had seen what their situation was reduced to, they sent two emissaries to the sultan to request terms of surrender. The sultan said, 'A horseman for a horseman, a turcopole for his equivalent and a foot-soldier for a foot-soldier. For any that cannot manage this the Jerusalem tarif applies.' The emissary looked and saw the battle for the breach fiercer than a blazing fire. He asked the sultan to stop the battle until he returned, but the sultan said, 'I cannot hold the Muslims back from this business, but go in to your comrades and tell them that they should retire to the citadel and leave my men a free hand in the town. There is no way of defending it any more.' The emissary returned with this message and the enemy withdrew into the Jaffa citadel, after several had been killed by mistake. Our troops made a victorious entry into the town and plundered many goods, a lot of crops, household furnishings and the remnants of the goods that had been plundered from **[225]** the Egyptian caravan. Terms were agreed in the manner the sultan laid down.

When it was Friday evening [31 July], a letter came to the sultan from Qaymāz al-Najmī, who was in the Jordan valley region[1] to protect it from the enemy forces that were in Acre, in which he reported that, when the king of England heard the news from Jaffa, he gave up his plan to go to Beirut and set out to return to Jaffa. The sultan was even more determined to complete the business and take over the citadel. I was one who did not think that granting terms was a good idea, for their capture had been imminent and it had been some time since our troops had won from the enemy any place ripe for plunder on which the sultan could let them loose. To take them by force of arms would have been something to excite the troops' zeal. However, the guarantees were given and terms agreed. Afterwards I was one of those who urged that the enemy be ejected from the citadel and it be taken over, fearing the arrival of a relief force. The sultan was also very eager, but our men on account of their fatigue were loathe to carry out his orders. Their armour,[2] the severe heat and the smoke from the fire had exhausted them, so that they had no strength left to move.

The sultan stayed on, trying to encourage them, until quite late at night, but, when he saw how tired the men were, he mounted up and rode to his tent by the baggage-train. We went with him and, after he had retired to his tent, I went to mine in an anxious state that kept me from sleep. As dawn approached we heard the bray of Frankish trumpets and realised that a relief force had arrived. The sultan summoned me immediately and said, 'Without a doubt a relief force has arrived by sea. We have troops on the shore who will prevent them from landing. The best thing now is for you to go to al-Ẓāhir and tell him to take up a position outside the South Gate. You, with those you think fit, will enter the

---

1 Reading *ṭaraf* with B, rather than *ṭarīq* (route).

2 In Arabic: *al-ḥadīd*, 'iron'. *RHC Or*, p. 328, interprets it as 'blessures', as does Wilson, *Saladin*, p. 366, 'their wounds'.

citadel and get their men out. Take possession of the money and weapons there and you yourself write a list of it all for al-Ẓāhir outside the town and he will get it conveyed to us.' To strengthen my hand in this task he sent with me 'Izz al-Dīn Jūrdīk, 'Alam al-Dīn Qayṣar and Dirbās al-Mihrānī. I set off straightaway, also taking with me Shams al-Dīn, the clerk of the Treasury, and came to his son al-Ẓāhir's position. He was asleep in his bivouac tent on a rise near the sea with our advance guard and wearing his quilted brigandine,[1] that is, in armour. May God not leave unrewarded their deeds done to bring victory to Islam! I woke him up and he rose with sleep still in his eyes. I went with him, while he was questioning me about the message from the sultan, until he took up his position as ordered. Then we entered Jaffa and, coming to the citadel, ordered the Franks to leave. They accepted the order and prepared to leave.

[226] How the citadel remained in enemy hands

This came about on the morning of Saturday 19 Rajab [1 August]. After they agreed to leave, 'Izz al-Dīn Jūrdīk said, 'None of them ought to come out until our men have left the town, for fear that they might lay hands on them.' Greed had already brought our troops into the town and 'Izz al-Dīn began to beat them soundly and drive them out, but there was no check on how numerous they were and they were not confined to one place. How was it possible to get them out! This situation lasted until the day was well advanced. I was criticising him but he did not change his plan, though time was passing. When I saw that no time was left, I said to him, 'Their relief force has arrived. It is best to hurry to get these men out. The sultan charged me to do that.' When he learnt the reason for my eagerness, he agreed to move them out and we went to the gate of the citadel which is close to the city gate where al-Ẓāhir was posted. We brought out forty-seven men with their horses, took down their particulars and sent them off.

After this group had emerged, the morale of the remainder stiffened and they resolved to hold out. The reason why those others had left was that they considered the ships that had come too few and they thought that there was no help for them there. They did not know, however, that the king of England was with that force. They also saw that they delayed disembarking until the day was far gone and they themselves were fearful of resisting, only to be taken and killed, so some of them did leave the citadel. Then later, the relieving force was strengthened and reached thirty-five ships. The spirits of those left in the citadel rose high and they showed signs and indications of resistance. One of

[1] In Arabic: *kazāghand*.

their number came out and told me that there was some confusion about what they intended to do. They took their shields and mantelets and climbed on to the walls. The citadel was of recent construction and not yet battlemented.

When I saw that the situation had come to this, I descended from the rise on which I was standing adjacent to the entrance of the citadel and I said to 'Izz al-Dīn, who was standing with his own troop below the rise alongside a detachment of soldiers, 'Take care. The enemy have changed their minds.' It was only just a short time, while I went outside the town to wait upon the sultan's son al-Ẓāhir, before the enemy had mounted their horses and charged out from the citadel as one man. They forced our soldiers out of the town. Our men were crowded together at the city gate with the result that many of them were close to meeting their doom. Some of them, the dregs of the army, remained in one of the churches, busy doing unacceptable things. The enemy pounced on them and slew them or took them prisoner.

Al-Ẓāhir[1] sent me to the sultan and I told him of the situation. He ordered the herald to summon the troops, the drum was beaten to call to arms and people rushed to battle from every direction. They charged into the town and confined the enemy, who were now convinced that they were lost, in the citadel. They deplored the slowness of the relief's disembarking and were very frightened. They sent their patriarch and the castellan,[2] who was of impressive build, as two emissaries **[227]** to the sultan, to seek pardon for what had occurred and to ask for the original terms. The envoys went to the sultan while the battle was raging.

The reason why the relief force refrained from landing was that they saw the town crammed with the Muslims' banners and men and they feared that the citadel might already have been taken. The sea prevented their hearing the shouts that came from everywhere and the great commotion and cries of 'There is no god but God' and 'God is great'. When those in the citadel saw how fierce the assault was and that the relief refrained from landing although they were now numerous, for the total had reached fifty-five ships, of which fifteen were galleys including the king's galley, they realised that those in the relief force imagined that the town had already been taken. One of the garrison entrusted his life to the Messiah and leapt from the citadel to the harbour side, which was sand and therefore did not injure him at all. He then ran at full speed to the sea. A galley put in for him and took him to the king's galley, where he told his story. Persuaded that the citadel was still in his men's hands, the king of England hastened to gain the shore. The first galley to deliver its men on land

---

1 I have omitted the designation of al-Ẓāhir as 'the sultan', which is in *Nawādir* and in B at this point. Whether it comes from the author or from a copyist, it reflects a view of al-Ẓāhir's position in Aleppo after Saladin's death.

2 The recently created patriarch was Ralph, bishop of Bethlehem, and the castellan was Aubrey of Rheims, see Nicholson, *Chronicle*, pp. 351-355.

was his. He was red-haired, his tunic was red and his banner was red, as was his device. In only a short time all the men from the galleys had disembarked in the harbour. All this went on before my eyes.

They then charged the Muslims, who withdrew before them and were cleared out of the harbour. I was on horseback so I galloped as far as the sultan and gave him this news. The two envoys were with him and he had just taken his pen in his hand to write their guarantee of safe-conduct. I whispered in his ear what had happened, so he stopped writing and kept them busy in conversation. Hardly a moment later the Muslims came fleeing towards the sultan, who shouted to those about him and all mounted their horses. He seized the envoys and ordered the baggage-train and the camp markets to move back to Yāzūr. All departed, but a vast amount of baggage was abandoned by them, some of the stuff that they had plundered from Jaffa but were unable to carry. The baggage-train reached [its new position], while the sultan stayed with a lightly equipped force and spent the night there. The king of England came to where the sultan had been when tightening the siege of Jaffa and ordered the defenders of the citadel to come out to join him. The mass of men with him was now large. Several of the mamlukes got to meet him and there was much conversation and merriment between them.

The renewal of peace talks

The king then asked for the Chamberlain Abū Bakr al-ʻĀdilī, who came to his presence along with Aybak al-ʻAzīzī, Sunqur al-Mashṭūb and others. He had made friends with several of the elite mamlukes and had knighted some of them. He was on very good terms with them as they met with him on numerous occasions. He had also made friends with several of the emirs, such as Badr al-Dīn Dildirim. When the group mentioned came before him, he was both serious and light-hearted. One of the things he said was, 'This sultan of yours is a great man. Islam has no greater or mightier prince on earth than him. How is it he departed merely because I had arrived? By God, I had not put on my breastplate and was not ready for anything. On my feet I only had sea boots. [**228**] How come he withdrew?' Then he said, 'By God, he is great. By God, I did not imagine that he could take Jaffa in two months. How did he take it in two days?' To Abū Bakr he said, 'Greet the sultan for me and say, "For God's sake grant me what I ask for to make peace. This is a matter that must have an end. My lands over the sea have been ruined. For this to go on is no good for us nor for you."' They took their leave of him and Abū Bakr came to the sultan to inform him of what had been said. That was towards the very end of Saturday 19 Rajab [1 August].

When the sultan had heard this, he gathered his councillors and the result was this reply: 'You originally asked for peace on certain terms. What was at dispute was Jaffa and Ascalon. But now this town of Jaffa has been laid to waste, so you will have from Caesarea to Tyre.' Abū Bakr went to the king and told him what had been said. The king sent him back with a Frankish envoy and the following message from himself: 'The Frankish custom is that when someone gives another some land, he becomes his vassal and servant. I ask you for these two towns, Jaffa and Ascalon, and their troops will be for ever at your service. Whenever you need me, I shall come to you as fast as possible and I shall serve you as you know how I can.' The sultan's answer to this was, 'Since you have opened this approach, I agree with you that we should divide these two towns into two lots, one of them for you, that is Jaffa and what is to the south of it, and the other for me, that is Ascalon and what is beyond to the south.'

The two envoys departed and the sultan left to go to the baggage-train in the encampment at Yāzūr. He posted the advanced units there and ordered the demolition of the place and of Bayt Dajan. He gave the sappers that job, guarded by the advanced units, and he himself travelled to Ramla, where he made camp on Sunday 20 Rajab [2 August]. The Frankish emissary came back with the Chamberlain Abū Bakr and the sultan ordered his honourable and generous reception. His message contained thanks from the king for the grant of Jaffa and a renewed request for Ascalon. Furthermore, 'If peace comes about in the next six days, he will leave for home, but if not, he will need to winter here.' The sultan gave an immediate answer and said, 'There is no way for us to cede Ascalon. However, his wintering in these lands cannot be avoided, because he has become master of them. He knows that when he goes away, they will necessarily be seized, and the same if he stays, God willing. If it is easy for him to winter here and to be far from his family and homeland, two months' travelling time away, when he is a young man in the flower of his youth and at a time when he seeks his pleasures, how easy is it for me to spend a winter, a summer, then a winter and another summer in the middle of my own lands, surrounded by my sons and my family, when whatever and whoever I want can come to me. I am an old man and I do not desire worldly pleasures. I have had my fill of them and have renounced them. In addition, the army that is with me during the winter is different from that which is with me in the summer. I also believe that I am engaged in the greatest service to God and I will continue in the same way until God bestows victory on whomsoever He wishes.'

When the envoy heard this, he asked to meet with al-'Ādil and was allowed to do that, so came to him in his tent. He had retired, because of an illness that had come upon him, to a place called Mār Ṣamwīl.[1] The envoy came to him with a small retinue.

The sultan then heard [**229**] that enemy troops had left Acre aiming to come to Jaffa to bring help. He summoned his advisers and held a council to discuss attacking them. The general opinion was that they should attack them, send the baggage-train away to the Uplands and move against them with a mobile force. If an opportunity presented itself, they should seize it, otherwise they should withdraw from them. This was preferable to waiting until the enemy's forces were concentrated and we would retire to the Uplands in the fashion of a defeated army. For the present, if we retired, it would be in a tactical fashion. The sultan ordered the baggage-train to leave for the Uplands on the evening of Monday 11 Rajab [3 August].

He himself set out without the baggage-train on the Tuesday morning [14 August] and stopped at al-'Awjā'. A report came to him that the enemy troops had arrived at and entered Caesarea, and that it had no further plans. He also heard that the king of England had camped outside Jaffa with a small band and a few tents. It occurred to him to seize this opportunity to make a surprise attack on his tents and win some advantage over them. He decided on that and set out in the first part of the night with Bedouin guides preceding him. They crossed the open country and came by the morning upon the enemy's tents. He found them to be few, about ten in number. The sultan was filled with eager anticipation and his men charged them as one man, but the enemy stood firm and did not move from their positions. Like dogs of war they snarled, willing to fight to the death. Our troops were frightened of them, dumbfounded by their steadfastness, and surrounded them in a single ring.

One who was present related to me, for I had moved back with the baggage-train and did not witness this battle, thank God, because of an indisposition, that the number of their cavalry was estimated at the most as seventeen and at the least as nine and their foot were less than 1,000. Some said 300 and others more than that. The sultan was greatly annoyed at this and personally went around the divisions urging them to attack and promising them good rewards if they would. Nobody responded to his appeal apart from his son al-Ẓāhir, for he got ready to charge but the sultan stopped him. I have heard that al-Janāḥ, al-Mashṭūb's brother, said to the sultan, 'Your mamlukes who beat people the day Jaffa fell and took their booty from them, tell them to charge.' At heart the troops were put out by the sultan's having made terms for Jaffa since they missed their chance of booty. What followed was a direct result of this. Understanding this, the sultan saw that to stand face to face with this insignificant detachment without taking any action was a sheer loss of face. It was reported to me that the king of England took his lance that day and

[1] Now known as Nebī Ṣamwīl (Prophet Samuel). Yāqūt, iv, p. 391, calls it 'a little town in the district of Jerusalem'.

galloped from the far right wing to the far left and nobody challenged him. The sultan was enraged, turned his back on the fighting and went to Yāzūr in high dudgeon. That was on Wednesday [**230**] 23 Rajab [5 August].

The army passed the night like a picketing force. On the morning of the Thursday [6 August] the sultan rode to Latrun, where he camped and sent for the army to come to him. We arrived at the end of the day, on Thursday 24 Rajab [6 August], and spent the night there. On Friday [7 August] in the morning he went to see his brother, al-'Ādil, to consult him. He came to Jerusalem, where he performed the Friday prayer, and then viewed and made arrangements for the building works there. That same day he returned to the baggage-train and passed the night there at Latrun.

The arrival of reinforcements

The first to come was 'Alā' al-Dīn, son of the Atabeg and lord of Mosul, who arrived midday on Saturday 26 Rajab [8 August] and was met at some distance with all honour and respect by the sultan. The latter received him in his tent, prepared a fine welcome for him and presented him with an excellent gift, before he proceeded to his own tents.

On this day the king's envoy came from him again, for al-'Ādil had given him an oral message to take to the king and he had gone back to Jaffa, accompanied by the Chamberlain Abū Bakr. The latter now returned and, coming before the sultan on this day, reported as follows: 'The king did not allow me to enter Jaffa, but came out to me and talked to me outside the town. What he said was, "How many times shall I throw myself at the sultan's feet, while he still refuses me! I was eager to return to my own country but now winter has set in, plans have changed and I have decided to stay. All talks between us are at an end."' This was his answer (may God forsake him).

The arrival of the Egyptian forces

The sultan remained at Latrun. When it was Thursday 9 Sha'bān [20 August], the troops from Egypt arrived and the sultan went out to meet them. With them were Majd al-Dīn Khuldirī, Sayf al-Dīn Yāzkūj and several of the Asadiyya. In attendance on the sultan was his son, al-Malik al-Mu'ayyad Mas'ūd.[1] They made a great show, unfurling their flags and banners, which made it a day to remember. The sultan received them, spread a meal and then they proceeded to their own encampments.

---

[1] Born in Damascus in Rabī' I 571/ September-October 1175 (*Rawḍ*, i, p. 276). He died in 606/1209-1210 (Maqrīzī, *Sulūk*, i, p. 171).

The arrival of al-Manṣūr, son of Taqī al-Dīn

By now al-Manṣūr had taken over the lands that he had been promised and had made all his dispositions. He came to join al-'Ādil's service on Saturday 11 Sha'bān [22 August], camped near him at Mār Ṣamwīl and paid him a visit. Al-'Ādil wrote to the sultan, telling him of his arrival, **[231]** and asked him to receive him with honour and respect and to look kindly on him. When the sultan's son al-Ẓāhir learnt of the arrival of al-Manṣūr, he asked his father for permission to meet him and to visit al-'Ādil. Permission being given, he went and found al-Manṣūr encamped at Bayt Nūbā. He called on him, delighted to meet him, and stayed with him until evening. That was on Sunday [23 August]. He then took him, travelling with a light escort, to the sultan's encampment.

We were with the sultan. Al-Manṣūr entered and the sultan showed him respect, rising and embracing him closely to his chest. He then burst into tears but mastered himself until, emotions overcoming him, he burst into tears again in a way that had never been seen before. For a good while all present wept in sympathy. He then put him at his ease and, having asked him about the journey, the audience ended.

His son al-Ẓāhir passed the night in his tent until Monday morning [24 August] and then returned to join his own force. They unfurled flags and banners, for he had a fine troop, which delighted the sultan. This was during the morning of Monday 13 Sha'bān [24 August] and he took up his position in the vanguard of the army close to Ramla.

The sultan moves to Ramla

When the sultan saw that his forces had assembled, he gathered his councillors and said, 'The king of England is seriously ill and the French without any doubt have set out to cross back over the sea. Their resources have dwindled. This is an enemy whom God has in his power. I think that we should march to Jaffa. If we find any opportunity, we can seize it. Otherwise, we shall return under cover of darkness to Ascalon. No reinforcements will reach it before we have already gained our objective there.' They considered this a good plan, so he ordered several emirs, such as 'Izz al-Dīn Jūrdīk, Jamāl al-Dīn Faraj and others, to set out on the eve of Thursday 16 Sha'bān [27 August] to form a sort of screen near Jaffa to discover through spies how many knights and men-at-arms were there and then to tell him. This they did.

Meanwhile, there was a steady stream of emissaries from the king of England requesting fruit and ice. In his illness God had burdened him with a yearning for pears and plums, which the sultan was supplying him with, while purposing to gain intelligence by the to-and-froing of the messengers. The information that was revealed was that in the town there were 300 knights at the largest estimate and 200 at the smallest, that Count Henry was going backwards and forwards between the king and the French to persuade them to stay, although they were unanimously determined to cross over the sea, and that they were taking no trouble with the city wall, but only concerning themselves with the citadel wall. The king of England had also asked for the Chamberlain Abū Bakr al-'Ādilī, with whom he was on very friendly terms.

Learning these reports, the sultan set out on the morning of Thursday [27 August] for Ramla [**232**] and made a halt there before noon. News came to him from some irregulars,who said, 'We raided Jaffa and no more than 300 knights came out, some of them on mules.' The sultan ordered them to remain in their position there and then the Chamberlain Abū Bakr arrived with an envoy from the king to thank the sultan for coming to his aid with fruit and ice. Abū Bakr mentioned that he had a private talk with him and that he said, 'Say to my brother (meaning al-'Ādil) that he should consider how he can influence the sultan to make peace and get him to give me Ascalon. I shall depart but he will remain here with this little band, quite able to take territory from them. My only aim is to establish my reputation amongst the Franks. If the sultan will not cede Ascalon, then let al-'Ādil take something from him to recompense me for my expenses on rebuilding the wall.'

After the sultan had heard this he sent them to al-'Ādil. With them was also Badr al-Dīn Dildirim al-Yārūqī's man, as a go-between. After they had gone the sultan confided to someone he relied upon to go to al-'Ādil and say, 'If they give up Ascalon, make peace with them, for the army is tired of constant campaigning and their resources are exhausted.' They left during the morning of Friday 17 Sha'bān [28 August].

Their agreement to cede Ascalon

At sunset on the aforementioned day Badr al-Dīn Dildirim sent from the advanced unit to say, 'Five persons have come out to us, one of whom is one of the king's commanders called Hawwāt [Howard?]. They say that they have something to say to me. May I hear their words or not?' The sultan gave his permission and at the time of the evening prayer Badr al-Dīn himself arrived and reported what they had had to say: 'The king has ceded Ascalon and given up his demand for compensation. His purpose to make peace is sincere.' The sultan sent him back with instructions to send a reliable person to take his hand on that and to say, 'The sultan has now called his forces together and is unable to discuss these matters with you unless he can trust you not to recant. If that is the case, then he can talk to you.' Badr al-Dīn went back to him on this basis and wrote to al-'Ādil with news of what had come about.

When it was Saturday 18 Sha'bān [29 August], Badr al-Dīn sent to say that someone he trusted had taken his hand on that and he took the territorial frontiers to be as had originally been agreed with al-'Ādil. The sultan summoned his clerks and recorded Jaffa with its district, left out Ramla, Lydda, Yubnā and Majdal Yābā, then noted down Caesarea and district, Arsūf and district, Haifa and district and Acre and district, and finally excepted Nazareth and Ṣaffūriyya. All was recorded in a document. A reply to the letter was written and sent [**233**] by the hand of Ṭurunṭāy with the envoy, who had come to draw up the terms along with Badr al-Dīn in the late afternoon on the Saturday. The sultan said to the envoy, 'These are the limits of the lands that will remain in your hands. If you can accept these terms, well and good! I give you my hand on it. Let the king send someone to take the oath. Let it be tomorrow morning. Otherwise, it will be understood that this is procrastination and temporising and the whole matter will be over and done with between us.' On this understanding they went off on Sunday morning [30 August].

When it was time for the late evening prayer on Sunday 19 Sha'bān[1] [30 August], someone came with news that Ṭurunṭāy and the envoys had come back and were seeking audience, which was granted to Ṭurunṭāy alone. He reported that the king had read the document and denied that he had given up compensation. The group that had gone out to Badr al-Dīn Dildirim reminded the king that he had done that, whereupon he said, 'If I said it, I will not go back on it. Say to the sultan, "Well and good! I accept these terms and I look to your noble generosity. If you give me something extra, it will be from your kindness and bounty."'

They went at night and summoned the envoys, who waited until the morning and were then taken before the sultan on the morning of Monday 20 Sha'bān [31 August]. They repeated what had been agreed on the part of their master and then they dispersed to their tents. The advisors and councillors came before the sultan and all was settled and the terms agreed. The Emir Badr al-Dīn Dildirim went to al-'Ādil and took the envoys with him as would-be petitioners for the addition of Ramla. He returned late in the evening on the eve of Tuesday 21 Sha'bān [1 September] and the draft treaty was drawn up, in which the conditions were recorded and a peace for three years from the date of the document, namely, Tuesday 21 Sha'bān 588[2] [1 September 1192]. 'Ramla is theirs and Lydda too' was an added clause. The sultan despatched al-'Adl, to

---

1 *Nawādir* and B mistakenly have Sunday 20 Sha'bān here. By the sequence of days, Sunday must be 19 Sha'bān.

2 *Nawādir* and B write Tuesday 22 Sha'bān both here and just above. Note that 'Imād al-Dīn himself drew up the treaty 'on Tuesday 21 Sha'bān ..., which corresponded to 1 September, for a period of three years and eight months' (*Fatḥ*, p. 436).

whom he said, 'If you are able to satisfy them with one of the two places or with condominium over them, then do so. Let them not have any say over the Uplands.' The sultan saw that this was for the best because of the weakness, scant resources and a longing for home that had overwhelmed our men, and also because of their lack of zeal at Jaffa that he witnessed on the day when he ordered them to attack and they would not. He feared that he might need them and find them gone. He decided to rest them for a while so that they might recover and forget this present state they had come to, and so that he might make the land productive again, supply Jerusalem with all the weapons that he could and have an opportunity to strengthen its defences. Part of the peace agreement was 'that Ascalon should be demolished and that our men and theirs should cooperate in its demolition for fear that he might take it over with defences intact and not demolish them.' Al-'Adl went with these terms and it was also stipulated that the lands of the Ismā'īlīs should be included. [**234**] The Franks made it a condition that the lord of Antioch and Tripoli should be included in this peace on the basis of the last peace we had made with that region.

The matter being settled in this way, the envoys left on Tuesday 21 Sha'bān [1 September] and the sultan laid it down that it was imperative to make a decision this day, either for peace or for hostilities, because he feared that these talks might be of the same kind as the king's previous talks and well-known prevarications.

The arrival of envoys from numerous quarters

On this same day the envoy of Sayf al-Dīn Baktimur, the lord of Khilāṭ, arrived declaring loyalty, common purpose and the dispatch of his troops. The envoy of the Georgians also came and one part of his communication concerned the monasteries they possessed in Jerusalem and their state of repair. They complained that they had been taken out of their hands and they requested the sultan from his good will to restore them to their representatives' hands. Another that came was the envoy of the lord of Erzerum, offering loyalty and service.

Account of the conclusion of the peace

When al-'Adl came to them, he was lodged outside the city in a tent until the king was told of his arrival. Informed of this, the king summoned him into his presence with the rest of the deputation. Al-'Adl proferred him the draft. The king, since he was sick in body, said, 'I have no strength to read this, but I herewith make peace and here is my hand.' Our envoys met with Count Henry and the others, acquainted them with the draft and they accepted an equal division of Ramla and Lydda and all the contents of the document. It was agreed that they would swear their oaths on Wednesday morning [2 September] because they had already eaten something on the Tuesday and it is not their custom to take an oath after eating. Al-'Adl sent someone to the sultan to tell him of this.

On Wednesday 22 Sha'bān [2 September] the company was summoned before the king. They took his hand and made their compact with him. He made his excuses, saying that kings do not swear and that he would accept that from the sultan. Then the following took the oath, Count Henry, his nephew who was his designated deputy on the Coastal Plain, and Balian, son of Barisan, son of the Lady of Tiberias. The Hospitallers and the Templars and all the Frankish nobles expressed their approval. During the remainder of the day they set out to return to the sultan's encampment, arriving at the last evening prayer. On the Frankish side came the son of Humfrey, Balian and several nobles, who were received with honour and respect. A tent that befitted their rank was pitched for them. Al-'Adl presented himself and recounted what had happened.

[**235**] During the morning of Thursday 23 Sha'bān [3 September] their envoys came before the sultan. They took his noble hand and received his oath to observe the peace on the agreed terms. They demanded that several persons swear, al-'Ādil, al-Afḍal, al-Ẓāhir, 'Alī ibn Aḥmad al-Mashtūb, Badr al-Dīn Dildirim, al-Manṣūr and every neighbour of their territory, such as Ibn al-Muqaddam, the lord of Shayzar, and others. The sultan promised them that he would send an emissary with them to all their neighbours to secure their oaths. He swore an oath to the lord of Antioch and Tripoli, but he made it conditional on their swearing an oath to the Muslims. If they did not, they would not be included in the peace. He then ordered the herald to proclaim in the encampments and in the markets, 'Listen all! Peace has been arranged. Any person from their lands who wishes to enter ours may do so and any person from our lands who wishes to enter theirs may also do so.' The sultan announced that the pilgrim route from Syria was now open and during that public session he conceived a plan to perform the Ḥajj. I was present throughout all this and when this thought came to him.

The sultan ordered that a hundred sappers should be sent to demolish the city wall of Ascalon, accompanied by a senior emir, and also to get the Franks out. A detachment of the Franks should be with them until the demolition was completed, as they feared it might be kept with defences intact.

It was a memorable day. Both sides were overwhelmed with such joy and delight as God alone can measure. However, God knows well that the peace was not what the sultan preferred, for he said to me in one of his conversations about the peace settlement, 'I fear to make peace, not knowing what may become of me. Our enemy will grow strong, now that they have retained these lands. They will come forth to recover the rest of their lands and you will see every one of them ensconced on his hill-top,' meaning in his castle, 'having announced, "I shall stay put" and the Muslims will be ruined.'[1] These were his words and it came about as he said. Nevertheless, he saw the advantage in making peace because the army was weary and showing signs of disaffection. The real benefit was in something that God knew of, for a little after the treaty his death occurred. Had that happened in the course of hostilities, Islam would have been in peril. The peace was nothing but a providential blessing for him (God's mercy be upon him).

Account of the demolition at Ascalon

On Saturday 25 Sha'bān [5 September] the sultan commissioned 'Alam al-Dīn Qayṣar to demolish Ascalon. With him he sent a company of sappers and stone-masons. It was agreed that the king should send people from Jaffa to be with him to oversee the demolition and to remove the Franks from the town. They arrived there on Sunday [6 September] and when they wished to start work, the troops who were there made excuses on the grounds 'that the king owes us some pay for a period of time. Either he pays us that before we leave or you pay it to us.' Later an emissary from the king arrived to order them [**236**] to leave, so they did. Demolition work started during the forenoon of Monday 27 Sha'bān [7 September] and was continuous after that. The men were given instructions about cooperating in the work. Each group was assigned a specific section of the wall and was told, 'Your leave begins when it is demolished.'

Account of the sultan's departure from Ramla

On Wednesday 29 Sha'bān [9 September] the sultan moved to Latrun. The two armies fraternised and a good many Muslims went to Jaffa in search of trade. A large host of the enemy came to Jerusalem to perform their pilgrimage. The sultan gave them every assistance and sent escorts with them to protect them until they were taken back to Jaffa. Many Franks did this. The sultan's aim in this was that they should fulfil their pilgrim duty and return to their own lands, leaving the Muslims safe from their wickedness. When the king learnt the great number of those who would make this pilgrimage, he bore it ill and sent

---

1 In this sentence the understanding of who says what differs from what is implied by the punctuation in *Nawādir* and from Wilson, *Saladin*, p. 387.

to the sultan, requesting him to stop the pilgrims and demanding that he should only allow individuals after the presentation of written authorisation from himself. The Franks from overseas learnt of this and were outraged and made every effort to visit Jerusalem.

Every day large numbers of them were arriving, officers, men of middling sort and princes concealing their rank. The sultan set about receiving honourably those who came. He offered food, met them with an easy manner and conversed with them. He told them of the disapproval of the king, but allowed them to perform their pilgrimage, announcing that he paid no attention to the king's prohibition. His excuse to the king was that if people had come such a great distance and God had given them the opportunity to visit this holy place, he did not find it permissible to prevent them.

The illness of the king had worsened, but he departed on the eve of Wednesday 29 Sha'bān [9 September]. It was said that he had died, but he and Count Henry with all the nobles went to Acre. In Jaffa only a very few remained, the sick and infirm.

The return of the armies of Islam to their homelands

When this matter was concluded and these peace terms settled, the sultan gave his men leave to depart. The first to leave were the troops of Irbil, who set out on 1 Ramaḍān the Blessed [10 September]. After them on 2 Ramaḍān [11 September] the troops of Mosul, Sinjār and Ḥisn [Kayfā] left. The sultan announced his plan [**237**] for the Ḥajj and strengthened his determination to fulfil his obligation in that respect. This was something that had occurred to me. I first made the suggestion on the day that peace was concluded. It made a great impression on him and he gave orders to his secretariat: 'If there are any troops who plan to go on the Ḥajj, record their names so that the number of those that will take the road with us can be reckoned.' Registers of what would be needed for the journey in the way of clothing and provisions, and such like, were drawn up and sent around the country for preparations to be made.

Account of the sultan's return [to Jerusalem]

When he had given the troops leave to depart and was sure that the enemy had been driven away to retrace their steps, the sultan decided to go to Jerusalem to prepare the material to restore it, to look to its welfare and to get ready to leave for the Ḥajj. He left Latrun on Sunday 4 Ramaḍān [13 September] and proceeded as far as Mār Ṣamwīl to visit al-'Ādil there, but found that he had already gone to Jerusalem. I was with the latter on a mission from the sultan, myself along with the Emir Badr al-Dīn Dildirim and al-'Adl. For a while al-'Ādil had been absent from his brother on account of illness. He was now making a recovery and we informed him that the sultan was coming to Mār Ṣamwīl to visit his sick-bed. He made a great effort, travelled with us and met the sultan in that place when he had just arrived and not yet dismounted. On meeting him, al-'Ādil dismounted and kissed the ground, before mounting again. The sultan beckoned him close and asked him about his health. Together they rode on to Jerusalem during the rest of that day.

The arrival of an envoy from Baghdad

When it was Friday 23 Ramaḍān [2 October] al-'Ādil prayed the Friday prayer and then set out to return to Kerak, having been given leave by the sultan, to look into its affairs and then to return to the eastern lands to govern them, for he had received them from the sultan. He had said farewell to the sultan, but when he arrived at al-'Āzariyya, he camped there and then a messenger arrived with news that an envoy from Baghdad was on his way to him. He sent to inform the sultan of this and said that he would meet him and find out the reason why he had come.

On Saturday 24 Ramaḍān [3 October] al-'Ādil came to an audience with the sultan and reported that the envoy had come to him from Ibn al-Nāqid[1] after the latter had taken the post of deputy vizier of Baghdad. The purpose of the communication was to urge him to reconcile the sultan's heart with the caliphal court, to act as intermediary between him and the August Divan, to criticise the sultan for delaying his diplomatic contacts with the Noble Threshold, and to propose the dispatch of Qāḍī al-Fāḍil to attend the Divan to establish terms of agreement which could be drawn up between it and the sultan only through him. Al-'Ādil had been promised great things by the Divan [**238**] if he could arrange this, and the Divan would owe him a favour that he could enjoy the fruit of subsequently. There were other matters of similar import.

The sultan had a notion to send an emissary to hear what the Divan had to say and to find out the effect of al-'Ādil's intervention in the dispute. Discussion of this went round and round and to and fro and in the end the sultan made up his mind to send Ḍiyā' al-Dīn al-Shahrazūrī. Al-'Ādil returned to his camp at al-'Āzariyya after this decision had been reached and informed the envoy that the sultan had agreed to send an emissary to attend upon the August Divan. On Monday [5 October] al-'Ādil set out to travel to Kerak,

[1] *Nawādir* gives the name as Ibn al-Nāfidh. However, other sources identify the deputy vizier as Sharaf al-Din al-Ḥasan ibn Naṣr Ibn al-Nāqid (died Ramaḍān 604/March-April 1208). See e.g. the unfavourable notice in Abū Shāma, *Tarājim*, pp. 61-62.

while Ḍiyā' al-Dīn set out en route for Baghdad on Tuesday 27[1] Ramaḍān [6 October].

The sultan's son al-Ẓāhir returns to his lands and receives the sultan's advice

The morning of Wednesday 28[2] Ramaḍān [7 October] the sultan's son, al-Ẓāhir, set out after saying his farewells and visiting the Dome of the Rock, where he prayed and beseeched God to do His will. He rode out, with me in attendance upon him, and said to me, 'I have just remembered what I need to consult the sultan about face to face.' He sent someone to ask permission for him to return into his presence. This was given, so he came before him. I was summoned, too, and the room was cleared.

Later the sultan said, 'I charge you to fear God Almighty, for He is the source of all good. I command you to do what God has commanded, for that is the means of your salvation. I warn you against shedding blood, indulging in it and making a habit of it, for blood never sleeps. I charge you to care for the hearts of your subjects and to examine their affairs. You are my trustee and God's trustee to guard their interests. I charge you to care for the hearts of the emirs and men of state and the magnates. I have only achieved what I have by coaxing people. Hold no grudge against anyone, for death spares nobody. Take care in your relations with people, for only if they are satisfied will you be forgiven, and also in your relations with God, for God will only be forgiving if you repent to Him, and He is gracious.'

This was said after we had broken our fast in his presence and some part of the night had elapsed. He said much in that vein but this is what I can relate from memory. His son remained with him until near dawn and then the sultan gave him permission to leave. He rose, went to him and said farewell. He kissed his face and rubbed his hand over his head. Al-Ẓāhir departed in a spirit of secure trust in God and took some sleep in the wooden tower that was the sultan's, where he used to sit sometimes until morning. I went part of the way in attendance on him and then took my leave. He travelled on, God willing, under God's protection.

[239] The departure of al-Afḍal

Al-Afḍal dispatched his baggage-train, but remained to consult the sultan through my agency about matters of business of his. He stayed until four days

1 *Nawādir* has '26' erroneously.
2 *Nawādir* reads '27'.

of Shawwāl had gone and then he set out on the eve of the 5th of the month [14 October] half-way through the night, in bad odour, and went with a small escort via the route through the Jordan Valley.

The sultan's departure from Jerusalem

The sultan continued to assign feudal grants to his men, to give them leave to depart and to prepare to travel to Egypt. His desires were concentrated on the Ḥajj, which was the greatest boon that had eluded him. He so continued until he received certain intelligence that the God-forsaken king of England's ship had set sail, on his way to his own lands, at the beginning of Shawwāl [10 October]. Thereupon the sultan formed his plan to enter the plain with a small retinue and to inspect the coastal castles, to go to Bānyās and then on to Damascus to remain there a few days. He would then return to Jerusalem on his way to Egypt to examine its affairs, establish its government and consider what would further its prosperity. He commanded me to stay in Jerusalem until his return to construct the hospital which he founded there and to administer the madrasa which he founded there.[1]

He left Jerusalem during the forenoon of Thursday 6 Shawwāl [15 October]. I escorted him as far as al-Bīra, where he halted and ate a meal. He then continued on his way until he had covered part of the route to Nablus. After a stop overnight, he then came to Nablus during the morning of Friday 7 Shawwāl [16 October]. He was met by a great crowd seeking redress from al-Mashṭūb and humbly protesting against his wicked stewardship of their affairs. The sultan continued to investigate their situation until the evening of Saturday 8 Shawwāl [17 October]. He then left and stopped at Sebastea to look into affairs there. On his journey he then came to Kawkab and carried out an inspection of the place. He ordered shortcomings there to be rectified. This was on Monday 10 Shawwāl [19 October].

Bahā' al-Dīn Qarāqūsh's exit from captivity

Qarāqūsh's release from captivity's noose took place on Tuesday 11 Shawwāl [20 October]. He appeared before the noble presence of the sultan, who was extremely delighted to see him. [**240**] The sultan and Islam owed him much. He asked the sultan for permission to go to Damascus to gather his ransom and permission was given. According to what I heard, the ransom was 80,000 [dinars?].

1 The hospital (*māristān*) took over a building near the Holy Sepulchre and the Ṣalāḥiyya madrasa for Shāfi'ī legal studies occupied the former Church of St Anne.

The prince presents himself before the sultan, seeking favour

When the sultan had arrived at Beirut, the prince, the lord of Antioch, came before the sultan, seeking favour. The sultan showed him much honour and respect and was very friendly towards him. He bestowed upon him al-'Amq, Azarghān and farms whose produce was worth 15,000 dinars.

The death of al-Mashṭūb in Jerusalem

Al-Mashṭūb had stayed behind in Jerusalem as part of the garrison assigned to it. He was not the governor. That post was held by 'Izz al-Dīn Jūrdīk, whom the sultan had appointed after the peace at the time of his return to Jerusalem[1] and after he had discussed it with al-'Ādil, al-Afḍal and al-Ẓāhir through me. They suggested him, as did the men of religion and piety, because he was very solicitous for, and of great service to, the righteous. The sultan commanded me to entrust the post to him on Friday at the Dome of the Rock. I gave him his post after the Friday prayer, having stipulated that he should show integrity and having told him what good trust the sultan had in him. He shouldered the task and undertook it in an exemplary manner.

Meanwhile al-Mashṭūb remained in Jerusalem as a part of the garrison, but he died on Sunday 23 Shawwāl [1 November] and was buried in his own house after prayers had been said over him in the Aqsa Mosque (may God have mercy on him).[2]

Account of the sultan's return to Damascus

The sultan's return there came after he had finished his inspection of all the coastal fortresses and ordered their shortcomings to be seen to and their garrisons to be put into good order and their full complement to be provided. He entered Damascus the morning of Wednesday 26 Shawwāl [4 November]. In the city were his sons [**241**], al-Afḍal, al-Ẓāhir, al-Ẓāfir and his young children. He loved this city and preferred residence there over all other places. He held a public session the morning of Thursday 27 Shawwāl [5 November], to which people came and satisfied their longing to see him. The poets declaimed their praises and both the elite and the generality attended that gathering. He continued at the customary times to spread the wings of his justice, to let fall the showers of his benevolence and favour, and to enquire

1 Jūrdīk replaced Ḥusām al-Dīn Siyārūkh, who had resigned (see *Fatḥ*, p. 442).

2 According to *Fatḥ*, pp. 443-442, Sayf al-Dīn 'Alī al-Mashṭūb died on Thursday 26 Shawwāl (Thursday would be 5 November!) and he is there described as lord of Nablus.

into the wrongs his subjects complained of until Monday 1 Dhū'l-Qa'da [9 November].

Then al-Afḍal gave a banquet for al-Ẓāhir. The latter, when he had reached Damascus, heard that the sultan was on his way there, so waited so that he could have the pleasure of seeing him again. It is as though his noble soul felt that the end of the sultan's alloted span was near. At that time he made his farewells many times, but kept coming back. When al-Afḍal gave him a banquet, he put on a fine show with all sorts of rarities, such as fitted his high aspirations. It was as though he wished to requite him for the service he had shown him at the time he went to Aleppo. The secular and religious notables attended and he asked the sultan to attend, which he did to mend his feelings. It was a memorable occasion, as I have heard.

The arrival of his brother, al-'Ādil

After al-'Ādil had investigated the state of affairs at Kerak and had given instructions for the improvement of what he planned to improve there, he set out to return to his Euphrates lands. He came to Damascus on Wednesday 17 Dhū'l-Qa'da [25 November]. The sultan had gone out to meet him and spent the time hunting around Ghabāghib[1] as far as al-Kiswa until their meeting, and then they went hunting together.

The sultan entered Damascus again towards the end of the day on Sunday 21 Dhū'l-Qa'da [29 November]. He stayed at Damascus, hunting with his brother and his sons, and all enjoying the neighbouring countryside and the haunts of his youth. It appears that he found some rest from all the constant toil and fatigue that had been his and from the sleepless nights and tiring days. This was like nothing else but a farewell to his children and the places that had provided him with so much enjoyment, although he was not aware of that. He forgot his intention to go to Egypt. Other matters came his way and different plans.

A letter of his came to me at Jerusalem, summoning me to his presence. There were heavy rains and much mud, but I left Jerusalem on Friday 23 Muḥarram 589 [29 January 1193] and I arrived in Damascus on Tuesday 12 Ṣafar [16 February], when the first groups of pilgrims had arrived on the Damascus road. The sultan made his entry into the city the late afternoon of Monday 11 Ṣafar [15 February] and I did not happen to appear before him to pay my respects until near midday of the day I arrived. I chanced to arrive when al-Afḍal was present in the northern vaulted chamber, attended by a large number of emirs and office-holders, who were waiting for the sultan's reception

[1] According to Yāqūt, iii, 771: 'It is a village where the district of the Ḥawrān begins, belonging to the district of Damascus, six leagues from the latter.'

to pay their respects. [242] When the sultan became aware that I was present, he called me in when he was alone before anyone else came to him. I entered and he rose to give me the most welcoming reception I had ever seen. He grasped me to him and his eyes filled with tears.

The sultan's reception of the pilgrim caravan

When it was Wednesday 13 Ṣafar {17 February}, he sent for me and I went to him. He asked me who was in the vaulted chamber. I informed him that al-Afḍal was waiting to attend on him with several emirs and notables in his train. He made his apologies to them through Jamāl al-Dīn Iqbāl.

On the Thursday morning {18 February} he summoned me early and, when I came to him in the garden portico where he was with his young children, he asked who was there to see him. He was told, 'The Frankish envoys and a group of emirs and notables.' He had the Frankish envoys called to that spot. A young son of his to whom he was greatly attached, called Emir Abū Bakr,[1] was with him and he was dandling him on his knee. When the boy's glance fell on the Franks and he saw how they looked, their shaven chins and their cropped heads and the unusual clothes they were wearing, he was frightened of them and started to cry. The sultan apologised to them and dismissed them after they had appeared before him, without hearing what they had to say.

He then said to me, 'Have you eaten anything today?' It was usual for him to be thus friendly. He then ordered, 'Bring whatever you have to hand.' They brought rice with leban and similar light dishes. He ate too and I had been thinking that he had no appetite. In recent days he was making excuses to people because it was difficult for him to move. It was as though his body was full and there was a lassitude about him. When we had finished eating, he asked, 'What news do you have of the pilgrim caravan?' 'I met with a group of them on the road,' I replied. 'Were it not for all the mud, they would have arrived today. However, they will come tomorrow.' 'God willing,' he said, 'we shall go out to meet them.' He commanded the roads to be cleared of water, for it was a year of copious rains and the water was running in the streets like rivers. I took my leave of him, not having found him to be as lively as I had known him.

He rode out early on the Friday morning {19 February} and I was just a little behind him. I caught up with him after he had met the pilgrims, amongst whom were Sābiq al-Dīn and Qarālā al-Yārūqī. He welcomed them, as he had great respect for such senior men. His son al-Afḍal then joined him to meet the

[1] In the list of Saladin's sons that 'Imād al-Dīn gives on the authority of the sultan himself there is only one with this name, al-Manṣūr Abū Bakr, but a note adds that he was born in Ḥarrān after (!) the sultan's death (quoted in *Rawḍ*, i, pp. 276-277).

company and began to engage me in conversation. I looked towards the sultan and could not detect that he was wearing his brigandine. It was not normal for him to ride out without it. It was a great occasion and to meet the pilgrims and see the sultan [**243**] most of the inhabitants of the city had gathered. I could not stop myself from moving next to him and speaking to him about his failure to wear it. He seemed to wake up and then asked for his brigandine, but the master of the armoury was not to be found. I was very disturbed by this and said to myself, 'A sultan demands what he normally cannot do without and cannot find it!' God planted a feeling of ill-omen in my heart. I said to him, 'Is there not a route that can be taken where there is no vast crowd?' 'Yes, of course,' he replied. He then went through the orchards making towards al-Munaybi'.[1] We attended him on the way while my heart was fluttering because it was full of fear for him. He came finally to the citadel and crossed over the bridge to enter, which was his normal route. This was the last of his mounted progresses (God bless him and sanctify his spirit).

An account of his illness

On the eve of Saturday {20 February} he experienced a great sluggishness and the night had not half gone before he was struck by a bilious fever, which was more internal than external. Saturday morning 16 Ṣafar [20 February] found him in a torpid state with the traces of the fever upon him. He did not reveal this to his people. I came to him along with Qāḍī al-Fāḍil, and his son al-Afḍal then entered. We sat with him for a long time and he began to complain of his disturbed state during the night, but he enjoyed our conversation until near midday. We left him, although our hearts remained with him. He commanded us to be present at the regular meal time in the service of al-Afḍal. That was not customary for the Qāḍī so he retired, but I went into the south vaulted chamber where the meal had been laid out. His son al-Afḍal had taken his seat in the sultan's place. I left as I did not have the stomach to take my place, so upset was I. Many wept that day, taking his son's sitting in his place to be a bad omen.

From that time on his illness began to worsen, while we kept up our visits at the two extremes of the day. We, that is Qāḍī al-Fāḍil and I, used to visit him several times a day and access was granted on certain days when he felt some relief. His illness was in his head. One of the ominous signs that his life was at its end was that his doctor, who at home and abroad knew his constitution so well, was absent. The doctors counselled that he be bled, so they bled him on the fourth day and his illness intensified. The moist humours of his body

1 One of the 'garden suburbs' of Damascus (see Kurd 'Alī, *Ghūṭat Dimashq*, p. 77).

became few and dryness came to dominate greatly. The illness continued to increase until he reached the extremity of weakness. On the sixth day of his sickness we sat him up and supported his back on a pillow. Tepid water was brought for him to drink after a laxative potion. He drank it and found it to be extremely hot and complained how hot it was. It was changed and offered to him again, but he complained it was too cold. He showed no anger and did not scold, but said nothing other than, 'Heavens above! Is nobody able to get the water just right.' Qāḍī al-Fāḍil and I went out and the former said to me, 'Just consider these qualities that the Muslims are on the point of losing. By God, had this been **[244]** a certain person, he would have banged the cup on the head of the man who brought it.'

On the sixth, seventh and eighth days his illness worsened and continued to increase. His mind wandered. On the ninth day a shaking began and he declined to take any drink. Rumour became rife in the town and people were fearful. They shifted their goods from the markets and were overwhelmed by more grief and sadness than can be expressed. Qāḍī al-Fāḍil and I used to sit together every night until a third of the night had passed, or something like that, and then we would go to the gate of his residence. If we found access, we would go in, look upon him and then depart, but otherwise, we would enquire how he was and then leave. We used to find people watching for us to leave to go home so that his state could be read from our faces.

On the tenth day of his illness he was twice given an enema, which eased him and provided some relief. He took a good quantity of barley water and people were very happy. We waited as usual until a certain portion of the night had past and then went to the gate of his residence, where we found Jamāl al-Dīn Iqbāl. We requested him to let us know the latest situation. He went in and then sent to us by al-Mu'aẓẓam Tūrānshāh[1] (may God restore him to health) to say, 'Perspiration has started on both his legs.' We thanked God for that and then begged him to feel the rest of his body and to tell us how it was perspiring. He examined him and then came out to us and reported that the sweat was copious. We thanked God for that and departed with happy hearts. On the morning of the eleventh day of his illness, which was Tuesday 26 Ṣafar {2 March}, we presented ourselves at the gate and asked how he was. We were told that the perspiration had become excessive, had soaked through his mattress and then the rugs and wetted the floor. The dryness of his humours had increased greatly, his strength had declined and the doctors feared the worst.

[1] This is a son of Saladin, born in Rabī' I 577/July-August 1181 and died in 658/1260.

Al-Afḍal exacts the people's oath of allegiance

When al-Afḍal saw what had befallen his father and was convinced that there was no hope for him, a start was made on asking people to swear allegiance. He held a session in the palace of Riḍwān,[1] known as his residence, and summoned the qāḍīs. A document was drawn up for him with an abbreviated oath, but one which met all requirements, containing an oath of allegiance to the sultan for the duration of his life and in the event of his death to al-Afḍal. He said to people in explanation that it was because of the sultan's serious illness and 'we do not know what may happen and we are only doing this as a precautionary measure according to the custom of princes.' The first person summoned to swear was Sa'd al-Dīn Mas'ūd, the brother of Badr al-Dīn Mawdūd, [**245**] the prefect. He hastened to take the oath without any preconditions. He then called upon Nāṣir al-Dīn, the lord of Ṣahyūn, who duly swore, adding that the fortress that he held should remain his. Then Sābiq al-Dīn, the lord of Shayzar, came and swore, but without mentioning divorce as a penalty. He made the excuse that he never swore on pain of divorce. Khushtarīn al-Hakkārī came and took the oath, as did Nūshirwān al-Zarzārī, on condition that he should have a fief that would satisfy him. Finally, 'Allakān and Mankalān swore. The table was then spread and all came and ate.

When the evening came, there was a renewed session of oathtaking. Maymūn al-Qaṣrī and Shams al-Dīn Sunqur the Elder were summoned and both said, 'We will swear with a stipulation that we will never draw a sword in the face of any of your brothers, but I will give my head to protect your lands.' This was what Maymūn said. Sunqur on the other hand declined for a while, but then said, 'You had me swear an oath for Latrun and I still keep to it.' Sāma attended and said, 'I have no fief. For what should I swear?' He was approached again and then he swore, but he made his oath depend on his being given a fief that would content him. Sunqur al-Mashṭūb presented himself and swore, having stipulated that he should be satisfactorily looked after. Then Ilyakī al-Fārisī came and swore, as did Aybak al-Afṭas, whose oath was subject to his being satisfied. He, too, did not swear that he would divorce if foresworn. The brother of Siyārūkh attended and took his oath, conditional on being satisfied. Finally, Ḥusām al-Dīn Bishāra, who was the commander of these men, came and swore. Not one of the Egyptian emirs attended and no pressure was brought on them. Only this small number took the oath and possibly some obscure persons followed a different line.

As for the text of the oath that was sworn and its clauses, the first was as follows: 'I from this time forward devote my duty and dedicate my true mind to

---

[1] This palace, perhaps named after the Seljuk prince, son of Tutush, was delapidated by the reign of Saladin's namesake and great-grandson and restored by him after 648/1250 (Ibn Shaddād, *Description de Damas*, p. 39).

al-Malik al-Nāṣir [Saladin] for the duration of his life and I shall not cease to bestow my efforts to protect his dominion with my person, my wealth, my sword and my men, obeying his commands and waiting upon his good pleasure, and then subsequently to his son al-Afḍal ʻAlī. By God, I shall be subject to his allegiance and I shall protect his dominion and his lands with my person, my wealth, my sword and my men. I shall obey his orders and his prohibitions. In this my inner and my outer self are as one. God is my witness in what I say.' Then came the 'exclusion clause'.[1] Such is the oath that was sworn to, I mean, its main import.

[246] Account of his death (may God have mercy on him, sanctify his spirit and give the Muslims a good successor)

When it was the eve of Wednesday 27 Ṣafar {3 March}, which was the twelfth night since he fell ill, the sultan's illness grew ever worse and his strength dwindled further. He fell into the beginning of the end from the first part of the night and his womenfolk intervened to keep us from him. I was summoned during that night, as were Qāḍī al-Fāḍil and Ibn al-Zakī, although it was not customary for the latter to attend at that time. Al-Afḍal proposed to us that we pass the night with him, but Qāḍī al-Fāḍil did not consider that to be a good idea, for people used to wait for us to come down from the citadel every night and he feared that, if we did not, it would be noised about the city and looting might possibly follow amongst the inhabitants. He thought it expedient for us to leave the citadel and for the Shaykh Abū Jaʻfar, the imam of the Kallāsa and a man of piety, to be called upon to spend the night in the citadel, so that, if death throes began during the night, he would be with the sultan, keep the women away from him, rehearse his confession of faith and keep God before his mind. This was done and we left the citadel, each longing to give his own life to ransom the sultan's.

He spent that night like one already passing into God's hands, while the Shaykh Abū Jaʻfar recited the Koran beside him and called God to his remembrance. From the eve of the ninth day his mind had been wandering, hardly being conscious except at odd moments. The Shaykh Abū Jaʻfar recounted that, when he came in his recitation to 'He is God than whom there is no other god, who knows what is invisible and what is visible,'[2] he heard him say, 'True!' Thus he was alert at the needful moment, a special consideration for him on God's part. Praise be to God for that.

---

1 In Arabic: *faṣl al-takhrīj*. Perhaps this was the clause that contained the penalties for breaking the oath, such as divorcing wives, manumitting mamlukes, going on Pilgrimage etc.

2 Koran lix, 22.

His death occurred after the dawn prayer on Wednesday 27 Ṣafar 589 {3 March 1193}. After dawn had broken Qāḍī al-Fāḍil made haste and was present for his death. I arrived when he was already dead and transported to God's favour and the seat of His grace. It was related to me that, when the Shaykh Abū Ja'far reached in God's word 'There is no god but He and in Him have I trusted,'[1] the sultan smiled, his face beamed with joy and he surrendered his soul to his Lord.

This was a day such as had not befallen the Muslims and Islam since the loss of the rightly-guided caliphs. The citadel, the city, the world was overwhelmed by such a sense of loss as God alone could comprehend. In God's name, I had heard from some people that they were desirous of ransoming those dear to them with their own lives, but I only ever heard such an expression as a sort of exaggeration or poetic licence until this day, as I knew for myself and for others that, had the purchase of his life been acceptable, we would have paid for it with our own.

His son al-Afḍal held a session for condolences in the north vaulted hall and the citadel gate was barred to all except the elite of the emirs and the turbanned classes. It was a terrible day. Each man's grief, sorrow, tears and cries for help kept him from looking at anyone else. In the chamber there was a ban on any poet reciting or any divine or preacher delivering any words. [**247**] His children came forth crying for help from people and men's hearts all but shrank away at their ghastly appearance. So things continued until after the midday prayer. Then the task of washing and shrouding the body was taken up, and it was only possible to provide items for his funeral, items that cost a pittance, by borrowing money, even for the cost of the straw with which the clay was mixed.[2] The jurist al-Dawla'ī washed his body and I was deputed to supervise his washing, but I did not have the strength to bear the sight. He was carried out after the midday prayer on a bier covered with a cotton sheet. That and everything necessary in the way of grave clothes to shroud him had been prepared by Qāḍī al-Fāḍil from a proper source he knew of.

At the sight of him cries and great lamentation arose, so much so that a reasonable man might have imagined that the whole world was crying out with one voice. The people were overwhelmed by a weeping and a wailing that distracted them from their prayer time. People delivered final benedictions over him in droves. The first to lead the people in prayer was the Qāḍī Muḥyī al-Dīn ibn al-Zakī. The sultan was then taken back to his residence in the garden, where he had fallen ill, and he was buried in the western portico there. He was lowered into his grave close to the time for the afternoon prayer. Later during the day his son al-Ẓāfir came down and condoled with the people for the loss and comforted their hearts. The inhabitants were too preoccupied with

---

1 Koran ix, 129, or xiii, 30.

2 For the bricks to line the tomb.

their weeping to bother with looting and mischief-making. Except for a few, no heart was not saddened and no eye without tears. People then went homewards most wretchedly and none of them returned that night. However, we came, recited some Koran and indulged our grief again.

That day al-Afḍal busied himself with writing letters to his uncle and his brothers to tell them of this sad event. The following day {4 March} he held a public session to receive condolences and flung open the citadel gate to the jurists and the ulema. Orators delivered eulogies but no poet declaimed. The session broke up at noon on this day, but people continued to come morning and evening to recite the Koran and say prayers for him. Meanwhile, al-Afḍal was fully occupied with his administration and diplomatic letters to his brothers and his uncle.

> Then these years and their players passed away,
> As though they all had been merely dreams.

God bless His prophet, our lord Muḥammad, and his family. These are the records of al-Malik al-Nāṣir Abū'l-Muẓaffar Yūsuf ibn Ayyūb (the mercy of God be upon him). I completed the collection of them the day he died. Through this I planned to win the favour of God by urging people to bless his name and to remember his excellent qualities. May God guide aright his successors that come after him and give him the reward that he deserves, through Muḥammad and his family. God is our sufficiency and an excellent steward is He!

Appendix

Our master and lord, the author, added:

A list of the cities and castles that God allowed to be conquered at Saladin's hands in Frankish territory from the year 583 [1187] until 586 [1191]

Tiberias on the Sea of Galilee, by the sword; Acre on the Mediterranean, on terms; Haifa on the coast, on terms; Nazareth, after which the Nazarenes [Christians] took their name; Ramla; Caesarea, by the sword; Arsūf, on terms; Jaffa (the city), by the sword; Ascalon, on terms; Gaza, on terms; Dārūm; Sidon on the coast; Beirut, on terms; Jubayl; Hūnīn; Jabaliyya; Tibnīn; Anṭarṭūs (apart from the taking of its keep), by the sword; Jabala, the city by the sword and the citadel on terms; Lattakia, the city by the sword and the citadel on terms; Sarafand; the city of Jerusalem (may God set it free); Nablus; al-Bīra in the district of Jerusalem; Ṣaffūriyya; al-Ṭūr; the castle of Dubbūriyya; al-Fūla; the castle of ʻAfarbalā; the castle of Jīnīn; Sebastea; Kawkab; the castle of ʻAfrī, north of Jerusalem; Bethlehem; the castle of al-ʻĀzariyya in the district of Jerusalem; the Red Tower near the latter; the castle of al-Khalīl; Bayt Jibrīn; Tell al-Ṣāfiya; the castle of Majdal Yābā; the citadel of Upper Jīb; Lower Jīb; Latrun; the Red Fort; Lydda in the district of Ramla; Qalansūwa nearby; Yubnā; Qāqūn; Qaymūn; the citadel of Kerak after a year and a half's siege; the citadel of Shawbak after a two years' siege; the castle of al-Salʻ; al-Waʻīra; the castle of al-Jamʻ; the castle of al-Ṭufayla; the castle of Hormuz, all these latter in Wādī Mūsā and al-Surāt; the citadel of Ṣafad; the castle of Yāzūr; Shaqīf Arnūn; the castle of Iskandarūna between Tyre and Acre; the castle of Abū'l-Ḥasan in the district of Sidon; Balda on the higher coast; Maraqiyya on the coast; the fortress of Yaḥmūr in Acre territory; Bulunyās between Jabala and al-Marqab; Ṣahyūn; Balāṭunus; the fortress of al-Jamāhiriyya; the castle of al-ʻĪdhū; Bakās; al-Shughr; Bikasrā'īl; al-Sarmāniyya; the castle of Burzey; Darbsāk; Baghrās near Antioch; al-Dānūr in the district of Beirut; al-Sūfand near Sidon.

Here ends this work. Praise be to God, Lord of all creation, and His blessings and His peace be upon our lord Muḥammad, his family and his Companions. Copying was completed on 12 Rajab the Blessed 626 [6 June 1229] at the hand of the poor slave in need of his Lord's mercy. God is our sufficiency and an excellent steward is He!

[The colophon in the Berlin Ms (B) reads as follows:

This copy was finished on Thursday 23 Sha'bān in the year 625 {27 July 1228} (may God grant it a fortunate completion). Through Him is our help and success, if God Almighty wills. Praise be to God alone and we take refuge in God from the Devil concerning any addition or excision.]

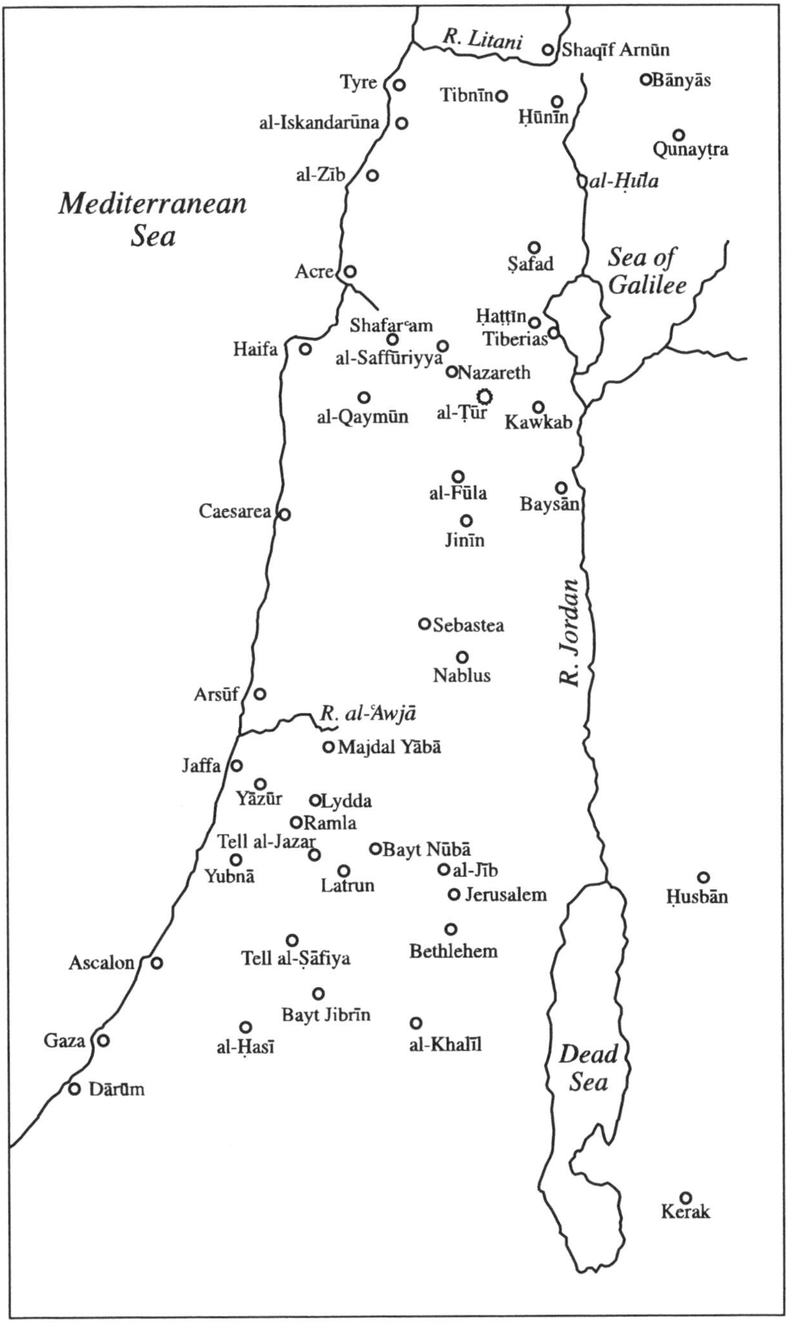

Map 1. Palestine and sites connected with the Third Crusade.

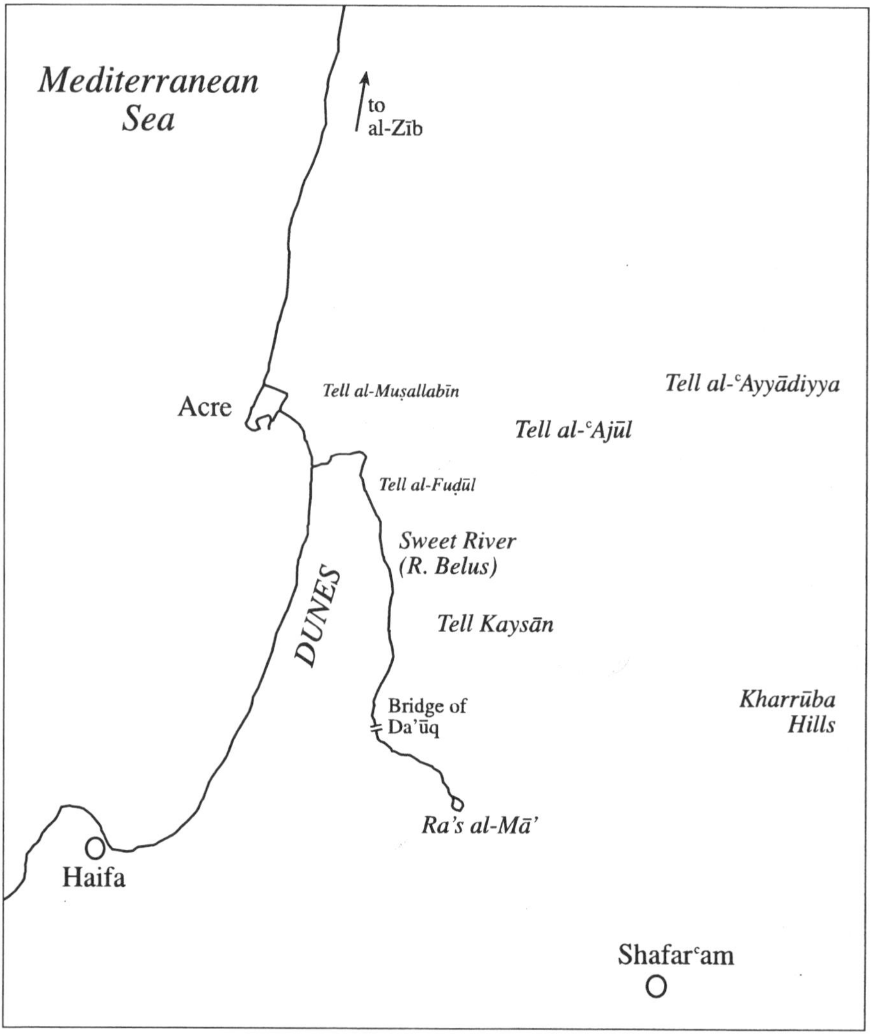

Map 2. The immediate surroundings of Acre.

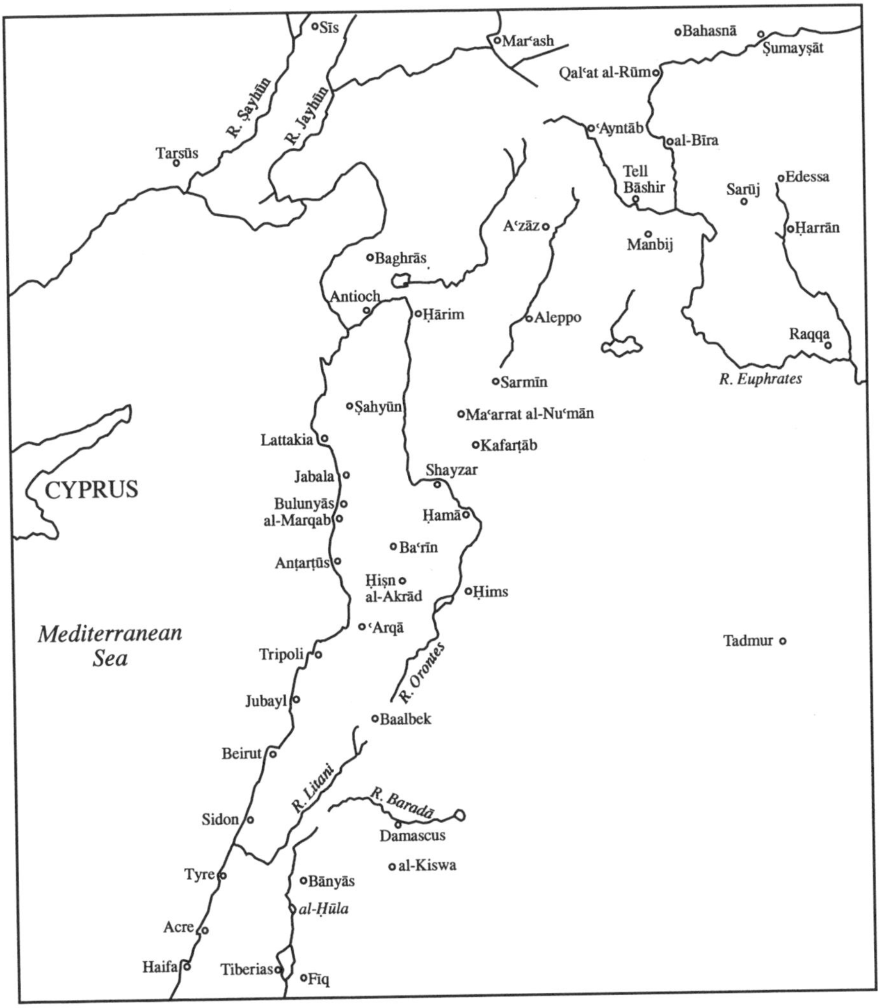

Map 3. Northern Syria and beyond.

Bibliography

Manuscript source

Bahā' al-Dīn Ibn Shaddād, *al-Nawādir al-sulṭāniyya etc.*, Berlin Ms. 9811, Wetzstein, 1893.

Primary Sources

Abū Shāma, *Kitāb al-rawḍatayn fī akhbār al-dawlatayn*, 2 vols., Cairo, Bulaq, 1870-1872.

Abū Shāma, *Tarājim rijāl al-qarnayn al-sādis wa'l-sābi' (al-Dhayl 'alā'l-rawḍatayn)*, Cairo, 1947.

Bahā' al-Dīn Ibn Shaddād, *al-Nawādir al-sulṭāniyya wa'l-maḥāsin al-yūsufiyya (Sīrat Ṣalāḥ al-Dīn)*, ed. al-Shayyāl, Cairo, 1964.

al-Bukhārī, *al-Jāmi' al-ṣaḥīḥ*, ed. M.L. Krehl, 4 vols., Leiden, 1862-1908.

al-Bundārī, *Sanā' al-barq al-shāmī*, ed. Fatḥiyya al-Nabarāwī, Cairo, 1979.

Ibn al-'Adīm, Kamāl al-Dīn 'Umar, *Zubdat al-ḥalab fī ta'rīkh Ḥalab*, ed. Sāmī al-Dahhān, 3 vols., Damascus, 1954-1968.

Ibn al-Athīr, 'Izz al-Dīn, *al-Kāmil fī'l-ta'rīkh*, Beirut, Dār Ṣādir edition, 1965-7.

Idem, *al-Ta'rīkh al-bāhir fī'l-dawla al-atābakiyya*, ed. 'Abd al-Qādir Aḥmad Ṭulaymāt, Cairo, 1963.

Ibn Khallikān, *Wafāyāt al-a'yān*, ed. Iḥsān 'Abbās, 8 vols., Beirut, 1977.

Ibn Shaddād, 'Izz al-Dīn, *La Description d'Alep*, ed. Dominique Sourdel, Damascus, 1953.

Ibn Shaddād, 'Izz al-Dīn, *La Description de Damas*, ed. Sami Dahan, Damascus, 1956.

Ibn Wāṣil, Muḥammad ibn Sālim, *Mufarrij al-kurūb fī akhbār Banī Ayyūb*, vols. 1-3, ed. J. al-Shayyāl, vols. 4-5, ed. Ḥ. Rabī', Cairo, 1953-77.

'Imād al-Dīn al-Isfahānī, *al-Fatḥ al-qussī fī'l-fatḥ al-qudsī*, ed. Carlo de Landberg, Leiden, 1888.

Idem, *Conquête de la Syrie et de la Palestine par Saladin*, trans. Henri Massé, Paris, 1972.

al-Khwārizmī, Muḥammad ibn Aḥmad, *Mafātīḥ al-'ulūm*, ed. G. van Vloten, Leiden, 1895.

Mālik ibn Anas, *al-Muwaṭṭa'*, trans. Aishe B. Bewley, London and New York, 1989.

al-Maqrīzī, *Kitāb al-sulūk li-ma'rifat duwal al-mulūk*, ed. Muḥammad Muṣṭafā Ziyāda *et al.*, 4 vols., Cairo, 1956-73.

Muḥammad ibn Taqī al-Dīn 'Umar al-Ayyūbī, *Miḍmār al-haqā'iq wa-sirr al-khalā'iq*, ed. Ḥasan Ḥabashī, Cairo, 1968.

Nicholson, Helen J., *Chronicle of the Third Crusade. A Translation of the Itinerarium Peregrinorum et Gesta Regis Ricardi*, Ashgate, 1997.

Ohta, Keiko, *The History of Aleppo, known as ad-Durr al-Muntakhab by Ibn ash-Shiḥna*, Tokyo, 1990.

al-Qalqashandī, Aḥmad ibn 'Alī, *Ṣubḥ al-a'shā fī kitābat al-inshā'*, 14 vols., Cairo, 1913-18.

Recueil des Historiens des Croisades: Historiens Orientaux, vol. iii, Paris 1884, pp. 3-374: *al-Nawādir al-sulṭāniyya wa'l-maḥāsin al-yūsufiyya.*

Sibṭ ibn al-Jawzī, *Mir'āt al-zamān fī ta'rīkh al-a'yān*, Hyderabad, 1951.

al-Tirmidhī, Muḥammad ibn 'Īsā, *al-Ṣaḥīḥ*, Bulaq, 1292/1875.

Wilson, C.W., *Saladin; or What befell Sultan Yûsuf*, Palestine Pilgrims' Text Society, vol. xiii: *The Life of Saladin*, London, 1897.

Yāqūt, Shihāb al-Dīn ibn 'Abd Allāh al-Rūmī, *Mu'jam al-buldān*, ed. F. Wüstenfeld, 6 vols., Leipzig, 1866-73.

Secondary Sources

Ahlwardt, W, *Verzeichniss der arabischen Handschriften*, part 21 of *Die Handschriften-verzeichnisse der königlichen Bibliothek zu Berlin*, Berlin, 1881-9.

Brockelmann, Carl, *Geschichte der arabischen Litteratur*, 2 vols. and 3 supplement vols., Leiden, 1943-49.

Cahen, Claude, 'Un traité d'armurerie composé pour Saladin', *Bulletin d'Etudes Orientales*, xii, 1947-8, pp. 103-163.

Chevedden, Paul E., 'The Hybrid Trebuchet: the Halfway Step to the Counterweight Trebuchet', in D.J. Kagay and Theresa M. Vann eds., *On the Social Origins of Medieval Institutions: Essays in Honor of Joseph F. O'Callaghan*, Leiden, 1998, pp. 179-222.

Clauson, Sir Gerard, *An Etymological Dictionary of Pre-Thirteenth-Century Turkish*, Oxford, 1972.

De Slane, *Catalogue des Manuscrits arabes de la Bibliothèque nationale*, premier fascicule, Paris, 1883.

Dozy, R., *Supplément aux Dictionnaires arabes*, 2 vols., Leiden, 1881 (reprint Beirut 1968).

Dussaud, R., *Topographie historique de la Syrie antique et médiévale*, Paris, 1927.

Elisséef, Nikita, *Nūr al-Dīn, un grand prince musulman de Syrie au temps des croisades (511-569 H./1118-1174)*, 3 vols., Damascus, 1967.

Encyclopaedia of Islam, ed. H.A.R. Gibb *et al.*, 2nd edition, Leiden and Paris, 1960-in progress.

Fihrist al-makhṭūṭāt al-muṣawwara, Arab League, Institute of Arabic Manuscripts, vol. ii, part 2: History, Cairo, n.d.

Freeman-Grenville, G.S.P., *The Muslim and Christian Calendars etc.*, Oxford, 1963.

Gibb, H.A.R., 'The Armies of Saladin', in *Studies on the Civilization of Islam*, ed. S.J. Shaw and W.R. Polk, London, 1962.

Idem, *The Life of Saladin from the Works of 'Imād al-Dīn and Bahā' al-Dīn*, Oxford, 1973.

Hill, D.R., 'Trebuchets', *Viator*, iv, 1973, pp. 99-116.

Hinz, Walter, *Islamische Masse und Gewichte*, Leiden and Cologne, 1970.

Holt, P.M., *Early Mamluk Diplomacy (1260-1290): Treaties of Baybars and Qalāwūn with Christian Rulers*, Leiden etc., 1995.

Kurd 'Alī, *Ghūṭat Dimashq*, Damascus, 1952.

Le Strange, Guy, *Palestine under the Moslems*, reprinted Beirut, 1965.

Lewis, Bernard, *Islam: From the Prophet Muhammad to the Capture of Constantinople*, vol. i: *Politics and War*, New York, Evanston, San Francisco, London, 1974.

Lyons, Malcolm Cameron, and Jackson, D.E.P., *Saladin; the politics of the Holy War*, Cambridge, 1982.

Pryor, John H., 'Transportation of horses by sea during the era of the Crusades: Eighth century to 1285 A.D.', *The Mariner's Mirror*, vol. lxviii, 1982, pp. 9-27 and 103-125.

Rogers, R., *Latin Siege Warfare in the Twelfth Century*, Oxford, 1992.

Richards, D.S., 'A Consideration of two sources for the life of Saladin', *Journal of Semitic Studies*, vol. xxv, 1980, pp. 46-65.

Salameh, Khader I., *Catalogue of Arabic Manuscripts in al-Aqsa Mosque Library*, part 1, Jerusalem, 1983.

Sivan, Emmanuel, *L'Islam et la Croisade: Idéologie et Propagande dans les Réactions Musulmanes aux Croisades*, Paris, 1968.

Trimingham, J. Spencer, *The Sufi Orders in Islam*, Oxford, 1971.

Wensinck, A.J. *et al.*, *Concordance de la Tradition musulmane*, 8 vols., Leiden, 1936-88.

Index

The Arabic article (*al-*) is not taken into account for alphabetical order. In princely titles 'al-Malik' has been omitted. Ignore 'ibn' except when it is given as the initial element of a name.

a. Persons and groups

b. Places